British Politics in the Global Age

To Lyn and Pat,
With thanks always for
your encouragement and
a time-saving word of
advice in return. Read
the last paragraph on
p. xv and you'll get the
most important message
of the book.

Love, Joel

British Politics in the Global Age

Can Social Democracy Survive?

JOEL KRIEGER

OXFORD

UNIVERSITY PRESS

OXFORD
UNIVERSITY PRESS

Oxford New York

Athens Auckland Bangkok Bogotá Buenos Aires Calcutta
Cape Town Chennai Dar es Salaam Delhi Florence Hong Kong Istanbul
Karachi Kuala Lumpur Madrid Melbourne Mexico City Mumbai
Nairobi Paris São Paulo Singapore Taipei Tokyo Toronto Warsaw
and associated companies in
Berlin Ibadan

Copyright © 1999 by Joel Krieger

Published by Oxford University Press, Inc.
198 Madison Avenue, New York, New York 10016

Oxford is a registered trademark of Oxford University Press

Published in the United Kingdom by Polity Press in association
with Blackwell Publishers, Ltd.

All rights reserved. No part of this publication may be reproduced, stored in a
retrieval system, or transmitted, in any form or by any means, electronic,
mechanical, photocopying, recording, or otherwise, without the prior
permission of Oxford University Press.

Library of Congress Cataloging-in-Publication Data
Krieger, Joel, 1951–
British politics in the global age : can social democracy survive?
/ Joel Krieger.
    p.   cm.
Includes bibliographical references and index.
ISBN 0-19-521574-5. — ISBN 0-19-521575-3 (pbk.)
1. Labour Party (Great Britain)   2. Great Britain—Politics and
government—1997–   3. Political planning—Great Britain.
4. Socialism—Great Britain.   5. Socialism—Europe.   I. Title.
UN1129.L32K/b   1999
320.941′09′049—dc21   99-26621
                                                          CIP

1 3 5 7 9 8 6 4 2
Printed in Great Britain
on acid-free paper

To Carol and Nathan

Contents

Preface

Since Tony Blair's election in May 1997, there is the unmistakable sense in the UK that something extremely interesting, elusive, and potentially significant is happening. Blair's stated willingness to experiment with ideas and policy, and his call to modernize almost anything in the grasp of government, have contributed to a sense of political renewal and intellectual ferment in the UK. For those dispossessed by the *longue durée* of archly conservative leadership, keen to try their hand at policy and theorizing about how left-of-center politics can take shape in an era of unprecedented globalization, the sense of challenge and readiness to take up the challenge is palpable. With center-left governments comprising a strong majority of EU Europe and growing concern about the potential global diffusion of an Asian economic crisis raising new questions about the durability of neoliberal orthodoxies, the UK's New Labour[1] model of government has garnered considerable international attention, and for good reason.

Blair's government is one of the first West European governments, and certainly the first in the UK, to experience from start to finish the full complement of new challenges that mark the emerging order of European politics. These transformative processes include globalization (a concept to be examined and clarified below) and European integration at a moment of tremendous uncertainty associated with the adoption of a single currency.

Equally significant, the Blair government faces a transformed domestic political environment. Traditional left versus right distributional politics no longer serves as the defining axial principle of competitive party politics and the reference point for social and economic policy orientations. Hence Blair's government must adjust to circumstances that preclude traditional social democratic mobilization and policy formation; it must operate within institutional arrangements, constitutional regimes, and a context of value changes and cultural cross-currents that make policy design extremely challenging and implementation far more complicated and dispersed than before.

Other European governments operate within the same complicated milieux, but Blair's New Labour is the first to tie its fortunes to the design and implementation of a new model of politics designed quite explicitly to conceptualize and manage these challenges. Indeed, looked at most favorably, New Labour's modernizing agenda self-consciously aims to come to terms with and effectively govern these transformations. It accepts globalization as a given and views its project quite sensibly: to preserve and enhance core values of equality and community, while accepting that the institutions and policies associated with social democracy are outdated. Viewed more critically, despite some impressive efforts to define, explain, and theorize New Labour's signature claim to represent a "third way" – a model of government not simply between, but beyond neoliberalism and traditional social democracy – the coherence and originality of Blair's project remain to be demonstrated.

Understandably, the phenomenon of New Labour has unleashed a furious debate, inevitably with partisan overtones. The debate has often focused somewhat narrowly on political agency, examining how the leadership qualities, aims, and ambitions of individual personalities contributed to the reconsideration of policy and the pressures for a modernization of the party. In addition, critics and supporters alike have looked to explain New Labour mainly by reference to the historical performance, aspirations, and strategic options facing the Labour Party. Advocates credit Blair with facing the stark fact that no Labour government has hitherto won two consecutive full terms in office, and with developing a bold strategy to modernize the ideology, organization, and program of Labour in order to break this discouraging legacy and to secure solid and enduring support for a revitalized center-left agenda. Detractors argue that New Labour modernizers paint an inaccurate, belittling portrait of their party's history to maximize the political impact of their claim to newness (Shaw, 1996); they also dismiss the claim that parliamentary socialism has failed or that socialist aspirations can be achieved within a framework fundamentally defined by market logics (Miliband, 1994; Panitch and Leys, 1997). In addition, in the debate about the importance and design of Blair's project, much is made of the relationship between New Labour and Thatcherism and the potential significance of the third way, viewed more or less locally, as a British invention.[2] In short, as provocative and insightful as the debates about New Labour and the third way have been, they are mainly focused on political leadership and party legacies, on internal developments in British politics without the benefit of comparative analysis, and on snapshot evaluations and often normatively loaded assessments of the Blair government.

The Approach: Political and Intellectual Challenges

This book asserts quite a different frame of reference and accordingly asks a different set of questions. Operating on the assumption that politics cannot be understood primarily as the exercise of political agency, it provides an account of the conditions that create the political space for a vibrant center-left politics in the UK. At the same time, I will argue that long-term political developments and structural changes in the organization of production, in collective identities and attachments, and in the processes of interest formation, give rise to a set of dilemmas that test the viability of center-left politics cast in the mold of New Labour. Thus, New Labour will be considered illustratively and comparatively for what it can tell us about British politics in the global age as well as for insight into the future of European social democracy.

In the chapters that follow, I set out to articulate a set of challenges that confront center-left politics in an era when the basic framework of postwar social democratic politics – class agency and national policy sovereignty – no longer holds. This is the primary intellectual challenge of the book. To develop a revitalized *social democracy for the global age* requires much more than finding an approach to economic policy that sets the right balance between regulation and deregulation, or implementing welfare reform that invests more effectively in human capital. The successful implementation of contemporary center-left politics requires a deeper understanding of core processes of change that operate well below the level of party platform and public policy. How have the interaction of global processes and domestic policies fundamentally reshaped the organization of production? How have the disparate work, family, public policy, and cultural experiences of women and ethnic minorities influenced the formation of collective identities and political agendas? What are the consequences for the UK's "imagined community" (Anderson, 1991) or the "four nations or one?" debate and the complex challenges of subsidiarity versus central authority in the UK and in the EU? How serious are the cultural and political reverberations of the UK's postwar history of immigration, nationality legislation, and unresolved tensions about nation and community?

A conception of social democracy for the global age, I suggest, cuts deep – it concerns the basic reorganization of politics in a global age of hybrid production systems, shifting context-dependent political identities, and brokered national sovereignty. In contrast to Blair's third way model of government, social democracy links politics crucially with material needs grounded in the diverse experiences of everyday life; it asserts that political preferences flow from interests and needs under-stood this way, and insists that political preferences have a collective, not merely an individual, basis. The mission of government is to recognize these transformations and to test the limits of political agency to resolve the ensuing dilemmas. Is it within the power of political agency to recon-nect politics to needs and collective agencies? This question poses the ultimate political challenge to government and the central challenge of this book.

The second critical aim of this book, therefore, is to identify and artic-ulate elements of an intellectual framework necessary for analyzing this new era of politics. This entails several steps. The conceptual argument of the book begins with an effort to lend analytic clarity to the much noted demise of social democracy both by distinguishing among three models of social democracy, and by analyzing New Labour in the com-parative context of the antecedents, strategic options, and dilemmas revealed by these alternative models of government. Secondly, I will offer a reconceptualization of class formation in the UK that recognizes the significance of foreign direct investment and the global diffusion of alternative enterprise-level strategies for technological and organiza-tional innovation. Thirdly, in an attempt to reconceptualize "identity politics," I will introduce the term "modular politics" to refine and empir-ically ground the complex interplay of gender, ethnicity, and work exper-ience in the formation of identities, interests, and political agendas. And finally, the term "globalization" begs for clearer conceptualization and more precise empirical application, so the book will also attempt to artic-ulate the relationship between global and domestic processes in a clear and grounded manner.

The term "globalization" is often applied as a general catch-phrase to identify the growing depth, extent, and diversity of cross-border con-nections that are a signal characteristic of the contemporary world. Discussion of the concept often begins with accounts of the increasing globalization of economic activities, seen in the reorganization of production and the global redistribution of the workforce (the "global factory") and in the increased extent and intensity of international trade, finance, and foreign direct investment (see, for example, Dicken, 1992; World Bank, 1995; Perraton et al., 1997). Usage of the term "globaliza-tion," however, has expanded to emphasize the diversity of processes operating on the global scale that deepen and intensify organizational, cultural, and legal relations and interactions. The term is also used to illu-minate other profound, although less immediately visible changes. The processes of globalization involve unsettling changes in "how social life is ordered across time and space." New applications of information tech-nology, such as the Internet and CNN, distort the traditional distinction between what is around the world and what is around the block, "stretching" connections across great distances (Giddens, 1990, p. 64ff.). In addition, "globalization" contributes powerfully to the dislocation of national cultural identities (Hall, 1992); it can inspire new models of "cosmopolitan governance" designed to extend democratic accountability and rights across national borders and throughout international and multilateral organizations (Held, 1995); it invites consideration of a global civil society (Lipschutz, 1992).

As this very brief and partial cataloguing of applications suggests, the term "globalization" is applied with enormous elasticity and, often, with too little precision. At the same time, an appeal to globalization is often used, in my view quite wrongly, to justify an intellectual retreat from attention to the context-rich study of specific countries or regions, and as an excuse for governments to blame particular problems, such as levels of unemployment, on "global forces" rather than accept responsibility for ameliorating structural problems in domestic economies (Hall and Tarrow, 1998). In the UK, for example, some have claimed that New Labour accepts the view that in the global era there is no alternative to welfare retrenchment, the acceptance of neoliberal orthodoxy in macroeconomic policy, and the sacrifice of an active role in industrial policy (see Grant, 1998; Hay and Watson, 1998b).

By contrast, I will assume, first, that despite global pressures of competitiveness and capital flows, governments always face alternative options with regard to macroeconomic, industrial, labor market, and social policy. In fact, a great deal of the book analyzes the interactive effects of global processes and domestic political initiatives, drawing on a range of comparative European experiences, and the study concludes by posing a set of five broad challenges to social democratic governance. Taken together, the comparative illustrations and the challenges should make it clear that alternatives are possible, indeed necessary, to a grounded and coherent center-left project (see Garrett, 1998). Secondly, I will use the term "globalization" or refer to "the global age" with specific, clearly delimited analytical aims in mind. For example, in part II, I will discuss the effects of specific aspects of global competition and foreign direct investment on the UK's system of production; in parts III and IV, I will trace the complicating effects of immigration, nationality policy, and the formation of diasporic identities on issues of identity and nationality in the UK today. In this way I hope to consider the implications of globalization for analyzing the prospects of a revitalized social democracy in a manner that is at once broader than capital flows and economic policy, and yet still analytically precise. If successful, the book should present a fine-grained analysis of British politics in the global age, giving due weight to global and cross-national pressures, but preserving ample sphere of maneuver for government and a host of political actors on the scene in the UK.

An Outline of the Book

Most critically, the organization of the book assumes an inherent connection between politics – party competition, policy regimes, intergovernmental affairs in the European Union – and the organization of production, the development of collective attachments, and the evolution of politically salient cultures and norms. No determinism should be read into this statement – the connections are reciprocal and the influences perpetually cross-cutting – but the assumed linkage fundamentally shapes the book. I assume that the New Labour project – what is possible, necessary, and paradoxical – is inherently shaped by radical changes in the structures and values that have traditionally grounded Labour politics. I will argue that these changes in production and identity formation, in politically salient cultural orientations, and in the decision-making capacity of the nation-state, are all influenced by the processes of globalization. These changes complicate the art of politics, creating opportunities and challenges for government and for political and social actors across the landscape, and they raise a profound question: is it within the power of political agency to resolve these contemporary dilemmas and forge a grounded and coherent progressive politics?

Part I draws on debates about social democracy to develop three alternative models of government defined by a set of key variables: agency, policy approach, institutional orientation, and political morality. Then, a comparison of New Labour and social democratic models of government helps identify the regime characteristics of New Labour, the strategic options it faces, and the choices it has made. The comparative analysis draws attention to critical paradoxes within the New Labour project and helps identify the dilemmas that a center-left political project must confront.

The three central sections of the book establish the conditions that give rise to these dilemmas. Part II investigates the way in which specific global processes reinforce domestic policy orientations to hasten the evolution of a distinctive post-Fordist British system of production. It considers how the organization of production forges individual and collective needs, and investigates the implications for political agency and interest formation. Part III extends this discussion of production, class formation, and the forging of political interests and agendas. It considers the specific ways in which deindustrialization and broader patterns of employment, as well as public policy, affect the experiences of women and ethnic minorities, and it looks at how these processes influence political dispositions and priorities. Part IV introduces the concept of "modular politics" to help illuminate the situational and context-dependent processes of identity formation, and it considers their implications for the normatively loaded issues of nationality and community in the UK.

The Conclusion returns to an evaluation of New Labour's governing project and a reconsideration of social democracy. The chapter reconsiders the dilemmas faced by New Labour and, more importantly, by any center-left project today. It integrates the analysis of New Labour's dilemmas and strategic options with an account of the developmental and structural conditions that give rise to these dilemmas and lays out the following set of challenges for New Labour and for center-left governance more generally:

Challenge 1: Enhance competitiveness while recollectivizing labor and transforming systems of production

Challenge 2: Design social policy that is responsive to the actually existing organization of production and social life

Challenge 3: Extend political recognition to modular communal identities

Challenge 4: Constitute British identity amidst competing territorial, ethnic, and supranational attachments and a complex patchwork of shared institutional authorities

Challenge 5: Reconnect politics to interests and collective attachments

I conclude by offering an alternative model of government: social democracy for a global age.

I am indebted to friends and colleagues who encouraged and assisted me in this project and offered critical advice: Marc Blecher, Sam Cohn, Peter A. Hall, David Held, Chris Howell, Peggy Kahn, Mark Kesselman, Marion Kozak, Andrei Markovits, Rianne Mahon, David Miliband, Craig Murphy, Pippa Norris, George Ross, Martín Sánchez-Jankowski, Susan Silbey, Sidney Tarrow, and Kent Worcestor. I would especially like to thank Samuel H. Beer. His account of British collectivism and the political contradictions that began to plague it in the 1970s inspired the ruminations that led to this project, and subsequent conversations, warnings, and exhortations, as always, proved invaluable. I am eager also to express my gratitude to Wellesley College, Norma Wilentz Hess, and the American Council of Learned Societies for generous support that greatly facilitated this effort.

Above all, I wish to thank my wife Carol Dougherty and our son Nathan Patrick Krieger. Carol meticulously read the manuscript and offered extremely helpful critical advice. Together they provided an extraordinary context that focused the mind and elevated the spirits, as my work on the book corresponded to their combined labor on a project immeasurably more valuable.

Part I
Situating New Labour

1

Social Democracy: The British Case in Theoretical and Comparative Perspective

To assess the viability of any center-left political project in the UK, it is imperative to come to terms, comparatively and conceptually, with the regime characteristics of the relevant governing model: European social democracy. Its rich and controversial legacy defines the heritage of an impressive range of governing projects in Europe, including – by provenance and by selective appropriation – Tony Blair's New Labour.

Is social democracy mortally wounded by the declining size and significance of the industrial working class, which robs social democracy of its historic agent? Can it resolve a contradiction at the core of contemporary social democracy "between commitment to economic globalization and the goals of egalitarian community" (Gray, 1997, p. 28)? Or does the future of social democracy rest on the strategic capacity of party leaders and activists to forge new electoral coalitions by pressing beyond traditional organizational, programmatic, and electoral legacies (Kitschelt, 1994)?

Given the historic importance of social democracy – and the evident stresses imposed on center-left government by neoliberal alternatives, the exacting demands of shifting constituencies, and the mountain of economic pressures constraining government largesse – it should not be surprising that debates about the future of social democracy have proliferated. A great deal of critical attention has been devoted to its meaning, practice, inclusionary and exclusionary boundaries, policy regimes, and organizational domains. An extensive and highly articulated literature addresses the daunting challenges facing center-left government and the dimming prospects of variants that aspire to preserve historical class associations and programmatic continuities.

In this chapter, I will clarify New Labour's model of government through a critical review of three alternative models of the organizational, electoral, and programmatic dynamic of European social democracy. In chapter 2, I will apply this framework to New Labour. This exercise should help map the political space and identify the range of strategic options available to a contemporary center-left government in the UK. It will establish a set of benchmarks from which to assess New Labour's appeal to and departure from social democratic traditions, and it will lend an important comparative dimension to analysis of New Labour. Finally, discussion of alternative social democratic models should help reveal, at least implicitly, the British Labour Party's motive and design in making itself over as New Labour. It will suggest that New Labour's organization and project lies outside the triangle of options described by these three models, and clarify the distinction between third way politics and social democracy, by offering an initial analytic assessment of New Labour's political project.

Here I develop three alternative social democratic models: *institutional-collectivist, analytical,* and *strategic adjustment*. It should be understood that there is considerable overlap among these models or interpretive schools, but the differences in emphasis which emerge critically implicate key variables that may be applied to analyze social democratic regimes (agency, policy approach, institutional orientation, political morality). My discussion begins from the most familiar alternative – what I call *institutional-collectivist social democracy* – which encompasses the British case. Table 1.1 summarizes these alternative conceptions of social democracy and compares them with New Labour.

Institutional-Collectivist Social Democracy

The institutional-collectivist model is a conceptual amalgam intended to represent base-line European social democracy, the broad conceptual frame for understanding British Labourism (or, as New Labour puts it more polemically, "Old Labour"). In general, the model describes the new political framework that developed in West European countries after the Second World War: a tacit alliance between the organized working class and large-scale business (Kesselman and Krieger, 1997b). From this perspective, the distributive cross-class growth coalitions and political bargains institutionalized in nationally specific "postwar settlements" set the framework for a general understanding of European party competition, political economy, and broad policy orientations.

The institutional-collectivist approach has dominated both the academic and the wider public discussion of social democracy in both the

Table 1.1 Comparison of New Labour and three models of social democracy

	Analytical	Strategic adjustment	Institutional-collectivist	New Labour
Agency	Industrial working class	Socioeconomic coalitions	Class actors mobilized by party and peak associations	Middle class down, middle England electoral coalition
Policy approach	Keynesianism	Strategic trade-offs	Postwar settlement, Keynesianism, and welfare state	"Third Way," Keynesianism, and business partnership
Institutional orientation	Tenure in office and centralized bargaining	Indeterminate relationship between institutions and party performance	Range in economic governance, social welfare, and labor regimes	Constitutional reform, reversal of statist centralization, and local participation
Political morality	Collective sovereignty	Equality, liberty, and community	Equality, class abatement, and collectivism	Equality, stakeholder society, Christian socialism, communitarianism, rights and responsibilities

United States and the United Kingdom. States intervened extensively to regulate economies, promote economic growth, and secure nearly full employment while expanding welfare provision. Within the model of institutional social democracy, Keynesian economics provides the rationale for a vigorous, activist governmental stance to assure aggregate demand through high levels of spending, which would in turn stimulate economic growth. As a result, the harmonious, positive-sum politics of class compromise became crystallized in the tacit agreements of the postwar settlement, and a period of sustained growth replaced traditional zero-sum conflict.

Despite changes in the economic context, both its normative and institutional dimensions contribute much to an understanding of center-left government. Its normative dimension is such standard fare of the center-left ethic that it requires only brief comment here. The institutional-collectivist model helped popularize the egalitarian ethic that inspires social democracy's resonant appeal to social justice. It also contributes the core concepts of collectivism, more recently recast as community – an important refinement for a more participatory age. Increasingly, the virtues of local communities and networks are counterpoised to traditional social democratic collectivism, which is associated with statist centralization and outmoded policy orientations (see Crouch and Marquand, 1995) – a victory for subsidiarity over federalism in the moral realm. In one form or another, collectivist appeals to a political morality based on egalitarianism and enhanced democratic participation continue to animate center-left politics, whatever reservations the overall model may inspire.

Regarding the institutional dimension, it is useful to emphasize this variable in a conception of social democracy to underscore how institutions shape, mediate, and refract political outcomes. First, the institutional-collectivist model of social democracy, more than the alternatives, permits the insights of historical institutionalism (Steinmo et al., 1992) to be explicitly applied to the analysis of social democratic regimes in critical policy areas, such as the welfare state or economic governance strategies (Esping-Andersen, 1985; Hall, 1986; Esping-Andersen, 1990). Secondly, by emphasizing the interactive effects of alternative institutional arrangements and normative claims, the model helps shed important light on the variation among social democratic regimes. By highlighting discrete elements of a policy mix of Keynesian economics and the welfare state, and by drawing attention to nationally specific institutional arrangements for governing the economy, the model provides a useful template for comparative European study, across a wide spectrum of cases, and has worked well for locating British politics within that framework (Hall, 1986; Marquand, 1988).

In fact, the institutional-collectivist model covers quite a range of empirical variation. At the height of the postwar settlement, there was extensive variation in the empirical application of the model in different countries in a host of dimensions: adherence to Keynesian principles; expression of collectivist principles; labor movement dynamics and the level and institutional form of labor inclusion in economic and social policy; approach to economic governance and the degree of state planning; levels of spending, institutionalization, universality, range of provisions, and comprehensiveness of the welfare state; and several more.

On one end of the spectrum of variants, the model includes – one might say embraces – the most robust case, Swedish social democracy. In the Swedish case, the electoral strength of the Social Democratic Party (SAP), combined with labor corporatism and solidaristic wage-bargaining strategies, led to a vast array of comprehensive, egalitarian, and universal welfare provisions (Esping-Andersen, 1990). The Swedish case also famously included an attempt at democratic control of investment through the Meidner Plan. It is therefore not surprising that when European comparativists speak of the "limits of Social Democracy" they point to Sweden, with the SAP so dominant for six decades until 1991, its high union density, and its impressive package of reform initiatives, as the *locus classicus* (Pontusson, 1992).

On the other pole, marginalized and neglected by many comparativists, one finds the "Labourism" that serves as the dramatic foil for Blair's modernization initiatives. Although seldom finding favor with academic observers smitten with the Swedish case, the UK, with its far more modest pretensions and its apparent solidity, nonetheless represents an important chastening alternative. In a Europe beset by restive constituencies and the neoliberal belt-tightening pressures imposed by the Maastricht convergence criteria, the terms of the EMU Stability and Growth Pact, and the anti-regulatory logic of intensified global competition, it becomes increasingly important to test the social democratic model to its *inner* limits. The British case represents a base-line social democratic model, in its heyday a significant and apparently durable achievement.

Social democracy in the UK

In its empirical expression in the UK, Samuel H. Beer captured the model in his classic study *British Politics in the Collectivist Age* (1969). As distinct from a liberal individualist model, collectivism meant, first, that the state assumed overall responsibility for economic governance and social welfare, and secondly, that the political instruments for policy making were collective: government operated by mobilizing powerful make-or-break constituencies, principally trade union and business confederations. At its high point, the collectivist polity claimed a symbiosis among its constituent elements. To borrow Beer's evocative language, the ideal foundations of the civic culture, a mix of deference and pragmatism, shaped – and were reinforced by – its choice mechanism (a hybrid system of parliamentary representation augmented by functional or corporatist representation). At the same time, relatively stable and unified producer groups (class actors) secured the social or class foundations of politics. Both party competition and policy debate operated smoothly within a classic European model of two-class/two-party competition. Collectivism likewise assumed the Keynesian paradigm of full employment, broad generalized consumption, and demand-driven growth, and presupposed expanding social provision within the limited horizons of a "residual" welfare state (Titmuss, 1958).

Accordingly, although it clearly represents a minimalist model, the UK's collectivism may be located within the general framework of social democratic compacts or policy regimes typical of the postwar settlement era preceding the oil shocks of 1973–4. It was weaker in its institutional reach (the National Economic Development Council was no Commissariat Général du Plan) and less robust in its policy aims (no serious consideration was given to worker participation, as in German co-determination or works councils, and never even a hint of collective share ownership through the build-up of wage-earner funds, as in Sweden's Meidner Plan). Moreover, although British tripartism, particularly in the area of incomes policies, involved the characteristic corporatist practice of state bargaining with peak associations, its episodic and one-sided nature (involving labor more than business) and the low durability of the bargains struck locate the UK very much on the edge of the corporatist model originally designed for Sweden, Austria, Switzerland, Belgium, and the Netherlands (see especially Schmitter, 1974; Goldthorpe, 1984).

In comparative terms, British social democracy is typically viewed as atheoretical, pragmatic, and insular, too closely linked to trade unions, and too preoccupied with public ownership as a reformist goal. It is considered to be non-interventionist in its approach to Keynesian demand management and unwilling to challenge the abiding neoliberal character of British economic management strategies (King and Wickham-Jones, 1998). All these policy orientations set British social democracy apart from its continental European counterparts.

The British case, however, represents an important alternative in part because its institutional underdevelopment was, in a sense, counterbalanced by its collectivist aspirations. It is worth recalling that a quite robust and well-articulated collectivist vision, consonant with this model, lies at the core of "Old Labour" political morality, and that the model in practice framed politics in postwar Britain for a quarter-century or more. The vision was perhaps captured best by C. A. R. Crosland, who wrote extensively in the 1950s of a new socialist society in the UK, distinguished by greater equality of incomes and opportunity, advanced by governmental intervention in economic affairs as well as by increased provision of social services. It heralded a normative shift in emphasis from property rights and competition to state responsibility for economic security and the virtues of co-operative action (Crosland, 1952, 1963). As Crosland explained, social democracy in the UK would be a hybrid: "non-capitalist to the extent that market influences are subordinated to central planning . . . [and] the power of the state is much greater than that of any one particular class"; socialist in its distribution of income; and "a pluralist society" (1952, pp. 38–45).

Animated more by ethical than institutional or policy aims, traditional social democracy in the UK has been identified with the normative goals of class abatement (Marshall, 1950), increased equality of both regard and outcome (Tawney, 1931), and a strong desire, as Crosland put it, "to replace competitive social relations by fellowship and social solidarity, and the motive of personal profit by a more altruistic and other-regarding motive" (1963, p. 54). British socialism is a rich hybrid, dominated by the standard welfare state traditions and statist collectivism associated with the postwar settlement. But it also draws its inspiration from a range of alternative appeals: the inspiration of syndicalist, anti-capitalist, working-class agitation mythologized by Chartism; the deeply religious appeals to "brotherhood" and altruism of the International Labour Party (ILP) tradition; the Fabian goal of collectivism in every sphere of social and economic life; and the Christian socialist aim of co-operative society based on communal (or community) ownership and devoid of the antagonisms fostered by competitive capitalism (Crosland, 1963). As will become clear in chapter 2, while rejecting the institutional dimensions of this model of social democracy, New Labour draws very strongly on normative claims in general, and on the Christian socialist tradition in particular.

The institutional-collectivist model: evaluation

A "big tent" approach that includes in one interpretive framework a significant range of labor regimes, institutional formats, strategies of economic governance, and delivery of social provisions, the institutional-collectivist model sacrifices sharp analytical boundaries or methodological coherence for the advantages of scope. For example, in explaining the evolution of institutional-collectivist social democracy, some studies have emphasized domestic political economy and institutional factors such as the specific organization of labor, capital, and the state, and the relationship between financial and industrial capital (Hall, 1986). Others focus on international political economy: for example, the collapse of the Bretton Woods arrangements and changes in the nature of capitalist production associated with the introduction of post-Fordist production systems (Markovits and Gorski, 1993). Still other studies pay more attention to fundamental attitudes and value changes in the political culture (Beer, 1982; Marquand, 1988). Indeed, some of the most interesting work crosses these somewhat arbitrary distinctions (Marquand, 1988; Hall, 1989; Markovits and Gorski, 1993). Many of the most insightful, context-rich studies of countries and regions within Europe have emerged from this approach.

The most glaring weakness of this model lies in the fact that social democracy in the form theorized by the institutional-collectivist model ceased to exist in pure form (if it ever existed) early in the 1970s. As is widely recognized, the postwar settlement and the social democratic regime identified by this model have experienced several phases of decline with little chance of renewal. Indeed, the model did not survive the oil shocks of 1973–4 in anything like its pure positive-sum form. Recently, the postwar settlement approach has been nourished by efforts to integrate new themes, such as the importance of collective identities that transcend and complicate class politics and the effects of international political and economic factors on a state's political institutions and processes (Kesselman and Krieger, 1997a). Nevertheless, despite the many efforts to analyze the denouement of the postwar settlement, no convincing positive account has been offered by the institutional-collectivism interpretation that effectively conceptualizes social democracy "after the fall."

The approach to the study of European politics based on the "rise and fall" of the postwar settlement and analysis of the institutional-collectivist social democratic regime associated with it therefore has important drawbacks. It leaves a legacy of primary emphasis on political economy constituted within a class-compromise model that cannot easily engage other dimensions of political contestation, such as the authoritarian–communitarian axis discussed below in the strategic adjustment model. It often accepts a focus on the nation-state as the unit of analysis, which does little to illuminate cross-border influences. In the end, it may be time to discard an increasingly time-worn assumption that contemporary politics can usefully be analyzed as a derivative development of bargains struck more than half a century ago.

Intensified by the end of the cold war, globalization and European integration, among other developments, have reduced the analytical utility of the postwar settlement model for the UK as for other national cases. Moreover, the weakening of boundaries between the national and transnational, together with complex questions about national identity and multinational states (like the UK, and many others), raises serious questions about the utility of a model designed for the comparative study of clearly rendered national (country) cases.

The institutional-collectivist model provides the classic base-line interpretation of European social democracy, including British Labourism, used by comparativists to illuminate the range of institutional and programmatic variation among country cases. By contrast, the next model emphasizes a core similarity that cuts across varied cases: the diminished numerical and strategic capacity of the industrial working class, social democracy's historic agent. Ironically, a heavily theoretical account that emerges from Marxist tradition provides the most powerful catalyst for practically minded center-left political elites to forsake working-class politics in the interests of electability.

Analytical Social Democracy

Analytical Marxism provides the methodological frame for one of the most sophisticated interpretations of social democracy, notable for its ability to combine careful historical and comparative study of the development of capitalism, critical application of both Marxist and analytical philosophy, and contemporary social scientific approaches such as game theory, rational choice analysis, and general equilibrium theory (see Mayer, 1994). The approach that I call, for purposes of comparison, *analytical social democracy*, is most fully articulated in the work of Adam Przeworski and his co-authors (Przeworski and Wallerstein, 1982; Przeworski, 1985; Przeworski and Sprague, 1986; Przeworski and Wallerstein, 1988; Przeworski, 1993).

Their interpretation emphasizes that "the degree of irrationality of capitalism is not given." Rather a kind of limited "functional socialism" is possible in developed capitalist countries that combine strong, well-organized unions engaged in centralized bargaining with social democratic governance strategies. Keynesianism provides the political and ideological framework for class compromise, and under propitious circumstances, investment, taxation, employment, and welfare policies contribute to favorable distributive outcomes. As Przeworski concludes, "the only countries in the world where almost no one is poor after taxes and transfers are countries that have pursued social democratic policies" (1993, p. 836).

Nonetheless, adherents of this approach recognize that social democracy is in trouble, due to a confluence of exogenous and endogenous factors that combine to erode central bargaining, to undermine the functioning of universalistic welfare programs, and to jeopardize the electoral base of social democratic parties. As a result, party strategy is locked into dire trade-offs. The numerical decline of industrial labor diminishes the traditional electoral base of socialist parties, even as cross-class electoral appeals "dilute the general ideological salience of class, and consequently, weaken the motivational force of class among workers." These workers are then more likely to stray to other parties that can appeal to them as individuals and citizens (Przeworski and Sprague, 1986, pp. 45–6).

It is important to add that, while Przeworski concludes that the social democratic model is no longer viable, he insists on the normative superiority of the ideal it embodies. He calls this ideal "collective sovereignty," understood as a set of democratic procedures by which people can alter existing institutions and determine the allocation and distribution of all available resources. Thus, analytical social democracy recognizes the quite debilitating dilemmas posed by electoral competition in a period of deteriorating performance in social democratic countries, but adherents insist nevertheless on the traditional normative commitments of socialism.

Przeworski and his colleagues deserve considerable credit for their elegant application of Marxist theory and contemporary social scientific methods to the analysis of social democracy. They are to be admired also for their honesty in disclosing the profoundly disquieting conclusions to which their analysis leads, while preserving the critical normative edge of their Marxian heritage. To its credit, analytic Marxism and its offshoot, analytic social democracy, offer an approach that selectively appropriates and, at the same time, challenges traditional Marxian analysis.

For example, Przeworski emphasizes the importance of alternative sources of collective identity and solidarity, such as race, nationality, gender, and religion. He moves a considerable distance from traditional Marxist understandings, insisting that the division of society into classes does not mean that politics will necessarily be defined by class. Likewise, Przeworski affirms that other sources of collective identity have as much claim to an "objective" basis as class, since they, too, are inherited by individuals and exist independent of will (1985, pp. 99–102). Whether or not one accepts the objective, as distinct from the "socially constructed," character of race, ethnicity, and gender, his insistence on the openness and fluidity of the process of class formation is refreshing. This claim, in turn, grounds Przeworski's critical insights concerning the strategic role played by political parties in forging collective identities, defining interests, and setting the policy and electoral-strategic terms in which class politics is fought in capitalist democracies.

It is important to recognize clearly, however, that Przeworski's openness extends only so far. At two important analytical junctures, the door is slammed shut. First, he insists on a narrow, conventional, and increasingly anachronistic definition of workers as "manual wage-earners employed in mining, manufacturing, construction, transport, and agriculture," in addition to those retired from these occupations or inactive members of their households (Przeworski, 1985, p. 104). Secondly,

Przeworski offers a traditional tableau from Marxist theory, harking back to Marx's own analysis of the events leading to the coup by Louis Bonaparte in 1851 (Marx, 1963), when he defines the competitive space on which party competition takes place: working-class parties represent the interests of workers, and bourgeois parties try to foist off their class interests as universalistic visions.

Thus, narrow and fixed definitions of class and conceptions of party competition reduce the applicability of what is otherwise a very rich theoretical framework. As a result, analytical social democracy is poorly equipped to ask important contemporary questions about the global division of labor and the sorting of labor market position and workplace experiences by race, ethnicity and gender. Paradoxically, Przeworski insists that the organization of politics admits the possibility of complicating collective identities, and that political parties play a big role in forging identities and defining interests that can inspire collective action, yet he bets very heavily on the increasingly suspect proposition that party competition nevertheless hinges on an immutable division of interest between manual labor and all other workers.

Evidence will be marshaled in part II to suggest how globalization and complex patterns of identity formation linked to decolonization and international structures of labor demand fragment class and influence the organization of politics. In chapter 10, I will discuss the implications of gendered identity formation, and the particular significance of the work and family nexus for the reconstruction of the competitive space open to political parties. For now, it is important to note that a significant alternative model of social democracy begins with quite powerful challenges to analytical social democracy's claim about what interests socialist parties can and cannot represent and how the competitive space for party politics is understood. The implications of this final model of social democracy for the center-left project in the UK today should become clear.

Strategic Adjustment Model

An alternative approach, introduced by Herbert Kitschelt, argues that social democratic parties have experienced considerable diversity in their electoral fortunes in the 1970s and 1980s, and that earlier claims about party dynamics, such as those offered by Przeworski and colleagues, cannot account for preference changes by voters and the newly configured "competitive space" now available to social democracy at the close of the century (Kitschelt, 1994). Applying social democracy as a generic concept to cover the range of West European parties that compete under social democratic, socialist, and labor banners, the *strategic adjustment* model applies systematic comparisons of the electoral trajectory of parties in nine countries to support an impressive set of counter-claims to the thesis of the demise of social democracy.

To emphasize here his disagreement with analytical social democracy, Kitschelt argues emphatically that no electoral trade-off consigns social democratic parties to defeat once they give up a claim that collective political agency is defined exclusively by traditionally understood class divisions. On the contrary, the fate of social democracy remains decisively in the hands of leaders and activists. Socialist parties are not locked into the tired framework of competition over distributive issues (the never-ending tug of war over the distribution of material resources shaped by industrial, taxation, fiscal, and social policy) and the ebb and flow of collective bargaining and industrial disputes. Instead, Kitschelt argues for a broader frame of reference in which politics turns on the salience of distributive choices relative to other priorities.

For Kitschelt, this means recognizing that the institutional arrangements that mobilized social democratic electoral support in the past, such as centralized labor movements closely linked to left governing parties (labor corporatism) together with universalistic, egalitarian, and comprehensive welfare policies, are as likely as not today to foster poor party performance. Success is readily available, however, to parties that can shift their focus away from representing the preferences of the traditional industrial worker understood exclusively in terms of putative distributional preferences. Instead, social democracy should forge the socioeconomic coalitions made possible by divisions identified in terms of education, occupation, gender and employment sector. These divisions shape consciousness and open voters more decisively to electoral appeals, Kitschelt concludes, than does traditional class identity: "Social democrats are no longer primarily the political agents of blue collar workers, but forge socioeconomic coalitions that include different segments of the labor market" (1994, p. 6).

Electoral advantage can therefore come quite readily to parties that can transform their strategies to take advantage of this wider scope of political preference formation and, in particular, not only appeal to voters on a left versus right distributive axis, but also take advantage of a second "communitarian division between libertarian and authoritarian demands" (Kitschelt, 1994, pp. 280–1). Thus, while loosening the linkage between class position and the "popular preference schedules" of voters, Kitschelt affirms a core assumption shared by all social democratic models. Political preferences follow interests shaped by everyday life experiences, the material consequences of occupational and sectoral structures, and economic group relations.

Much is gained in explanatory power by expanding the frame of reference of social democracy in the manner that Kitschelt has done. To its credit, the strategic adjustment model of social democracy is empirically grounded and fully consonant with the emergent pattern of normative claims and tactical overtures of actually existing social democratic parties in Europe. Moreover, it complicates politics in the best sense, by exploring the complexity of individual and collective preference formation with rich empirical referents. There seems little doubt that winners and losers in the electoral market place can be explained to an important degree by their differential ability to recognize and exploit the complicated and shifting matrix of voter preferences explored in this model.

Kitschelt rightly argues that as the trade-offs faced by party strategists have become more complicated than analytical social democracy recognizes, it becomes increasingly difficult to plot interests and values on a single axis. In fact, it seems increasingly unrealistic to suppose, as analytic social democracy must, that distributional preferences are defined exclusively by narrowly defined class position. The other assumption of Przeworski and colleagues is likewise suspect: that distributional preferences are more salient than other kinds of appeal, whether to insecurity and fear of "the other" or to local participation in the provision of social services. What about the blue-collar worker marginalized by "post-Fordist" production and tempted by the authoritarian appeal of a xenophobic party? How should an analysis of social democracy treat the highly educated technical worker in an internationally competitive sector, who may support reduced public expenditure and lower taxes, contemplate a center-right alternative, and support more community participation in educational or health care provisions? Kitschelt's approach applies an impressive range of cases, shows a grasp of both strategic and conceptual dilemmas, and adds considerable clarity to our understanding of the behavior of social democratic parties.

Of course, with this strategic adjustment approach, a different kind of clarity is lost. There is disconcerting vagueness in what might be called the political morality of social democracy. Kitschelt argues that social democratic parties must not confine themselves to the traditional pursuit of equality, but should balance equality with liberty and community. He argues that they should "consider the liberating potential of market transactions that free citizens from collective dependency relations and allow them to develop a measure of personal accountability and control," and take up "individual choice and self-governance concerns" (Kitschelt, 1994, p. 299). Thus despite a progressive orientation and an explicit insistence that social democracy affirm tolerance for cultural diversity, the normative stance seems inchoate, perhaps intentionally so. The strategic considerations of cross-class vote maximization and broad coalition building take precedence over the traditional core egalitarian or redistributive values of parliamentary socialism. The strategic adjustment approach, therefore, makes it very difficult to analyze social democracy in all its dimensions, including normative legacies and aspirations as well as political and institutional expressions.

In the end, according to the strategic adjustment model, social democracy assumes a nominalism, as the term is *de facto* applied to any party that carries a labor, socialist, or social democratic label. In an era marked by sizable disjunctures between the historic legacy of party names and programmatic orientations, boundary issues arise that the strategic adjustment approach is not well suited to resolve. Put differently, it would seem that its conceptual frame could not engage in a very interesting way a question implicitly posed by New Labour: can strategic adjustments, hybrid normative orientations, organizational makeovers, and programmatic innovations place a labor party outside the pale of social democracy? As we shall see, a party's strategic adjustment to place the institutions and normative orientations that have historically defined social democratic politics at arm's length contributes very substantially to political volatility and creates a set of challenges, not only for New Labour, but for left-of-center social democratic politics more generally.

Social Democracy Versus the Third Way

These three alternative models of social democracy help situate New Labour by analyzing historical antecedents, identifying critical strategic choices, and identifying both the enormous challenges and creative possibilities facing contemporary center-left politics. Of course, New Labour has laid claim to an original and ambitious modernizing agenda that exhibits some considerable ambivalence about the label "social democracy." It is clear, therefore, that no "off-the-rack" model of social democracy fits New Labour without significant alterations.

Nevertheless, the Blair government operates within a context that is framed in several important ways by the experiences of previous social democratic governments in the UK and in Europe more generally. First, the Blair government draws quite consciously on the deeply resonant normative claims of British socialism. Secondly, its efforts to innovate are inevitably limited by the institutional and policy legacies of traditional social democracy (Labourism) identified in the institutional-collectivist model. Thirdly, New Labour faces a range of dilemmas in going beyond a working-class base, which have been analyzed in very different terms – and with sharply contrasting conclusions – by Przeworski and Kitschelt, respectively. Clearly, New Labour is willing to take the risk identified by analytical social democracy that a dilution of the ideological salience of class encourages working-class voters to stray to other parties. It is betting that bold leadership, a host of successful and wide-ranging modernization initiatives, and strong economic performance will secure continued support from a middle-down coalition. As much as anything else, New Labour is defined by its strategic adjustments – a willingness to look in novel ways in what Kitschelt calls the "competitive space" opened to center-left parties that can make the most of a wider scope of political preferences, beyond left and right as traditionally defined in distributive terms.

The discussion in this chapter has presupposed that the debate about social democracy can help frame an analysis of New Labour's project and its attendant dilemmas. It provides a much needed benchmark for assessing what about social democracy is dead and what is very much alive – and which species of social democracy is at issue. It also makes clear that a new social democratic project, however labeled and described, can draw from a rich and varied European legacy. Some parts of this legacy, above all the fundamental role of working-class agency and the distributional politics and institutional arrangements that historically follow, are hotly contested. It is important to recognize, however, that despite the considerable variation across the three models of social democracy, one critical point is not in doubt. Social democratic politics crucially links politics with needs and material interests. What is more, political preferences flow from interests, and interests have a collective, as well as an individual, basis.

This kind of analysis of social democracy, one that infuses debate in the United States and Europe, has largely been crowded out in the UK by controversies about the third way. Clearly, the third way has provided New Labour with an original intellectual and policy framework, and has influenced thinking in the United States and, notably, that of German Chancellor Gerhard Schröder. The very originality of the third way project, however, means that the debates about social democracy and the third way are, for the most part, incommensurable: to an important degree they lack a common basis, standard, or measure of comparison.

The debate about social democracy assesses the electoral viability and programmatic vitality of center-left politics, defined by abiding interests achieved through the institutionalized collective organization of working-class agency. It is grounded in concrete comparative studies of historical antecedents. By contrast, the third way represents an intellectual framework and programmatic overture designed to transcend both traditional social democracy and neoliberalism, largely freed of interests and detached from institutionalized agency outside of government. Its calling card is modernization and invention, spurred by the demands of globalization and competition, positioned beyond the reach of antecedents. The third way aspires to innovative, progressive politics, and in its most articulated expression – although less consistently in its governmental application and "spin" – it theorizes a renewal of social democracy that draws, at least illustratively, on comparative insights (Giddens, 1998).

That said, there is a crucial parting of the ways between social democratic and third way politics. The debate about social democracy, whatever else it subjects to critical scrutiny, accepts the linkage between interests and political projects. In contrast, the third way not only presupposes the death of social democracy, but discloses a more radical break – and a different kind of break – with traditional politics than what is usually meant by referring to it as a politics beyond left and right. In fact, Tony Blair's third way severs the historic ties between political projects and material interests, whether understood by reference to class or any alternative schema for describing collectively distributed social and economic inequalities, group solidarities and attachments, and constituencies. What is this distinctive model of government that has emerged to frame New Labour's political project? How can comparative analysis from the perspective of alternative models of social democracy help reveal both its characteristics and the dilemmas it faces?

2

New Labour: Regime Characteristics, Strategic Options, Dilemmas

In rejecting a politics grounded in collective agency, attachments, and interests, while drawing upon the normative claims and heritage of social democracy, the third way politics of Tony Blair and New Labour retains an enigmatic quality. In addition, New Labour's modernizing agenda and the intellectual ferment it has inspired assure that major areas of policy remain in flux.

That said, some of the core defining features of the government's approach are clear. Blair has committed government to an ambitious program of modernization defined by a set of challenges – to develop top quality public services, especially in education and health; to take tough action on crime; to forge a new partnership with business; to introduce radical constitutional reforms; and to reconfigure the UK's relationship with Europe. In institutional and policy terms, New Labour's signature innovations are intended, in a variety of ways, to reverse the tendency of previous Labour governments in the UK to provide centralized "statist" solutions to all economic and social problems. Blair promises new approaches to economic, welfare, and social policy, shaped by the notion of a "stakeholder" society.

In electoral terms, New Labour rejects the notion of interest-based politics. In 1997, Labour enjoyed its electoral triumph because it was able to gain support across the socioeconomic spectrum from the middle class down. In organizational terms, it rejects the historic ties between Labour governments and the trade union movement, choosing instead to emphasize the virtues of a partnership with business. At the same time, New Labour is working to reinvent an ethos for the Labour Party, emphasizing the signal role of local communities and the responsibility of individuals and families. As a result, it may draw as much from communitarianism as from social democracy, and it contains strong elements of Christian socialism.

Chapter 1 analyzed three models of social democracy by reference to a set of key variables: agency, policy approach, political morality, and institutional orientation. In this chapter, we will analyze New Labour in the same terms – in effect, ideal-typically. The aim here is not to provide an exhaustive inventory of Blair's project, but to identify critical elements of an emergent model of politics, emphasizing traits that distinguish it from the three models of social democracy. What are the regime characteristics of the center-left governing model that New Labour represents – the dilemmas and the strategic options it faces? How does it aim to reorganize politics and construct a distinctive governing model in order to meet the challenges of a global era?

In this chapter, each component of New Labour's governing model is briefly considered in turn. In the concluding section, I will discuss the dilemmas presented by the three models of social democracy analyzed in chapter 1 set against Blair's own view of the dilemmas faced by New Labour.

Agency

In terms of agency, New Labour has done more than simply redefine and expand its constituencies beyond the blue-collar worker. While the strategic adjustment model links preference formation to social structure, thereby associating electoral and socioeconomic coalitions,[1] New Labour associates agency more or less exclusively with a very broad-based electoral coalition that defies socioeconomic definition. Recognizing that the traditional solidary working-class core of the Labour Party has no more socialist exit option, New Labour very effectively positioned itself in 1997 to concentrate on "swing" voters: those who had voted Conservative in 1992 but had seriously considered voting for Labour. As Blair acknowledged, the target voters were "middle income, middle England," an expression that connotes a milieu and set of aspirations that distance the party from traditional solidary working-class constituencies.[2] Although the term applied by Labour Party strategists is a "middle-down coalition," it is more an arithmetic aggregation of voters than a true coalition in the sense of an alliance or fusion of interests.[3] It pinpoints an electoral strategy – to "represent the great majority of the public, not an assemblage of minorities" (Seyd, 1998, p. 60) – without claiming to constitute a socioeconomic coalition defined by interests and empowered by institutional linkages. As corroborating evidence, Labour's target voters in 1997 were almost indistinguishable from those of the Conservatives and Liberal Democrats: ABC1s[4] and homeowners (Sanders, 1998).

Of course, political agency involves more than voter profiles. It also involves the collective organization of interests, and in this regard New Labour's message is also extremely clear. New Labour quite categorically asserts a different relationship with organized labor than that of any previous Labour government. The government's arm's-length, potentially hostile relationship with trade unions is expressed in a variety of ways: symbolically in the courting of business elites, materially in the party's reduced financial reliance on unions, and institutionally in the rejection of any "labor inclusion" model of corporatist bargaining (see Howell, 1998). As a net result, organized labor has lost the capacity to set agendas and shape policy.

Nothing speaks more clearly to New Labour's approach to agency than its industrial relations project. Blair could hardly be more categorical in insisting that the Conservative reforms on the industrial relations system that eviscerated "trade union power and privilege" in support of managerial flexibility are, in his view, irreversible. In a signed article placed for maximum political effect in the mass circulation *Daily Mail* during the heat of the 1997 election campaign, Blair made this commitment unmistakably clear:

> There will be no return to the trade union laws of the 1970s. Laws banning secondary and flying pickets, on secondary action, on ballots before strikes and for union elections – on all the essential elements of the 1980s laws – will stay. If anyone, in the trade unions or elsewhere, thinks we have transformed the Labour Party in order to go back to those days, they should wake up. It won't happen.

In this maximum-impact public forum, Blair promised no return to the closed shop, but he did defend New Labour's pledge that workers should have the right to choose to have union representation in accordance with a majority ballot. He noted that New Labour's policy on union recognition was broadly based on legislation in the United States, drawing a parallel with the National Labor Relations Act, and added that the right of workers to organize and bargain collectively was "a principle enthusiastically endorsed by Ronald Reagan when he was the US President – a man not even the Tories could claim was a soft touch for union power." In a remarkable statement to reassure an electorate that might be jittery on this issue, Blair insisted that despite the promise concerning union recognition under New Labour, "Britain will remain with the most restrictive trade union laws anywhere in the western world" (Blair, 1997).[5]

Union recognition and regulation, and the construction of a New Labour industrial relations regime, speak directly to the core issue of class agency. The White Paper *Fairness at Work*, published in May 1998, stands as the central testament of New Labour's approach to these issues.

Although subject to modification, Blair has made clear that it stakes out the whole legislative agenda in this area until the next election (Department of Trade and Industry, 1998).[6] How should this key document be assessed?

Fairness at Work helps establish a framework for enhanced individual rights and benefits of workers in important domains such as unfair dismissal, maternity and parental leave, and the minimum wage, bringing the UK closer to European norms. With reference to the collective rights of organized labor that are more critical to the question of political agency, however, the implications are more ambiguous.

The central gain for organized labor concerns union recognition. Highly politicized during the campaign, union recognition remains a contentious test of government–union relations. Labour's election manifesto included an apparently straightforward commitment: "Where a majority of the relevant workforce vote in a ballot for the union to represent them, the union should be recognised." Predictable complications began soon after the election, when the Prime Minister asked the Trades Union Congress (TUC) and the Confederation of British Industry (CBI), the traditional peak association adversaries in corporatist bargaining, to negotiate implementation. Agreement foundered on a number of points, and especially on the matter of balloting rules. Should a ballot for union recognition require a "Yes" vote by a majority of those eligible to vote (the CBI position) or by a majority of those casting ballots (the TUC position and the normal practice in ballots for union recognition elsewhere: for example, in the United States and in the election of MPs). *Fairness at Work* proposes a compromise: union recognition will require a majority of those voting, but a minimum of at least 40 percent of those eligible to vote. In addition, the White Paper hands unions a critical asset. It allows "card-check" recognition: union recognition will require no ballot where a union can establish that a majority of the employees are union members.

This blend of improved individual and collective rights benefits employees and unions and, in Blair's words, attempts to "change the culture of relations in and at work – and to reflect a new relationship between work and family life" (Department of Trade and Industry, 1998, Foreword, p. 1). Apart from safeguards afforded those engaged in lawful industrial action, however, the capacity of unions to strike or otherwise advance collective aims remains fundamentally unchanged. In fact, the Prime Minister's foreword makes it clear that the government's program for promoting partnership between employers and employees delivers on his *Daily Mail* campaign pledge. As Blair puts it, "Even after the changes we propose, Britain will have the most lightly regulated labour market of any leading economy in the world" (Department of Trade and Industry, 1998, Foreword, p. 1).

It seems clear that, where questions of agency blend into its legislative agenda for consolidating an industrial relations regime, New Labour has gone far to confirm the loss of working-class and trade union power that was the preoccupation of eighteen years of Conservative government. It has transformed the historic collaboration between party and unions within the labor movement into a frosty arm's-length relationship that severely strains any social democratic project.

Viewed retrospectively, New Labour's electoral triumph in 1997 may lend an air of inevitability to the government's decision to open an historic chasm between the party and its social base. We will argue, on the contrary, that New Labour's strategy to bypass interest-based, institutionally grounded socioeconomic coalitions in favor of middle-class, middle England is neither inevitable nor necessarily durable. New Labour rejects not merely "Old Labour" class politics, but all politics connected to occupational or socioeconomic positions and grounded in collective attachments, needs, and material interests. This approach has far-reaching consequences that this book will endeavor to examine. For a start, it contributes to an historic level of electoral volatility that may imperil New Labour's future success. More profoundly, New Labour appears to reject conventional class-based agency without substituting a richer, more differentiated framework for reconnecting politics with actually existing interests and group attachments. Much of the analysis of the book is intended to illuminate these interests and attachments, their fluid context-dependent character, and the new – and rather uncharted – political terrain they constitute. In the final chapter, we will return to a set of challenges that point toward a social democracy for a global age, one that insists on grounding politics once again in enduring needs and interests, but interests understood in a different way.

Policy Approach

The subject of intense scrutiny and debate, both from within and outside the government, the orientation of New Labour policy has been clearly articulated in several critical areas. We briefly discuss in turn the government's economic and social policy orientations.

Economic policy approach

Time will tell whether New Labour thinking on macroeconomic policy, backed by new political will, can provide the cohesion previously lacking in postwar British economic management strategies. On the one hand, much has been made of the influence of revitalized Keynesian ideas and reform proposals (Hutton, 1995). On the other, critics consider New

Labour economic policy evidence of a neoliberal ascendancy and the sign of a new cross-party political settlement engineered by Labour (Hay, 1998). It should come as no surprise that there is evidence for both claims.

For example, the new spending plans for social services announced by the Chancellor of the Exchequer, Gordon Brown, in July 1998, to which I will return briefly below, can be read as a sign of a Keynesian redirection or, at least, correction, in public spending. At the same time, the neoliberal direction of policy has been clear from the earliest days of New Labour government. The first shot fired in the Blair revolution, the announcement within a week of the election by Gordon Brown that the Bank of England would be given "operational independence" in the setting of monetary policy, is quite significant in this regard. The decision transfers out of cabinet a critical, and highly political, prerogative of government and in this sense flies in the face of New Labour's promises to expand the democratic accountability of government. In addition, with Brown attuned to the pressures of international financial markets and the control of inflation and stability as the key goals of macroeconomic policy, the transfer of authority over monetary policy consecrates a marketization of economic policy – a neoliberal turn in policy – more generally.[7]

New Labour's economic policy, like its social policy discussed below, is strategically eclectic. Within the mix, it is probably fair to say that neoliberalism dominates and that Labour macroeconomic policy displays a high order of convergence with Conservative policy (see Howell, 1998; Hay, 1998). That said, when it comes to New Labour's economic policy orientation the whole is greater than the sum of its parts – or at least it is different in political motif.

To apply the logic of alternative social democratic models, New Labour challenges the economic and social policy orientations of the Keynesian welfare state, which figure so prominently in the institutional-collectivist model, for at least two distinct reasons. First, a modernized Labour Party will not give into trade unionist pressures. Secondly, and more interestingly, Keynesianism is suspect because it treats national economies as if they are essentially contained within national borders, emphasizing the domestic economy over international trade and investment (see Giddens, 1998, p. 16). In contrast, New Labour's economic policy orientation is implacably global.

It is not enough, however, to note the incomplete ascendancy of neoliberalism or the terms of New Labour's resistance to Keynesianism. It must be added that the New Labour policy orientation also rejects the hard edges of Thatcherite neoliberalism, its mean-spirited, anti-egalitarian streak and its resentful dismissal of the welfare state for its almost unmitigated destruction of initiative and autonomy. New Labour's claim to originality begins here with the government's central preoccupation with the implications of globalization for its governing project and its aim to reconstitute social policy as a means of personal renewal in the service of competitiveness.

For New Labour, globalization means that government cannot control demand, so it must focus on supply-side interventions. Since capital is international, mobile, and not subject to control, industrial policy and planning are futile. Rather, government can enhance the supply of labor through skills-based education and training; it can maintain the labor market flexibility inherited from the Thatcher regime, and help attract investment to the UK. Strict control of inflation, low taxes, and tough limits on public expenditure help promote both employment and investment opportunities (see Driver and Martell, 1998, pp. 32–73). At the same time, industrial policy is directed at enhancing the competitive strength of key sectors and developing a "partnership" with business through R & D, training, technology, and modernization policies (Reynolds and Coates, 1996). Blair, his economic policy team and his supporters hope that this approach helps build a stable and competitive economy, one in which all Britons have a "stake." New Labour refers to its vision as "the stakeholder economy" or "the stakeholder society," a key ingredient in New Labour's political morality to which we will return below.

Social policy approach

To an important degree, differences in economic doctrine are not what matter most in policy terms. In fact, British governments in the past have never followed any economic theory consistently in the making of economic policy, whether Keynesianism or monetarism, and today the economic policy of New Labour is, by its very nature, pragmatic and eclectic. The political consequences of economic orientations are more significant: each economic doctrine helps justify a broad moral and cultural vision of society, provide motives for state policy, and advance alternative sets of values. Should the state intervene to reduce inequalities through the mildly redistributive provisions of the welfare state and sustain the ethos of a caring society (collectivist social democracy)? Should the government back off and allow the market to function competitively and thereby promote entrepreneurship, competitiveness, and individual autonomy, recognizing that there will be losers as well as winners (Thatcherite neoliberalism)? Or should the government help secure an inclusive stakeholder economy, in which business has the flexibility, security, and mobility to compete, and workers have the skills and training to participate effectively in the global labor market (New Labour)? These alternatives make clear that economic management strategies are closely linked to social or welfare policy.

As with economic policy, social policy has provided an opportunity for the government to balance pragmatism and innovation in an effort to implement a new modernizing approach. Thus, the Blair government rejects the attempted welfare retrenchment of Conservative governments, which seemed punitive and ideologically driven, and did little to create opportunities; it also rejects the egalitarian traditions of the UK's collectivist era, which emphasized entitlements and normatively embraced redistributive measures to reduce class-based inequalities. Instead, New Labour focuses its policy on training and broader social investment applied individually as an alternative to neoliberalism and institutional-collectivist social democracy.

Following his New Democratic counterpart in the United States, the Prime Minister promises to create a modernized, leaner welfare state, in which people are actively encouraged to seek work. New Labour's reform initiatives emphasize efficiencies and attempts to break welfare dependency, linking social policy to the trademark themes of business partnership, community, and the determination to associate rights with responsibilities. As Blair put it at a conference on social policy and economic performance in Amsterdam in January 1997, the modern welfare state must "combine opportunity and responsibility as the foundation of community" (quoted in Deacon, 1998, p. 307).

At the center of the policy, efforts to spur entry into the labor market combine carrots and sticks. The positive inducements include extensive training programs, especially targeted at youth, featuring the "New Deal" initiative with £3.5 billion earmarked to tackle unemployment. In addition, the government provides incentives to private industry to hire new entrants to the labor market, as well as extensive wage subsidies. But there are also negative inducements. New Labour's welfare regime requires strict positive compliance, with eligibility restrictions and reductions in coverage providing quite formidable sources of compulsion (see Shaw, 1998). As part of the New Deal program, those between eighteen and twenty-five claiming the dole for more than six months stand to lose all benefits if they decline all options for work or training offered under the government's welfare-to-work plan. Moreover, as with the Conservative Jobseekers' Allowance, the New Labour initiative stipulates that those individuals considered "vulnerable" (pregnant women or those with dependants) lose 40 percent of their entitlement should they fail to satisfy the terms of their "welfare to work" contracts (Hay, 1998). As the government's Green Paper on welfare reform makes clear, New Labour's social policy approach combines three distinct formulations about the aims of welfare: it can promote a self-interested social well-being through incentives; it compels compliance with social norms; it provides a means for moral regeneration (Deacon, 1998). Above all, the New Deal affirms a substantial commitment to improve the skills and increase the employability of youth, although its success in moving the unemployed and economically inactive beyond a revolving door of low-paying jobs and benefits and into solid employment remains to be seen (Oppenheim, 1998).

This hybrid approach clearly marks a significant departure from the traditional institutional-collectivist view of welfare provisions, following T. H. Marshall (1950), as a modern extension of citizenship rights. It can be read positively as a communitarian appeal to " a greater sense of mutual obligation" (Deacon, 1998, p. 311). Alternatively, one can see in the strict compliance and compulsion components of the program the elements of a more authoritarian approach, a position located on the wrong end of Kitschelt's communitarian axis of party competition (defined by libertarian versus authoritarian orientations).

Wherever one places the emphasis, it seems clear that Labour's "New Contract for Welfare" puts a new signature on social policy. At the same time, New Labour draws political strength from the "Old Labour" legacy of commitment on the "caring" social policy issues. Like everyone else on the political scene, New Labour strategists know full well that the government must operate within a context set by the institutional and policy legacies of social democracy. For example, with 87 percent of Britons having no private health insurance, an overwhelming majority of them rely exclusively on the National Health Service (NHS), the "jewel in the crown" of Old Labour's welfare state, for their health care – and nearly everyone receives most of their critical care in NHS hospitals. They also know that in the 1997 general election many millions of voters, all across the political and occupational spectrum, in all regions, and across all age groups, were deeply concerned about public services and the future of the welfare state; they blamed the Conservatives for problems in these areas and even blamed Tory social policies for increases in crime. Polls made clear that by 1997 the health service had knocked employment out of first place as the most urgent issue on people's minds. It is a measure of the concern that people had for the caring issues that a majority of the Conservatives' own supporters worried about what might happen to health and other social services with another Tory government (King, 1998b).

Under these circumstances, reform of the NHS, for example, is unlikely to satisfy the pledge of radical reform of the welfare state and, indeed, policy in this area may not differ a great deal from what might be expected under a traditional Labour government riding an economic upswing. This context helps explain the curious *trompe l'oeil* quality to New Labour's social policy agenda: attention is directed toward underspecified commitments to radical welfare state reforms, and the spotlight is cast on modernizing, communitarian alternatives to statist solutions and a redesign of welfare policy. All the while, party leaders and British voters alike recognize that a significant element of Labour's appeal is actually based on Labour's social democratic institutional-collectivist legacy of commitment on the "caring" social policy issues.

It is interesting to consider in this light the much heralded spending plans for social services announced by Gordon Brown in July 1998. The plans call for a three-year increase in public expenditure of more than 10 percent – with dramatic increases in cash spending for education and health care. The announcement generated quite a furor, with observers divided on the merits of the plan and its implications. Does it represent a return to big government and a retreat from the fiscal conservatism that Blair and Brown promised? Or is it great political theater with relatively modest budgetary or policy implications? After all, due in large part to the aging population, social expenditures, and especially health care costs, increased under the Conservatives, and the strong economy should be able to float the increases without undue difficulties. Or does the spending review illustrate a distinctive New Labour approach, increasing health care out of necessity and expanding education to achieve the critical goal of a high-skilled, competitive workforce for a global age? Uncertainty about this initiative illustrates a basic paradox at the heart of New Labour's policy: what is most distinctive about New Labour and potentially most radical rests on a foundation of conservative (neoliberal) economics and traditional institutional-collectivist social policies and appeals.

Areas such as social and welfare policy provide important additional information about the government's policy approach. The commitment to no increase in income taxes for the duration of Blair's first government (a key part of the campaign's "five-year pledge") combined with a categorical refusal to run up deficits for traditional "spending" programs means sharp limits on social democratic efforts to reverse welfare retrenchment. For example, there is little likelihood that the Blair government will substantially restore the real value of state-provided pensions or reverse the Conservative reform initiative to effectively wind down the State Earnings Related Pension Scheme (SERPS) (see Pierson, 1994, pp. 58–64). More broadly, Brown's third budget announced in March 1999 appeared to signal a decisive shift in social policy from universal to means-tested benefits.

As the discussion thus far should make clear, the political valence of Blair's government in some key areas of economic and social policy has shifted decisively from that of its Labour Party predecessors. Its pre-eminent concern to strengthen competitiveness by reinforcing core elements of the inherited Conservative industrial relations regime renders the notion that unions might evolve into an "internal opposition" by no means a fanciful one. New Labour's commitment to partnership with business and its resolve to ensure fiscal stability, combined with its approach to economic and social policy, place it outside the boundary of all three models of social democracy. Like the economic policy orientations that emphasize neoliberal policy directions and preserve much of the industrial relations regime inherited from the Thatcher era, the social policy orientations of New Labour invite serious reflection on the ultimate consequences of New Labour's strategic adjustments for the consolidation of a center-left project.

Political Morality

As noted in chapter 1, British social democracy has not been as impressive as its French, German, or Swedish counterparts in developing innovative policy or institutional capacities for achieving significant reforms. In an important sense, the "comparative advantage" of British social democracy lies in the ethical dimension, which gives it, paradoxically, both depth and ambiguity. New Labour is making good use of this opening as it works to reinvent an ethos for the Labour Party: in Blair's words, "to define a new relationship between citizen and community for the modern world" (1996, p. 215).

New Labour's political morality draws on the egalitarian legacies of the institutional-collectivist model of social democracy. At the same time, the normative claims of New Labour are at a carefully measured distance from the party's heritage: its class abatement motif and any redistributive design or solidaristic basis in a class-conflict model. Thus, Blair affirms a commitment to the normative values of socialism, but interprets what that means in a way that studiously avoids class as a reference point. For Blair, class is not the source of social solidarity or the binding attachment that drives politics. Class neither defines a politics framed by group-based inequalities nor inspires ameliorative social mobilization.

In a carefully crafted and quite influential speech to the Fabian Society to mark the fiftieth anniversary of the 1945 general election, Blair argued that the "ethical basis of socialism" – and not what he called the "economic dogma" – is the only socialist foundation that has stood the test of time and survived the collapse of communism. Blair then described his conception of the normative basis of New Labour's concept of socialism:

> This socialism is based on a moral assertion that individuals are interdependent, that they owe duties to one another as well as themselves, that the good society backs up the efforts of the individuals within it, and that common humanity demands that everyone be given a platform on which to stand. It has objective basis too, rooted in the belief that only by recognising their interdependence will individuals flourish, because the good of each does depend on the good of all. This concept of socialism requires a form of politics in which we share responsibility both to fight poverty, prejudice and unemployment, and to create the conditions in which we can truly build one nation. (Blair, 1995)

Blair's remarks capture New Labour's core normative themes: interdependence (rather than conflict); commonality of values and aims defined in terms of community or humanity (but never in class terms); and the responsibility of individual citizens (rather than – or linked to – their rights or entitlements). There is considerable variation in the explicit language and in the choice of normative traditions invoked to supply the political morality in New Labour's model of government. Indeed, Blair and his supporters are likely to revise, discard, and introduce new catchwords as conceptions gel and as popular response may warrant. Despite these variations, however, the underlying motifs of New Labour's political morality seem quite consistent.

The core normative claims are sometimes associated with the stakeholder notion, a vision of society as a joint stock enterprise operating on behalf of all paid-up members or shareholders. All who play by the rules and contribute stand to gain. The stakeholder concept emphasizes the importance to society of rules and responsibilities as well as the benefits of membership (in family, company, community, nation). It tends to gloss over the structured inequalities in the distribution of the "shares" or "stakes" (Finer, 1997).

Alternatively, the language and framing of New Labour's normative dispositions may draw on Christian socialist traditions, which have played an important role in the development of Blair's political thinking. Blair attributes his rejection of both a narrow Tory view of self-interest and the determinism he associates with Marxism to his Christian values. In addition, he explicitly equates what he considers the ethical basis of socialism, "the view that better social conditions enhance personal responsibility," with Christian socialism (Blair, 1996, pp. 57–61).

In the end, the critical focus that Blair places on the new relationship between citizen and community, emphasizing localism, deliberation, and individual or family responsibility, makes the collectivist core of New Labour as communitarian as it is socialist (see Etzioni, 1995). For Blair, the community is constituted by a dense network of rights and responsibilities and bound together by the mutual obligations imposed on individuals as family members, employers and employees, teachers, councilors, taxpayers and neighbors.

This perspective has far-reaching policy implications. With reference to education policy, for example, there has been a great deal of discussion about increased community-based participation, local authority control, and efforts to encourage parents to take more direct responsibility for schooling. In addition, drawing on its communitarian disposition, New Labour's approach to law and order includes expanding police–community partnerships and improving relations with ethnic minority groups. It considers tough action on crime as part of its approach to community, which emphasizes the responsibilities of individuals and citizens and insists that people play by the rules or face the consequences. In an interesting twist, since a visit to New York in 1996 by Labour's Shadow Home Secretary to examine that city's success in reducing street crime, Tony Blair has adopted the "zero-tolerance" approach trumpeted by New York's Republican mayor, Rudolph Giuliani (Benyon and Edwards, 1997). Like the stakeholder and Christian socialist perspectives, New Labour's communitarianism asserts a relationship between individual and society or humanity. In Blair's famous phrase, everyone is part of "one nation, one community" (Driver and Martell, 1998, p. 28). The perspective intentionally sidesteps class and implicitly effaces gender, ethnicity, and indeed all group attachments and any endemic patterns of group-based inequality.

Other areas of public policy raise questions about the implications of New Labour's "no rights without responsibilities" communitarian approach. In practical terms, what does it mean to put concern for the family at the center of policy? The UK has the highest divorce rate in Western Europe and very nearly the highest rate of female labor participation. Yet child care remains overwhelmingly a private responsibility. Like other parents, although more acutely, single mothers therefore experience the gap between child care need and public provision of care even more acutely than other parents. In the late 1980s, the issue of support for single mothers in the UK came on the public agenda – as it had earlier in the United States – as a defining idiom of the problem of "welfare dependency." Initially, for the purposes of social policy, single mothers were treated as mothers, and the Conservative government launched a dramatically unsuccessful effort to secure greater financial contributions by absent fathers through the Child Support Agency. Subsequently, greater attention was paid to single mothers as paid workers, and the Major government proposed that special benefits and premiums to lone parents be withdrawn, an approach implemented by the Labour government (Lewis, 1998).

As the controversy that erupted in December 1997 over a quite limited reduction in single-parent benefits vividly illustrates, ambiguity in normative dispositions can become heavily politicized. Those who interpreted the cut in benefits as punitive – or as insufficiently sensitive to the difficulties that lone mothers face in balancing work and family responsibilities – accused Christian socialists in high places of pressing a male breadwinner model of the family (Lloyd, 1997). The accusation was just as vigorously denied, and supporters of Labour's egalitarian concern for women could point to the *Childcare* Green Paper with its promise of generous tax credits, the National Childcare Strategy which aims to subsidize the cost of child care and increase its supply (Oppenheim, 1998), and the host of "family-friendly policies" in the *Fairness at Work* White Paper (Department of Trade and Industry, 1998, ch. 5). The normative overtones of New Labour's family policy stir controversy in part because they reflect powerful cross-currents of values and policy directions. It is probably fair to offer three observations. First, there are a variety of perspectives on the family within New Labour, some privileging traditional family forms and others not. Second, the principle of gender equality is broadly affirmed. Third, key policy makers are nonetheless concerned about the proliferation of lone-mother families. For some, attention to single mothers flows from practical concerns about the economic circumstances normally faced by single-parent families and the child-rearing challenges posed by absent fathers. For others, the concern reflects more normatively loaded preferences for two-parent families.[8]

Although battles are still being fought for the normative and policy directions of New Labour, any signs of a familist undertow in social policy, with its indications of special support for two-parent families, are quite significant. If confirmed, these normative orientations, like the authoritarian elements of its welfare reform, pull New Labour's communitarianism to the right. Once again, as with agency and economic policy approaches, New Labour crosses the boundary of social democracy: even the strategic adjustment model – the most normatively amorphous of the three models – presupposes movement towards left-libertarian, not right-communitarian politics (see Kitschelt, 1994, pp. 280–7).

More generally, the communitarian focus on the responsibilities of families, much like the equally bromide appeals to community and the stakeholding society, raises a serious question about whether the normative framework supplied by New Labour is sufficiently rigorous or substantial to guide policy and frame public debate. To take the example at hand, whether punitive or practical, questions can be raised about a family policy that begins with cuts in lone-mother benefits before comprehensively addressing the fundamental issue of child care – a matter that is, as one observer put it, "fundamental to the ethics of the modern state" (Lewis, 1998, p. 13).

We will return below to the implications of New Labour's vision of family and community. In chapter 5, we will investigate the actual experiences of work and family that frame the lives of British women, then reconsider the gendered implications of social policy, and the dilemmas posed by New Labour's family policy and employment policy, and the inadequate treatment of a set of problems associated with the work–family nexus. In chapter 9, we will consider some political consequences of New Labour's communitarian perspective, particularly in the context of ethnic minority communities. And in chapter 10, we will return to consider these themes in challenge 2 and challenge 3.

Institutional Orientation

We come at last to the institutional orientation, which includes some of the most radical and potentially transformative elements of New Labour. New Labour's institutional and constitutional innovations are intended, in a variety of ways, to reverse the statist tendencies of institutional-collectivist social democracy and, in some cases, to reconfigure profoundly the territorial dimensions of UK politics. The reform initiatives are especially noteworthy for their tendency to devolve centralized powers, from the limited decentralization of housing and education to the potentially far-reaching rearticulation of governance within the UK. Constitutional reform promises measured devolution to Scotland and Wales, and the settlement regarding Northern Ireland sets in motion institutional changes with significant constitutional and practical ramifications, including a Northern Ireland assembly, an intergovernmental council, and a set of cross-border executive bodies.

It should be noted, moreover, that although much of New Labour's agenda concerning subcentral government is focused on the political role of nations within the UK, devolution within England is also on the agenda. The Blair government's program includes the quick formation of regional Development Agencies and, in the long term, the introduction of regional assemblies. At the same time, changes in the governance of London are on the fast track. New Labour has no plans to reconstitute the Greater London Council or to return to city government the powers currently enjoyed by quangos and by London's boroughs, but the formation of a city-wide strategic authority with extensive powers and the direct election of an American-style mayor represents a significant reform. Although New Labour appears genuinely ambivalent about decentralization, with the loss of central government direction and control that it entails, the Blair government has generally emphasized greater local democracy and accountability (see Holliday, 1997; Driver and Martell, 1998, pp. 140–5). It is important to add that the decentralizing logic of the institutional reforms, combined with the informality and potential transparency of the participatory processes, clearly locates New Labour's institutional policies on the left of the libertarian–authoritarian dimension, as predicted by the strategic adjustment model.

With the Conservative Party staunchly defending a centrally governed four-nation union, ironically, from their position in Parliament after the 1997 election as an England-only party, these institutional and constitutional issues promise to differentiate the two major parties most sharply. An important part of New Labour's agenda to modernize the UK for a global age, these institutional reforms signal bold leadership. They represent an ambitious, laudable, and yet potentially risky effort to articulate new administrative and representative structures to make sense of complicated cross-currents of central authority and subsidiarity.

Time will tell whether these initiatives extend democratic accountability and effectively modernize the institutions of government, or whether they destabilize politics by fostering multiple regional and national identities from below the level of the United Kingdom, even as the ever-shifting and tense relationship between the UK and the EU complicates UK identity from above (see Sanders, 1998). There is little question, however, that they represent a bold and radical agenda for institutional change that touches important issues of national identity, sovereignty, and political community. We will return in chapter 3 to the UK's EU dilemmas, now focused acutely on the question of participation in the single currency initiative, and we will further consider the implications of this complex interplay between subcentral, UK, and supranational government in chapter 10 in the context of challenge 4.

Finally, without diminishing the potential significance of New Labour's institutional reform agenda, one can also note its electoral utility in mobilizing support for a purportedly radical, modernizing agenda when, in fact, quite a few positions – on taxation, unemployment, law and order, and social policy, among other areas – departed little from those of the Conservatives and Liberal Democrats. "With the abandonment of social democracy, Labour had little to offer in the economic and social field," observed Patrick Seyd. "Institutional reforms provided a substitute sense of radicalism, required to satisfy part of its electoral constituency" (Seyd, 1998).

Social Democratic and Progressive Dilemmas

As a heuristic exercise,[9] it is interesting to reflect on the dilemmas that alternative models pose for New Labour: the strategic options they pose, the tensions to which they give rise, and the motivation they provide for the redesign of the Labour Party's political project. In sum, how does the UK's New Labour measure up against the three models of social democracy that have been presented?

To begin, it is easy to see that New Labour rejects any explicit association between class agency and party constituency, refusing to be trapped in the downward spiral of electoral trade-offs to which Przeworski consigns social democratic parties. It quite consciously breaks the linkage between party and class, making clear that New Labour's modernizing appeal, above all, denies that the party is the representative of the working class. At the same time, it reduces the salience of distributive politics with its forthright insistence on fiscal prudence and steady-state taxes. In another development predicted by the strategic adjustment model, Blair raises the visibility of positions on the progressive end of the libertarian–authoritarian dimension, emphasizing the importance of decentralized, informal, participatory processes.

That said, I have argued that New Labour departs from the behavior predicted by the strategic adjustment model in at least three dimensions. First, in terms of agency, New Labour rejects socioeconomic coalitions that are at least partly grounded in labor market relations in favor of nondescript middle-down electoral coalitions focused on swing voters. Secondly, the policy approach advanced by New Labour moves decisively toward market solutions and business partnerships. Thus it is not merely that New Labour reduces the salience of the distributive dimensions of party competition. Rather, critical elements of social and economic policy are located on the conservative side of the policy spectrum. Thirdly, we come to the normative orientations of New Labour. How do we assess its abstract appeals to community (ignoring the endemic social and ethnic divisions within communities), appeals to stakeholders (neglecting the structural inequalities in the distribution of shares), and appeals to family (privileging two-parent families and insufficiently addressing the needs of working women)? There are battles to be fought, but immanent within New Labour is a normative tilt toward right communitarianism. Thus, to the limited extent that Kitschelt provides an exclusionary boundary for his model of social democracy, Blair's New Labour crosses it, by adopting some critically important positions that do not lie on the "progressive half" of the distributive and communitarian dimensions and by going further than Kitschelt's model would suggest to break with labor as a source of political agency (Kitschelt, 1994, p. 296).[10]

What can be said of New Labour's relationship to base-line traditional social democracy? In fact, New Labour's relationship to the institutional-collectivist model of social democracy is more interesting than it might at first appear. Invariably associated with "Old Labour," this model of social democracy appears as the dramatic foil for Blair's modernizing agenda. In terms of institutional arrangements, New Labour's signature innovations are intended, in a variety of ways, to reverse the tendency of Labour to "provide centralised, 'statist' solutions to every social and economic problem" (Mandelson and Liddle, 1996, p. 27): for example, with reference to education and housing. But historic legacies and voter expectations make difficult a radical break with the policy approaches and institutional orientations of the institutional-collectivist model. As a consequence, New Labour exhibits some critical areas of continuity with the traditional collectivist-institutional model of social democracy, such as dedication to the caring issues, expansive commitments to health care and education, and a taken-for-granted egalitarianism in its normative orientations.

Comparisons with social democratic models help reveal a set of paradoxes and dilemmas at the heart of the New Labour model of government. Its normative appeals and positions on distributive politics are scattered across the ideological spectrum, lending an aspect of perpetual ambiguity to a very intentionally crafted governing model. Elements of family policy and welfare reform reflect a right-communitarian (authoritarian) disposition, while institutional reform exhibits a left-communitarian (libertarian) orientation. At the same time, by relying on a merely arithmetic middle-down aggregation of voters rather than an institutionally grounded interest-based coalition, New Labour faces the dilemma of mobilizing support for its extensive reform agenda without recourse to any organized collective agency outside party and government.

Then there is the ultimate paradox. What is most radical about New Labour – whether the institutional and constitutional reforms or the potentially bold welfare and public expenditure initiatives – rests on neoliberal economics and traditional social democratic normative appeals. As one observer put it, the Blair government faces hard questions stemming from the "obvious, if unacknowledged, tension between the conservatism of New Labour's economics and the radicalism of its politics" (Marquand, 1997, p. 335). It faces a disjuncture between social democratic commitments to broad egalitarian measures and social justice aspirations on the one hand, and on the other, the hard-bitten consequences of "workfare" compulsion, tight limits on public expenditure, and a one-sided industrial relations regime (to be discussed further in chapter 4) that reinforces managerial prerogative and contributes to the erosion and decline of standard full-time employment. Can New Labour "define a new relationship between citizen and community" while preserving a very traditional hierarchical and restrictive relationship between worker and manager?

Labour's dilemmas and paradoxes are analyzed differently by New Labour insiders, less in comparative terms and more from the perspective of Labour's historic performance both inside and outside government and an analysis of Labour's strategic options for crystallizing the enduring majority support it has never enjoyed. What motivates New Labour's ceaseless efforts to modernize and reinvent center-left politics in the UK? By his own account, Blair is driven to resolve the "progressive dilemma" posed by David Marquand in his study of the challenges faced by Labour ever since it replaced the Liberals as the main anti-Conservative alternative in the UK's competitive party system:

> The Labour Party has faced essentially the same problem since the 1920s: how to transcend Labourism without betraying the labour interest; how to bridge the gulf between the old Labour fortresses and the potentially anti-Conservative, but non-Labour hinterland; how to construct a broad-based and enduring social coalition capable, not just of giving it a temporary majority in the House of Commons, but of sustaining a reforming government thereafter. (Marquand, 1991, p. 207; quoted in Blair, 1995)

To resolve the dilemma, New Labour is willing to gamble that cross-class appeals (really non-class appeals), animated by a new political language of modernization and third way politics beyond left and right, have sufficient mobilizational capacity to sustain popular support and fundamentally recast British politics. It is willing to bet that the "labour interest," historically identified in terms of class, occupation, and socioeconomic position, has transmogrified (or, to use a suitably modernized term, "morphed") into the interests of individuals as stakeholders, who are determined to acquire their fair shares of a globally competitive economy. Blair's New Labour operates on the assumption that appeals to modernization, backed by new orientations in economic, welfare, and social policy, together with effective mobilization of the community to fight crime and revitalize democracy and thoroughgoing institutional and constitutional reforms, will secure a long-term electoral majority – without a proper, organizationally rooted, collectively defined, interest-based social coalition. From the perspective of New Labour, globalization means that the reforms needed today are every bit as far-reaching as those embraced by the "new Liberals ... who were both liberals with a small 'l' and social democrats, also in lower case, living on the cusp of a new political age" in the period after the Liberal coalition splintered in 1916 and Labour assumed the leading role of anti-Conservative reform party.[11] Blair stakes his claim to leadership on the bold hope that his New Labour will have better staying power and ultimately more programmatic success than what was then "literally 'new Labour'" (Blair, 1995).

Can a center-left politics cut off from its historic agency conceived in class terms provide a policy agenda – and the collective instruments for securing and administering that agenda – that rivals the durability of social democracy? In rejecting social democracy and especially in forsaking the party's historic reliance on class agency and socioeconomic coalitions, New Labour has left behind more than policies and ideology: it has rejected a way of organizing politics. Can the Blair government, despite the formidable challenges it faces, organize politics on its own terms, sustain its initiative despite the evident paradoxes, and resolve its acknowledged and unacknowledged dilemmas? What are the implications of this project for the durability and salience of center-left politics?

Part II
The Organization of Production

3

Social Democracy, Class, and National Policy Sovereignty

By all accounts, British social democracy[1] (viewed as a center-left project) presupposed the organization of politics according to class[2] in the design of a two-party dominant system, in explaining voting behavior, in the institutionalized expressions of the most powerful interests in society, and in public debates over economic and social policies. Yet in each of these dimensions the claim that class decisively shapes structure, agency, and institutions is subject to increasing skepticism. Parties can no longer rely on relatively unified, coherent class-based constellations for electoral support; nor can their programs be plotted on a single left versus right axis defined by reference to the distribution of economic rewards and the collective goods of the welfare state. Above all, it is hard to envision any return to policy debates driven explicitly by mobilized class-based interests, expressed through the associational politics of the Confederation of British Industry (CBI) or the Trades Union Congress (TUC). It is evident that the significance of class for the organization of politics in the UK invites serious reconsideration.

I think it important to add that social democracy presupposed a second, equally critical constituent element: a taken-for-granted assumption of sovereignty, understood as effective governmental or state control over policy-making processes, especially with reference to economic policy, and a reasonable purchase on outcomes.[3] In effect, the *Westminster model* of British representative government was nestled within an interstate system that has been called the *Westphalian model* (referring to the Peace of Westphalia of 1648, which ended the German phase of the Thirty Years War). The model assumes a world of autonomous sovereign states, operating by national interest, with diplomatic relations and recourse to force, but with minimal cooperation (see Held, 1995, pp. 77–83). Even as modified by participation in international organizations such as the United Nations or NATO, the model does not accommodate the growing challenges to sovereignty that flow from the global reorganization of production and the growing significance of the European Union's economic and monetary union (EMU). Because autonomous control over policy was taken for granted, this important threshold condition warranted little or no discussion in analysis of social democracy, or in the political negotiations and bargaining of the postwar settlement era more generally. As with the unquestioned assumption that social class provides the basic template for the organization of politics, specific processes associated with globalization challenge the claim of national policy sovereignty and distinctive national economic models.

Are we entering a new era of politics? The organization of politics has changed, I will argue, as a consequence of processes broadly linked to globalization that have fundamentally eroded the two foundational principles of center-left politics: first, the class basis; and second, the capacity of national governments to control policy levers and "govern the economy" (Hall, 1986) through alternative policies and national models. Class, pure and simple, will never again play the dominant political role it has in the past, nor will governments enjoy autonomous policy control. Yet, the experiences of work continue to shape individual and collective needs and policy agendas in very powerful ways, and the scope of government to respond to this emergent patchwork of interests – or to spurn it – remains great.

Class and the Organization of Politics

In fact, although the class basis of social democracy was almost uniformly assumed, even before the current period of intensified international trade and foreign direct investment, the claim always required a hefty suspension of disbelief. For many in government and trade unions, a few core male manufacturing industries were allowed to stand symbolically for the whole of a segmented and highly sex-segregated labor force. Moreover, the ability of the TUC either to affect distributive policies or to enforce bargains could seldom be detected. In addition, open ruptures between the labor movement and the Labour Party, over the "Alternative Economic Strategy," party governance, the role of the annual party conference (see Panitch and Leys, 1997, pp. 66–85), and the débâcle of the Social Contract in the run-up to Thatcher's initial electoral victory, underscore the fact that significant differences in policy, goals, and the balance of institutional power have been endemic to social democratic politics in the UK.

Looked at in comparative perspective, the inadequacies of incomes policies that lacked the solidaristic support of Scandinavian wage-bargaining agreements and the liberal orientations of the welfare state[4] may be seen to contribute in critical ways to the failures of British labor (Pontusson, 1988). It never achieved hegemony, the relationship between the trade union movement and Labour Party was subject to considerable vacillation, and the mobilizational capacity of class actors lacked the organizational underpinnings found elsewhere. Hence, it is not surprising that Labour was poorly positioned to withstand the onset of economic hard times. Not only did the British Labour Party suffer the sharpest decline in support of any party on the left between the beginning of the postwar period and the end of the 1980s, but the Labour vote within the traditional manual working class fell very sharply during the same period (from 63 percent in 1951 to 40 percent in 1992) (see Crewe, 1992). Thus, important questions arise about the class organization of politics in the social democratic UK, with reference to a string of key assumptions about unified agency, interest mobilization, electoral competition, and the setting of policy agendas.

It would be tempting to conclude that the class basis of British social democracy was simply overblown. As the illustrations above suggest, in analytical terms the claim is at least subject to important qualifications. It is impossible, however, to ignore the central importance of class for the base-line organization of politics in the UK for much of the postwar period, as seen in the elemental organization of the party system, the distributive design of the postwar settlement, the brutal industrial disputes of the Thatcher era, and the struggle over legitimating motifs for government policy (e.g. Keynesianism versus monetarism, egalitarianism versus the entrepreneurial culture). How, then, on balance do we assess the continuing significance of class for the organization of politics in the UK – and for the future of a center-left project? How is class, grounded in workplace experiences, politically actualized?

To begin, I will argue, following Przeworski, that the organization of politics in terms of class is not inevitable or inexorably linked to capitalism, despite the critical understanding that class position "structures the daily experience of individuals, generates a certain kind of knowledge, endows people with interests, and under some circumstances may even evoke an understanding of a shared lot" (Przeworski, 1985, pp. 99–100). Changing circumstances very much complicate the processes of class formation, viewed as the active forging of collectivities (see Wright, 1985, p. 10), the sorting and prioritizing of interests and preferences, and the setting of political agendas. These changes open up and recast the political consequences of class formation.

By now, the processes of class decomposition are well known: the reduction of the manufacturing workforce associated with deindustrialization, the declining ratio of employment in high union density occupations, the expansion of the service sector, the growth of part-time workers, increased labor market participation by women in non-standard forms of employment, displacement of jobs through an international division of labor, and so forth. All these processes, taken together, fragment class into a coterie of working people, their daily experiences differentiated by conditions of employment in a variety of dimensions.

Technological change and the globalization of capital intensify the differentiation in actual experiences of work, which takes many forms, including the sorting of jobs by race, gender, and ethnicity (to be discussed in chapter 6). This process both reflects and crystallizes alternative schemes of collective identity and interest formation, and further complicates the contradictory class locations endemic to contemporary capitalist development. Thus the process of class formation is at the same time a process of class fragmentation that enhances what is often termed *identity politics* – the politics of gender and sexual orientation, race, ethnicity, and nationality, etc., which include both work-related and quite autonomous cultural components. Taken together, the proliferation of alternative systems of collective identity contributes to what I call "modular politics" and vastly complicates the work of government.[5]

Class had anchored the political system; the decomposition of class cuts the system adrift. As John Gray put it succinctly, "social democracy is now a political project without a historical agent" (1997, p. 13). However, we have seen that any claim of unitary and coherent agency always glossed over divisions, since class formation is continuously in flux, shaped by the actual empirical relations and nitty-gritty experiences of the workplace, and complicated by the shifting relationships and policy agendas of workers, unions and social democratic parties. Put another way, the assumption of the working class as unitary agent of social democratic politics should be reconsidered in light of a set of structural and institutional changes both at the level of class formation and with reference to the changing capacities of states as actors within regional and global systems.

For a start, it seems necessary to treat with considerable skepticism any assumption that the organization of politics by class is inevitable, and to reject a mythic account of unified class interests and coherent and strategically articulated collective aims. It seems equally appropriate, however, to insist that how production is organized and how work is therefore experienced have profound practical consequences for the organization of politics.

As Przeworski (1985) observed about class position, daily work experience critically shapes the knowledge, sense of shared fates, collective identities, priorities, and potential for political mobilization of given congeries of individuals. I will assume that work experiences play a very important role in constructing commonsense understandings about the social world, constituting strategic policy agendas, defining interests, and framing ideological dispositions and preferences. In this specific sense, by shaping understandings, policy agendas, interests, dispositions, and preferences, the experiences of work structure political agency: work both enables and constrains the exercise of politics.[6] Emergent forms of work organization, workplace relations, and local divisions of labor therefore contribute to the of politics in critical ways, by structuring the experience of work, although there is no automatic translation of class position or work experience into the realm of politics. As will be discussed in part III, the politically formative influence of labor is by no means exclusive, immutable, or autonomous, but the influences are significant, if not easy to infer from the general characteristics of a production system. Above all, entering into the analysis of the political consequences of production, it is necessary to preserve a tolerable level of agnosticism about how production is organized and what consequences the actually existing organization holds for the potential political agency of working peoples to set strategic political agendas and frame what comes to constitute the commonsense understandings of politics.

As we look much more closely into the changed production systems and the new forms of work organization driven by globalization, what prospects of collective organization and agency will we find – and what auguries for the political project of New Labour or alternative center-left projects? In order to understand the contemporary development of systems of production, their implications for the actual empirical transformation of work experiences and in turn for the organization of politics, we must first consider how the regionalization and globalization of the economy have affected national economic policy sovereignty, the second critical assumption of the social democratic model.

Policy Sovereignty, National Models, and the Organization of Politics

The challenges to national policy sovereignty exerted by external transnational processes involve both a regional and a global dimension. Each has quite significant implications for class formation and the reorganization of work in the UK, and holds important clues about the challenges – and the opportunities – that any center-left government would face in reorganizing politics in the UK.

The regional dimension

The increased significance of the European Union's role in trade and in macroeconomic and monetary policy, and its potential (post-Maastricht, post-Bosnia) participation in foreign policy and security matters (not to

mention the issue areas of the Social Charter) present important challenges to any principle of effective national policy control. The endemic
crises in UK–EU relations during the governments of Thatcher and
Major overshadowed the fierce distributional politics, the hard-edged
class politics of the Conservative UK. The tortuous saga of economic and
monetary union, involving the UK's spectacular departure from the
Exchange Rate Mechanism (ERM) in the débâcle of Black Wednesday
(16 September 1992), and the all-encompassing challenges that EU
policy brought to Thatcher and Major, underscore the domestic political
consequences of the partial externalization of policy control. For a
decade, the seemingly endless backbiting and rebellion over the Social
Charter and Maastricht within the Conservative ranks kidnapped two
premierships and fixated governments.

Likewise, despite growing signs that the question has shifted from
whether to when the UK will join the euro, the single currency may well
prove a serious challenge to New Labour's managerial skills and unity.
Key members of the government support British participation in the
single currency, and the decision to free the Bank of England from direct
government control was a very powerful indication that Blair and Brown
intend to create the proper conditions for British entry. Quite rightly, the
decision is not being taken lightly.

For those countries that join the euro club, the European Central
Bank acquires critical economic policy powers that will reduce national
sovereign control over monetary and fiscal policy. Taking the logic at
least a few steps further, many observers have noted that monetary union
is a process that is likely to make comprehensive European integration
all but irreversible. This prospect has inspired significant resistance
within New Labour, not to mention among the Conservative opposition,
which will surely make it a leading campaign issue in the next general
election.

In time New Labour will have to face these issues, and the divisions
that will almost certainly follow, head on. After all, the Maastricht Treaty
did call for eventual political union. The issues swirling around British
participation in the single currency are profoundly political, the tide of
European integration is rising, and the matter of the UK's participation
in the euro seems likely to create significant political pressures for New
Labour. We will return to the issue of British participation in the single
currency in chapter 10 (challenge 4).

Beyond the euro, there is yet a deeper level of politics at play in the
post-Maastricht EU intrigues. EMU and the underlying problems of
the UK's participation in the EU, with its complex (and legally superordinate) institutional arrangements, present another formidable challenge to a class-based model of social democratic governance. To the
extent that divisions over the European Union fundamentally reshape
British politics and party competition, they displace traditional class-

distributional politics as the central organizing principle, and they do so for good reasons.

The post-Maastricht agenda for increased economic and monetary union, focused on the introduction of a single currency, will fundamentally influence the UK's ability to compete internationally and sustain its own model of economic development. It will hold significant consequences for price stability, and for the capacity of national government to manipulate interest rates and exchange rates to cushion declines in demand and thereby limit unemployment. In addition, the euro will create pressure for coordination of tax policies (see Miles, 1997; Feldstein, 1998). Economic and monetary integration, therefore, has potentially quite significant repercussions for standards of living and distributional politics at home.

The capacity of government to master intra-EU diplomacy, to insert national goals into collective regional policy making and to develop consistent policy at each new stage of integration takes on ever greater importance. Indeed, controlling the terms of the debate and defining national interests with regard to critical EU policies may well become the litmus test of a party's and a government's credibility and electability, as the ability to govern the national economy and mobilize the support of unions and business was in the heyday of the social democratic polity. Distributional politics shifts from the arena of the nation-state to that of Europe, and issues of institutional and constitutional reform become politicized in a new way. Insofar as the EU impinges significantly on national sovereign control over policy, the validity of the institutional-collectivist model of social democracy is jeopardized, as is the capacity of the government to govern by striking bargains with the representatives of labor and capital. To the extent that exchange rates or social policy is determined in Brussels, why should business or labor direct their energies to Whitehall or Westminster?

The regionalization of policy by the EU is therefore an important contributing element to the reorganization of politics, as a central axis (perhaps *the* central axis) of party cleavages shifts from domestic distributional politics to the politics of European integration, and EU policy impinges on key areas of economic and social policy that were the traditional focus of social democratic distributional politics. To take a critical example, the macroeconomic and social policy orientations mandated by the EMU convergence criteria – deficits below 3 percent of GDP, inflation rates no more than 1.5 percent greater than the average of the three members with the lowest rates, and so forth – play havoc with the postwar settlement distributional bargains that underlie social democratic politics. Throughout the run-up to the initial launching of the euro on New Year's Day 1999, the neoliberal, market-driven agenda for deepening European integration tended to nullify the full employment, Keynesian welfare state policy regime. Unless and until the terms of the

Stability and Growth Pact are changed to emphasize employment over price stability and subject the European Central Bank to political control, the tendency of the EMU to circumscribe the options of center-left governments will continue. The regional dimension, however, is but one part of a broader externalization of politics linked to the processes of globalization. To what extent is it still possible to talk of national models and systems of production?

Globalization and national systems of production

Until recently, the stock-in-trade of comparative studies in political economy, the resilience and continued effectiveness of national systems of production, has been challenged by a "hyper-globalization" school that claims the demise of national policy controls and national economic models (Ohmae, 1991, 1995; Reich, 1991).[7] Kenichi Ohmae, the most influential advocate of the claim that radical mobility of factors of production has effectively swamped the capacities of the nation-state, argues that the "information-led transition to a genuinely borderless economy" raises "troubling questions about the relevance – and effectiveness – of nation states as meaningful aggregates in terms of which to think about, much less manage, economic activity" (Ohmae, 1995, p. viii).

In response, an impressive set of international scholars has attempted to reassert the importance of non-market institutions and governance mechanisms that tend to preserve a measure of national diversity, within a context in which economic coordination also occurs simultaneously at other levels: in sectors, regions within countries, and transnational regions (such as the EU), and also at the global level (Hollingsworth et al., 1994; Berger and Dore, 1996; Hollingsworth and Boyer, 1997). Hollingsworth and Boyer (1997) emphasize the importance of coordinating mechanisms as alternatives to markets. They contend that institutions or structures of a country or region that coordinate capitalism shape and are shaped by social systems of production (SSPs) comprised of: industrial relations systems; the patterns of relationships among firms within a sector and between firms and suppliers or customers; vocational training and educational systems; state structures and policies; corporate organization; idiosyncratic customs, values, norms, moral principles, and laws, and so forth. Because the institutions are "embedded in a culture in which their logics are symbolically grounded, organizationally structured, technically and materially constrained, and politically defended," nation-states and (probably to a lesser extent) transnational regions have different trajectories of development and exhibit different social systems of production (Hollingsworth and Boyer, 1997, p. 2). Hence diversity is preserved within a complex and indeterminate interplay of the processes of globalization and the powerful embeddedness of institutions that are viewed as the properties of particular national systems of production.

A compatible research program led by Suzanne Berger and Ronald Dore contrasts their approach to "the perspective from Ohmae's garden," insisting that there is real diversity among national production systems, in which "institutional constellations and cultural legacies provide distinctive strengths and weaknesses." For them, "the core issue is whether or not Japanese lean production, German high-skill, high-quality social market economy, Italian industrial districts, U.S. flexible mass production, and others are fundamentally different systems capable of achieving similar results in markets through quite different mechanisms" (Berger and Dore, 1996, p. 21). They strenuously resist any convergence hypothesis, while some authors see functional equivalence across national models and others see specific comparative advantages.

Taken together, the findings and analyses of these two impressive research teams make important contributions to our understanding of the interplay of institutions and processes that shape production systems and models at multiple levels. In particular, their insistence on the diversity of national experiences is an important and compelling antidote to unbounded (for Ohmae, borderless) globalism. Nevertheless, they leave unresolved a set of questions of great importance here, since they fail to address the empirical realities of how production is organized in the UK and how the organization of production shapes the political space available for center-left political mobilization.

It is worth noting that, in their quick inventory of national production systems, no British system is identified by Berger and Dore. To be sure, selectivity is appropriate and other national models have routinely acquired a more elevated comparative status, but a more serious issue may at least be worth considering. As the prime location for foreign direct investment attracted by the single market program of the EU (Lord, 1996), and as a leading beneficiary of the anti-regulatory bias of intensified foreign investment associated with the processes of globalization more generally (Streeck, 1997), the UK increasingly exhibits a hybrid economic model. Particularly in some sectors (automobiles) and regions (the north-east and Wales), where intensive Japanese direct investment brings with it the overlay of a powerfully articulated system of production on a more weakly institutionalized British model, the specificity or "embeddedness" of a British system of production should be assessed critically.

Although the "embeddedness of institutions" recognized by Hollingsworth and Boyer (1997) has much to recommend it, particularly as a counterweight to the hyper-globalization approach, both the preconditions needed to sustain embeddedness and the degree of nationally specific resilience to cross-border, transplant, or global logics of production are, of course, empirical questions. Considerable variation is to be expected and, as I hope to demonstrate, one of the signal features of the British system of production, in combination with specific government policies, is that entrepreneurs and political leaders have colluded to render it more porous than some others may be or, in my view, than the UK should be. As a consequence, the British economy has been rendered especially vulnerable to a core feature of globalization, the *disembedding of social institutions*, identified by Giddens as "the 'lifting out' of social relations from local contexts and their rearticulation across indefinite tracts of time-space" (1991, p. 18).

Although Giddens initially had in mind more abstract systems of exchange, and expert systems involving technical knowledge and guidance about social relations, it seems clear that the globalization of economic relations presents a significant challenge to country or regional coordinating mechanisms that constitute production systems. On the one hand, several components of what are said to be nationally based SSPs – for example, corporate organization, vocational training, chain-of-production relationships among firms, suppliers, and customers, relationships among firms within a sector, and aspects of industrial relations systems – are portable and accompany direct investment and transplant operations. This is all the more clear if one looks at the disembedding of practices and local understandings from national systems: thus training, supplier and client company relations, and shopfloor work relations can be transformed locally (as with Nissan's venture in Sunderland or Sony's in Bridgend). These changes can occur whether or not a British national system of vocational training or industrial relations is transformed, or a broad pattern of arm's-length buyer–supplier relationships is changed more generally (see Morris and Imrie, 1992). On the other hand, the diffusion of computer-based technologies, intensified global competition, rapid production cycles, the introduction of new forms of work organization, and alternative organizational principles that govern enterprise coordination and workplace relations contribute a genuinely global dimension to production systems. It is not too much to say that any reasonably cosmopolitan management team has a vast menu of options from which to select the most propitious combination of enterprise organization and competitive strategies, which articulates the best available mix of production methods, market scope, and production scale.

It is this rather chaotic mix of transplanted elements of alternative national production systems, distinctive but weakly institutionalized British mechanisms for non-market coordination of the economy, and the global diffusion of strategic production alternatives that frames the organization of production in the UK today. Colin Crouch and Wolfgang Streeck (1997) have recently argued that globalization has eroded the capacity of the nation-state to sustain institutional diversity and distinctive niches, institutional cultures, and governance arrangements (see also Grant, 1998). In the British case, it seems clear that pre-existing institutional legacies, reinforced by Thatcher-era industrial, labor market, and industrial relations policies, among others, have opened the UK to more than its share of international influences. As a result, with Blair trumpeting the success of the UK's business partnership approach and deregulated labor market, the British economy has finally acquired the status of a model for emulation: neoliberal post-Fordism. Is there no alternative? Chapter 4 will explicate the actually existing organization of production in the UK and then consider its implications for center-left governance and the organization of politics. Drawing on comparative European cases, our analysis throughout will emphasize the alternatives to neoliberal production systems, a theme to which we will return in chapter 10 (challenge 1).

4

Globalization, Post-Fordism, and the British Model

Experiences of labor help shape understandings about the social world, frame ideological dispositions, create the potential for solidarity, constitute interests, and in that sense structure political agency. But what shapes the experiences of labor in the UK? To address this question, I will consider the interactive effects of national and cross-national factors on emergent forms of production and work organization. This process, I will suggest, has led to the emergence of what might be called a hybrid transnational production system in the UK, resulting in part from intensified foreign direct investment (FDI). After tracing the comparative and global dimensions, the chapter will detail the British model of production. It will conclude with a discussion of the implications of production for the organization of politics in the contemporary UK.[1]

Post-Fordism: Challenges and Alternatives

Micro-level work organization, the point of production, distills all the formative influences of a system of production in a particularly acute form, absorbing the impact of global, regional, and national forces, and refracting them through industry-specific and plant-specific cultures and practices. Working from the outside in, we can begin by noting the broad imperatives, driven by processes of global competition and technological innovation, that shape production systems and strategies.[2]

Post-Fordist flexibility and national variation

An extensive European literature suggests that under intensified competition, spurred by the diffusion of computer-based technologies and rapid product cycles, industry is facing the challenge of thoroughgoing technical and organizational change on a continuous basis.[3] Pressures for technological innovation challenge the traditional departmental and hierarchical patterns of enterprise organization, forcing management to consider quite radical organizational makeovers in order to respond to the changing competitive environment: changed work designs to mobilize new forms of skill, and a reconfiguration of relationships between different phases of production.

Thus, a simple truth lies behind the debate over Fordism and alternative post-Fordist production systems, such as flexible specialization and lean production. Viewed narrowly as a production system (rather than as a regime of accumulation and a mode of regulation), Fordism presupposed a particular Taylorist model of work organization. Despite the necessary caveats about variations due to national alternatives in institutions and cultures, and the dependence of Fordist enterprise on non-Fordist economic sectors (Gordon, 1993), as the term is generally used Fordism involved a rather fixed equation. It wedded a specific design of the labor process (fragmented semi-skilled or unskilled labor inserted into assembly-line production and using dedicated machinery) to a particular competitive strategy (the production of standardized goods for mass markets, made price-competitive by economies of scale) (see Charles, 1995, p. 239).

However controversial or analytically limited the distinction between Fordism and post-Fordist flexibility, this much can safely be said: Fordist strategies are being superseded by flexible technologies and organizations that attempt to create a capacity for perpetual innovation. But there is no single determinate direction, form, or content for flexible production systems. At least as a simplification, a tendency toward convergence on the "one best way" was powerfully inscribed in the global competitive dynamics of Fordism: economies of scale, efficiencies in assembly-line production, and mass-market price-competition. By contrast, the current industrial regime is marked by the malleability of new technologies, and this, coupled with the continuous pressure to innovate, encourages the proliferation of quite distinctive production and organizational strategies, each potentially competitive within a volatile and multipolar competitive environment.

In general, within a European context of organized, highly skilled labor and quality-competitive production, the search for competitive advantage spurs management to consider forms of work and production organization that explicitly overturn the principles of Fordist production: economies of scope rather than scale; skill enhancement and multi-skilling; team working within a context of reduced hierarchy and more fluid coordination of functions within the enterprise; new production methods geared to shorter production runs; increased product variety with speedier responses to market impulses. Competitive strategies entail choices about the trade-offs between standardized and non-standardized production strategies, typical size of production runs (scale), and the range of products manufactured in a given unit (scope). At the same time, management must consider a menu of quite comprehensive options concerning how to integrate different phases of production, the relationship of the labor process to other operations, the level and range of skills and responsibilities expected of shopfloor personnel, the distribution of work tasks and responsibilities, and the relationship between authority and expertise throughout the enterprise as a whole (Gordon and Krieger, 1992; R. Gordon, 1995). Circumstances and strategies differ, and in this domain it is clear that the principles of diversity and subsidiarity prevail, albeit within a general trend toward flexible post-Fordist alternatives to standardized mass production. As the discussion below will indicate, some important patterns emerge that permit a greater appreciation of distinctive features of work organization in the UK.

Strategic choices at the enterprise level are necessarily influenced both by specific sectoral considerations and by national institutions and industrial cultures, as both Fordism and post-Fordist alternatives locate production narrowly defined within a larger context. Considered broadly as an economic and social system, Fordism blurred the distinction between enterprise management and the broader social environment (Maier, 1987, p. 53). Viewed from this perspective, classic Fordism included a set of non-market coordinating mechanisms to sustain the conditions of production, but often at some remove from the factory itself: industrial relations systems, Keynesian demand management, social policies associated with the welfare state, and the distributive bargains and public policy framework of the postwar settlement. Similarly, post-Fordist production strategies are integrally shaped by the diversity of contemporary non-market coordinating mechanisms identified by Hollingsworth and Boyer (1997), from industrial relations and vocational training systems to norms and laws that shape production practices to the range of state structures and policies.

A recent comparative study of the crisis and future prospects of social democracy in four of the most advanced cases (Austria, Norway, Finland, and Sweden) confirms that changes in the international economies since the 1970s – including the rise of post-Fordist production systems – have eroded the institutional moorings of the social democratic model. Huber and Stephens (1998) argue that financial deregulation and the multinationalization of capital have robbed governments of key policy instruments, such as generous reinvestment in production, that have traditionally sustained the social democratic model. The study illustrates the run-on effects of changes in the global economy and in production systems on what I have called the organization of politics. Although there is no clear-cut or necessary connection between systems of production and governing models, it is quite clear that the eclipse of Fordism compromises social democracy and that the proliferation of post-Fordist production scenarios contributes to the weakening of political instruments for consensual economic management. This global era finds a growing range of variation in production as well as in the non-market mechanisms for coordinating production.

The diversity that may be found in the coordinating mechanisms present in the member countries of the European Union inevitably complicates an understanding of general trends towards economies of scope, skill enhancement, or flexibility in the use of computer-based technologies. Thus, it is safe to say that there is a trend toward "post-Fordist" flexibility, but it is much trickier to identify what that flexibility means in practice. The heterogeneity of national production systems and industrial cultures means that the flexibility that post-Fordism entails is subject to considerable variation. It is at this juncture, where global pressures for fast-paced innovation and national industrial cultures, industrial relations systems, market niches, and expressly political decisions by governments come together, that important variations among countries take form. Since all policy decisions that shape production and influence competitive strategies are inherently political, such variations are inevitable, even though the discourse of globalization may provide government with the justification to claim otherwise (see Hay and Watson, 1998a).

Flexibility in anthropocentric production systems

In several European settings, significant examples may be found of what a series of studies commissioned by the Forecasting and Assessment in Science and Technology (FAST) program of the European Communities have termed "anthropocentric production systems" (APS) (see Gordon and Krieger, 1992; Lehner, 1992; Charles, 1995). Although the APS concept has distinctive meanings in different countries, in empirical terms it has come to assume a set of interdependent elements: a flexible approach to automation that supports human intervention and decision making; decentralized organization of work, with flat hierarchies that devolve considerable power and responsibility to the shopfloor; systems design that integrates the labor process of direct manufacturing personnel with off-the-floor operations; continuous training and upskilling of manufacturing workers through work-based learning; and product-oriented integration of the entire production process, from research and development to manufacturing, marketing, and customer service (Krieger, 1992c; Lehner, 1992).

Despite receiving considerable attention in EU technology and industrial policy circles and some wider public recognition, particularly in

Germany, the diffusion of APS in European industry has been slow and uneven, for a number of reasons. In many cases, both the technology design for computer-integrated production and management strategies for its adoption display a bias toward Taylorist work and firm organization. In addition, in many European countries, institutionalized rigidities in status and wage systems hinder flexible deployment of production workers. In addition, "low-trust" industrial relations impedes organizational innovation and makes the necessary redesign of jobs extremely difficult. In many countries, weak vocational training results in severe shortages of multiskilled labor capable of system-wide problem solving. Finally, where production remains oriented toward standardized price-competitive mass production, incentives for implementing APS, which is oriented towards diversified-quality batch production, are relatively weak (Lehner, 1992).

Predictably, where specific elements of national institutions and industrial cultures create a propitious setting, post-Fordist flexibility includes APS elements, however episodic, uneven, and contested their diffusion. Thus, as one observer involved in EU studies of APS observes, " 'the Swedish model' still represents the best example of anthropocentric production" (Charles, 1995, p. 247). This claim can certainly be justified by reference to the innovations in production design and work organization introduced by Swedish car makers, including Saab and Scania, but especially Volvo. These developments were made possible by a unique combination of factors during the period of Social Democratic ascendancy. Strong economic competitiveness created the space for experimentation with alternatives to the much heralded system of lean production introduced by Toyota (Womack et al., 1990). At the same time, institutionalized co-determination agreements signed by Volvo and its union in 1983 and modeled on the national peak level co-determination agreement of 1982 should be understood as but one achievement of a broader labor offensive begun in the 1960s and spurred to new reforms by the return to power of the Social Democrats in 1982. The Volvo Development Agreement provided for routine participation by unions in the planning of new plants, and affirmed participation by employees in decisions about work organization and technological innovation (Pontusson, 1992).

In two landmark plants, Kalmar (in production from 1974 until 1994) and Uddevalla (which operated from 1989 to 1993), Volvo consolidated a long series of experiments with alternative forms of work organization.[4] The innovations at Uddevalla were the most far-reaching. The assembly-line process was dissolved in favor of "parallelized production," in which small teams of highly skilled workers assembled entire cars in one place, and where emphasis was placed on "whole-car competence." At the same time, an integrated approach to assembly replaced short-term repetitive tasks with longer job cycles, as long as four hours compared to the two-minute assembly operations in a traditional plant. This movement toward "job enlargement" was combined with job rotation in a decentralized enterprise organization that explicitly excluded traditional first-line management, giving responsibility for such matters as quality control and maintenance to team representatives, in principle on a monthly rotation (Berggren, 1992; Pontusson, 1992). The combination of diffused control and responsibility, flattened hierarchies, and production islands represents the most comprehensive model of APS applications (see Gordon and Krieger, 1992). Symbolically, the 1999 sale of its car division to Ford marked Volvo's demise as APS innovator.

Examples of anthropocentric production can also be found in Germany, especially in the machine tool industry, where works councils make it possible for trade unions to support new experiments in "skill-based manufacturing" and production workers are viewed as "thinking and acting subjects." Recognizing the competitive advantages of introducing more integrated problem-solving approaches to help secure a "quality production" model, German industry appears more willing to support new forms of work organization involving increased group work, job enlargement, participation, and decentralized organization with diffused responsibilities (Brodner, 1986; Kern and Schumann, 1987; Lehner, 1992; Charles, 1995). Other cases of human-centered work organization may be found scattered throughout EU Europe. In Italy, for example, Lamborghini "systematically followed an anthropocentric strategy in the organisation of its production" (while Fiat retains a Taylorist approach and Alfa Romeo is taking a position between its two competitors). Rates of experimentation remain fairly high in Denmark and France and, except in Greece and Portugal, interesting examples of APS may be found nearly everywhere in the countries of the European Union (Lehner, 1992). How does the UK organization of production fit into the broader European pattern?

Post-Fordism in the United Kingdom

Some experimentation with APS may be observed in the UK, but it is quite limited, and found disproportionately in high-technology firms, the investment goods sector and, not surprisingly, foreign-owned companies (Lehner, 1992). The obstacles to the development of anthropocentric production are significant, stemming from specific features of the British system of production. In fact, the basic theme of post-Fordism and the organization of production in the UK is the transformation of flexibility into a management prerogative that shapes the work organization, thereby ultimately affecting the organization of politics in the UK. Two broadly defined aspects of the organization of production in the UK are especially telling, and will be discussed in turn: industrial organization and competitive strategy; and labor market policy and industrial relations.[5] Taken together, they decisively shape the organization of work and lend a characteristic appearance to post-Fordist flexibility in the UK.

Industrial organization, competitive strategy, and the British model

As is widely noted, British industrial organization is more polarized than that of its other European counterparts, with little integration between the concentrated corporate sector and the sector comprised of small and medium-sized enterprises (SMEs), which experienced a boom, especially in small firm growth, in the 1980s (Charles, 1995; Lane, 1995). Although the 1988 Enterprise Initiative reduced government support for industry in general, SMEs, which were viewed by the Thatcher government as "the stormtroopers of its enterprise initiative," received extensive targeted support in the form of Department of Trade and Industry (DTI) grants and loans, on the one hand, and substantial tax credits through the Business Expansion Scheme, on the other (Sharp and Walker, 1994, p. 418).

Despite the sustained policy support for SMEs, their record in the UK does little to support a "flexible specialization" thesis which points to the collective strength of dynamic small firm collaborations in regional agglomerations (Piore and Sabel, 1984; Lane, 1995). Industrial districts in which SMEs combine "productive decentralization and social integration" serve as highly competitive and innovative collective entrepreneurs in the Third Italy (Best, 1990). SMEs likewise establish niche capabilities or otherwise contribute to competitive strengths, often through ongoing integrated relationships with larger corporate firms, in Germany and Japan (Sharp and Walker, 1994; Lane, 1995). In the UK, the SME story is quite different. Despite the deliberate and highly ideological targeted support for SMEs, in the late 1980s overall UK support as a percentage of GDP was less than half that of the GDR; moreover, whereas 20 percent of the German support for SMEs went to research and development, only 2 percent of British support was directed there. As one study observed, "confronted by recession and aggressive competition from, amongst others, foreign firms, too many British companies cut out R & D altogether and resorted to the low price, low cost, low productivity route to competitiveness" (Sharp and Walker, 1994, p. 419). Indeed, although the UK exhibited the greatest increase in the formation of small firms in the 1980s, SMEs have done little to regenerate economic competitiveness, as one might expect, through the formation of local production systems or industrial districts.

It seems that even a rare exercise of substantial government support, advanced as part of a broader initiative to encourage a shift from collectivism to the enterprise culture, was not enough. It could not overcome a set of institutional, strategic, and industrial-cultural deficiencies: weak ties between SMEs and banks, which limited timely access to financial support for necessarily risky investments for new technologies; growing concentration and "predatory" practices in the corporate sector; reliance on less skilled workers; production of standardized goods with low to medium technology content and price-competitive rather than quality-competitive production; and restrictive trade union practices that tend to impede fast-paced innovation (Ramsey, 1991; Buxton et al., 1994b; Charles, 1995; Lane, 1995; Zeitlin, 1995).

Within a context set by competition among EU members and intensified pressures of globalization, this pattern of industrial organization and competitive strategy, combined with developments in labor markets and work relations since the 1980s, has produced a particular national production model. Drawing on a "relatively cheap, easily disposable and segmented workforce," the UK has become a specialized producer of relatively low-wage, low-technology, low-value-added products (Nolan and Harvie, 1995).

Labor market policy and industrial relations

With the weakening of trade union "power and privileges" through a well-known set of legislative restrictions and showcase industrial defeats from 1980 onwards, declining union membership, and increasing anti-union action by managers through the withdrawal of union membership, the nature of industrial relations has changed significantly. Unions can call strikes only under specified balloting procedures, including a postal ballot and a week's prior notification before any strike action; employers may dismiss striking workers and hire alternative workers for the duration of the dispute; the closed shop has been abolished; the number of pickets who can be active at the premises of a firm directly involved in the dispute can be limited and secondary pickets are illegal; unions have lost their immunity from civil damage suits and, as a consequence, industrial disputes place union funds at risk to court orders (as in the 1984–5 miners' strike) (Johnes and Taylor, 1996).

Not surprisingly, as union capacities in general have declined, and strike rates have plummeted, the role of unions in the labor market has commensurately weakened and negotiations over the organization of work have been fundamentally decollectivized. Although pay bargaining in the UK has traditionally taken place at the national level, union strength has been expressed most forcefully at the local level, in increasingly anachronistic and tenuous efforts to dig in to protect the exclusive terrain of jobs, and to secure the rights of occupational or work groups over certain tasks and technologies based on skill and craft definitions from an earlier system of production. Many of the intense industrial battles of the 1980s were demarcation disputes as management sought with considerable success to remove these elements of inflexibility. It is far less clear, however, that evolving skill requirements have been met or that occupational profiles that can make the most use of new technologies have been introduced (Dankbaar, 1994).

Whatever the pay-off in increased competitiveness, the process of change in the industrial relations system is quite pronounced. The trend towards firm-specific pay agreements and collective bargaining systems may be readily observed (Rubery, 1989). Increasingly, the weakening of the collective organizations of labor, combined with the increasing competitive demands for rapid firm-level responses to international competitive pressures, has encouraged employers to localize and modify agreements and to buy out restrictive practices: in effect, to individualize industrial relations (Howell, 1997).

The resulting flexibility has been extensive (one study found that during the 1980s three-quarters of all collective bargaining groups implemented changes in work practices) (Ingram, 1991; Howell, 1997). Equally important, flexibility in the UK has been quite one-sided, emphasizing the replacement of standard employment by part-time work, and the fragmentation and erosion of a union-based regulatory system for job demarcation and control. In comparison to France, Germany, or Sweden, the system of labor market regulation is notable for the absence of both legal restrictions or effective political or social constraints on the managerial exercise of flexibility.

When employers decide to introduce substantial changes in work organization in response to competitive pressures, management prerogative is unchecked by legislation, union power, and sectoral or national standards for regulating the labor market. As a result, even in the unionized sector, British firms exercise increased control over work organization and conditions with impunity. They can increase *functional flexibility* by reducing job demarcations, which, due to the historical importance of craft distinctions in the organization of unions, is a greater challenge to the collective organizations of labor in the UK than comparable changes would be elsewhere. At the same time, management prerogative largely controls *numerical flexibility* through changes in working time arrangements as well as *wage flexibility*: for instance, through productivity incentive agreements. Such incentive agreements further fragment bargaining systems and decollectivize the terms of employment. They also set the interests of workers who enjoy a favorable strategic position in more competitive sectors or firms against others with less advantageous locations in the system of production (Rubery, 1989).

The very fragmentation of industrial relations systems, the firm-specific nature of competitive pressures and strategic responses, and the extraordinary diversity in patterns of work organization make it difficult to generalize with confidence about national patterns of work organization. On balance, British industrial workers have experienced modest gains in task integration and upskilling, there is debate about the effect of functional flexibility on the prospects of job enlargement, and there is some moderate reduction in the traditionally rigid horizontal division of labor. Nevertheless, by contrast to Germany, for example, where management is no longer uniformly committed to Taylorist–Fordist approaches to work organization and a significant minority of workers have participated in post-Fordist forms of work organization, the conditions for innovation in the UK are far less auspicious. Traditional hierarchical approaches are entrenched, preventing significant movement toward the post-Fordist reorganization of work (Lane, 1995), and the innovation in work organization, such as it is, remains driven by management prerogative.

Transnational Production Systems: The Japanization of British Industry?

With its emphasis on price-competitiveness, fairly low-value-added products, and the ready availability of a relatively low-cost, easily dismissed, poorly organized and segmented labor force, operating within a fragmentary, individualized, and very weakly regulated system of industrial relations, the British production system reveals a distinctive pattern. This is a far cry from Uddevalla or the experiments with anthropocentric production systems in German machine tool companies or car production at Lamborghini.

As competitive pressures and firm-specific competitive strategies are shaped by institutional, organizational, and cultural elements of national production systems, it becomes clear that globalization cuts both ways in the UK. It acutely influences the way British firms and institutions reorganize production to meet competitive pressures and, at the same time, makes the British production system into a very powerful magnet to attract foreign direct investment (FDI). Importantly, state policy initiatives regarding industrial relations and labor markets – begun by Thatcher and thus far accepted by Blair – have the same double-edged results: the weakening of labor and the one-sided unregulated imposition of flexibility serve management interests at home and, at the same time, attract eager investors from abroad. What are the consequences of the particular pattern and sources of FDI for the organization of production in the UK?

FDI: the UK's most favored nation status

For a start, FDI favors national systems like those of the UK (and the United States) which rely more on private contractual and market-driven arrangements and less on state capacity and political or institutional arrangements. Reasonably enough, foreign investment tends to steer clear of production systems like that of Germany or the Scandinavian countries, which rely more on citizenship status, institutionalized coordination, and state-sponsored arrangements. Thus, globalization increases the mobility of capital and labor across borders and expresses its deregulatory and anti-institutional bias in quite dramatic patterns of FDI (Streeck, 1997). It seems likely, therefore, that patterns of foreign direct investment tend to erode negotiated coordination between nationally based capital and labor, challenge progressive distributive bargains more generally, and punish countries with more egalitarian policy legacies and institutional capacities.

In the UK, FDI focuses in a particularly acute way the interaction of national and European Union policies with broader global processes, in this case in a singularly compatible manner. From the mid-1980s onward, the single market initiative of the EU has attracted foreign investment by according insider status to non-EU-based companies, so long as minimum local content requirements are met; and, since 1979, British governments have, for both pragmatic and ideological reasons, promoted the UK as a magnet for foreign investment. For the Thatcher and Major governments, FDI was a congenial market-driven alternative to state intervention as a means to improve sectoral competitiveness, especially in the automobile industry. It had the added benefit of exposing UK producers to "lean production" techniques, and management cultures and strategies that reinforced government designs to weaken unions and enforce flexibility. It appears thus far that New Labour will continue this approach and eagerly help business, whether domestic or foreign, to help itself – an approach that emphasizes the very important role of productive investment (see Hay and Watson, 1998b).

With the UK in the 1980s attracting more than 40 percent of total US and Japanese investment in Europe, and foreign-owned companies accounting for approximately one-quarter of manufacturing output and nearly 30 percent of capital investment in British manufacturing firms, the results of the UK's effort to turn the single market program into an FDI initiative are impressive (Lee, 1996). Flows of inward direct investment to the UK have been second only to the United States during most of the last decade and are equally impressive when viewed in relation to GDP: FDI stocks as a percentage of GDP exceed those of any other G7 country, while both inward and outward direct investment flows as a percentage of GDP in the UK are more than double those of its closest G7 competitor (Treasury, 1997). In addition, FDI seems to be highly productive: labor productivity in foreign-owned manufacturing subsidiaries in the UK is reported to be approximately 40–50 percent higher than that in British-owned firms (OECD, 1996).[6] Finally, FDI appears to be growing, with direct investment by foreign companies in the UK increasing by £16.1 billion in 1996 (the highest total since 1990), and earnings from FDI reaching a record £14.4 billion (Office for National Statistics, 1997a) despite declining Asian investment.

In fact, the UK's success in attracting FDI (measured both in stocks and in flows) and its status, at the same time, not only as the most attractive host country, but as the main foreign investing country among the fifteen members of the EU, raises an important note of ambiguity about the definition of the British economy. Some have asked bluntly whether it is useful any longer to speak of *British* industry (Ackroyd et al., 1988, p. 12). As one observer has put it, do we define the UK economy "as British companies, even though so much of the capital stock located in Britain is owned by companies domiciled abroad, while, conversely, so many foreign assets make up the balance sheets of British firms?" (Lord, 1996, p. 226). Equally significant, the international mobility of capital and, as should become clear below, the proclivity of foreign capital to bring with it distinctively un-British industrial cultures, industrial relations systems, and patterns of work organization, lend empirical clarity to the disembedding of social institutions, identified by Giddens as a core feature of globalization and "high modernity." In a very explicit way, what has been termed the "Japanization of British industry" (Oliver and Wilkinson, 1992; Morris, 1994) through direct investment and the subsequent emulation of Japanese industrial practices by UK companies indicates "the 'lifting out' of social relations from local contexts" (Giddens, 1991, p. 18) and their reinsertion elsewhere with potentially significant political results.

The application of Japanese management practices

The extent of Japanization, what it means, and what implications it holds for British industry have been subjected to very extensive debate and exhaustive research. Following Oliver and Wilkinson (1992), the discussion here will be limited to the application of specific Japanese management practices to British industry, emphasizing work organization and industrial relations practices.[7] Both *direct Japanization*, which refers to changes in organizational behavior resulting from direct investment, and *mediated Japanization*, which involves the transfer of elements of Japanese manufacturing systems to non-Japanese-owned firms as a result of emulation and competitive pressures, will be considered (see Ackroyd et al., 1988; Morris, 1994). A comprehensive review of this literature, which would go beyond the scope of this analysis, should not be necessary to substantiate a simple claim that Japanization has contributed in important ways to the contemporary evolution of the actually existing organization of work and production in the UK.

Due to such factors as low costs, political climate, government-sponsored financial incentives, reduced trade union power, and a large pool of potential non-unionized recruits, the UK has been the favored location in Europe for Japanese FDI, with annual FDI flows into the UK more than four times those of Luxembourg, its nearest European rival, and eight times those of Germany (Oliver and Wilkinson, 1992; Morris et al., 1993). Quite predictably, Japanese manufacturers have concentrated their investments in regions with high unemployment and relatively cheap labor, notably the north-east and Wales (Oliver and Wilkinson, 1992). The influence of Japanese direct investment on UK industry may be illustrated by the experience in Wales, the region with the greatest proportional share of Japanese FDI, where direct investment by Sony, as early as 1974, tended to attract additional Japanese investment in consumer electronics and components manufacturing. Then, a brief reprise of the most prominent case of Japanese FDI in the UK, Nissan Sunderland in the north-east, and discussion of UK emulators in the automobile industry, will help illuminate the broader pattern.

The influence on work organization and industrial relations in Wales

Comprehensive field research sponsored by the Welsh Development Agency and conducted by researchers at the Cardiff Business School suggests that since the early 1980s Japanese manufacturing has transformed both work organization and industrial relations in Wales (Morris et al., 1993). Among the twenty-two companies included in the study, team-based organization (found in eighteen firms) and just-in-time production (found in fifteen companies) ranked first and second as the most consistently applied transfers in work organization practices. Related changes in work organization were also introduced in 50 percent or more of the companies that were studied (quality circles, statistical process control, individual fault tracing).

Taken together, the effects are interesting and somewhat paradoxical: individual autonomy is reduced in favor of team responsibility, but both teams and individual operators are subjected to incessant discipline (hour by hour, or literally minute by minute). In addition to obsessive concern with efficiency and precise time measurement of task-cycles through traditional industrial engineering techniques, task rotation is very limited (in some plants there is no rotation), and the tasks performed by individual operators (particularly in the leading electronics plants) are often short and repetitive (consisting of a sequence of operations taking some thirty seconds while a component passes on the line). Thus the transfer of Japanese management practices involves greater group responsibility than would be found in traditionally managed British factories, but at the same time, the preoccupation with time measurement of tasks, minimal job rotation of short-duration repetitive tasks, and the tendency to organize work operations on production-line principles, as the Welsh researchers conclude, "suggests a degree of continuity with, certainly not a complete break from, Taylorist or Fordist principles" (Morris et al., 1993, p. 71).

Receptivity to flexibility and diligent work habits were the main criteria for selection of shopfloor workers, and extensive training and appraisals tended to generate a disciplined workforce. Within a context set by considerable job insecurity and declining union membership, both recruits and unions (and the TUC) were prepared to acquiesce to the critical demands of Japanese-style production and the flexible, disciplined deployment it required. Above all, this meant a broad scope of management prerogatives, since day-to-day union involvement in the allocation of work tasks would entail unacceptable inefficiencies, and very stable industrial relations, since just-in-time production orientations increase the multiplier effects of even short or episodic work disruptions. Japanese investors tended to favor industrial relations systems without unions in new towns and semi-rural locations, and single-union agreements in locations with strong union traditions like Wales (Morris et al., 1993).

Trade unions were recognized in nearly all the Japanese-owned companies (22 of 24 studied), but the agreements differed quite markedly from the typical British pattern. Despite the dominance of multiple-union representation in British manufacturing enterprises, all but three of these agreements were single-recognition deals. Moreover, in a dramatic departure from traditional UK practices, of eighteen collective bargaining agreements made available to the Welsh research team, fifteen contained flexibility clauses that granted management unrestricted rights to deploy labor, with complete flexibility of jobs and duties to meet the needs of the company. In addition, fourteen contained "continuity of production" clauses, which eliminate strikes or other industrial action and refer disputes to binding arbitration. Increasingly, agreements include pendulum arbitration, in which the arbitrator must find wholly in favor of one party or the other – a process that tends to lead disputants to moderate positions and to look for the center ground (Oliver and Wilkinson, 1992). Finally, management prerogatives for extensive direct communication with the shopfloor workforce (backed by agreements in about 60 percent of the cases) reduce the traditional role of shop stewards as the go-between in management–labor interactions, and as the potential mobilizing force for worker resistance or militancy. Without exaggerating their significance (and in numerical terms the influences remain quite limited), these changes in work organization and features of the emergent transplant industrial relations system in Wales may suggest some broader patterns in the organization of production in the UK.

Nissan Sunderland

The influences of Japanese direct investment on work organization and industrial relations in Wales seem broadly to match those of corresponding investment elsewhere, notably in the north-east with the Nissan plant in Sunderland, which was opened formally by Margaret Thatcher in September 1986, to considerable fanfare. Sunderland represented the second-largest investment in Europe by a Japanese company, and Nissan UK is considered the most complete case of Japanization in the country (Garrahan and Stewart, 1992; Oliver and Wilkinson, 1992).

Peter Wickens, the Director of Personnel and Information Systems for Nissan UK, characterized the Nissan approach to production organization as a "tripod" of work practices grounded in teamwork, quality, and flexibility – a carefully articulated application of the principles of lean production pioneered at Toyota (Wickens, 1987). Both in theory and in practice, each element involved a strong departure from British industrial traditions. As in the Welsh transplant companies, teamwork involved enhanced group responsibility, but with greater control and initiative from team leaders. Cutting against the grain of traditional British skill and task demarcations, flexibility at Nissan required a bare minimum of job classifications and assignment governed by management prerogative. Responsibility for quality devolved onto both individuals and groups – a demanding and, apparently, stressful process (Garrahan and Stewart, 1992; Morris, 1994).

These practices have been aided by a supportive industrial relations context. At Nissan Sunderland there is a single-union agreement, with little opportunity for bargaining between management and union. Rather, collective bargaining is conducted with a Company Council, which represents all groups of employees (manual and non-manual, union and non-union), within a context set by a "minimum disruption" agreement and a stipulation that the union support flexible working practices and productivity goals. The system weakens the union and provides the industrial relations stability required for just-in-time production (Garrahan and Stewart, 1992; Oliver and Wilkinson, 1992).

The implications of Nissan UK remain controversial. Some see in Nissan UK a region-saving injection of very substantial investment (projected at £610 million) by a world-class company that brings with it a production model that combines the efficiency of lean production with a more European attention to the quality of work life (see Charles, 1995). Others see paternalistic management control, intensified assembly-line work, and subservient trade unions imposing the forced flexibility of managerial control over labor on a region softened up by deindustrialization and the erosion of trade union power (Garrahan and Stewart, 1992; Sadler, 1992). In their extensive and critical study of Nissan UK, Garrahan and Stewart turn the managerial "tripod" popularized by Wickens on its head, arguing that "the 'Nissan Way' rests upon control through quality, exploitation via flexibility, and surveillance via teamworking" (1992, p. 139).

Broader implications of FDI in the UK

Beyond the continuing controversy about the merits of the Nissan Way lies an important recognition shared alike by critics and supporters of Nissan's approach, as well as by observers of the Japanese management practices in British industry more generally: in terms of industrial relations and work organization, the British motor industry could not compete without emulating Japanese practices. Although competitive pressures from Nissan were only a small contributing factor, by the 1980s a multitude of factors were contributing to the rapid decline of the British car industry. The strategy of merging the whole of the UK's automobile industry into British Leyland in 1968 left it ill equipped to face the challenge of heightened import penetration, stagnant home demand, and the policy of leading international producers to coordinate production and marketing regionally within an international division of labor (Church, 1994; Foreman-Peck et al., 1995). This global strategy did little to staunch the bleeding of the UK's quickly failing indigenous motor car industry. As one observer put it, "the Trojan horse effect of tied imports and heavily-sourced cars which only appeared to be British was thus partly responsible for Leyland's inability to generate sales at levels which would support scale economies in production," and contributed to a deepening trade imbalance (Church, 1994, p. 116).

Faced with deteriorating competitive conditions, particularly *vis-à-vis* Japanese imports and transplants, since the 1980s each of the three leading non-Japanese producers in the UK – Rover, Ford, and General Motors (GM) – has attempted with varying degrees of success to emulate Japanese work organization and industrial relations practices.[8] As is well known, the most radical makeover in industrial relations was attempted by Michael Edwardes at Rover (formerly British Leyland), where very aggressive efforts were undertaken to assert managerial prerogative in work organization, including closure threats, successful confrontations with shopfloor unionism and the shop steward organization, and insistence upon the claim that the determination of work practices was a managerial function, not subject to negotiation. In a clear example of emulation, job classifications were substantially reduced, and team-working and quality control initiatives were implemented. In a context set by traditional British management attitudes and hierarchies and a confrontational management style, results were mixed (Foreman-Peck et al., 1995). Since 1992, however, with Edwardes gone, and after extensive union consultation, Rover has more successfully introduced a package of Japanese-inspired changes, including binding arbitration, flexibility agreements, acceptance of a single bargaining unit, and elimination of remaining job demarcations (Morris, 1994).

Nissan Sunderland has cast a huge shadow over its UK competitors, with the Chairman of Vauxhall (a GM subsidiary) claiming that the Nissan plant in Sunderland enjoyed an advantage of £250 to £500 per car, and a plant convenor of the Transport and General Workers' Union (TGWU) at a Vauxhall factory claiming that all Nissan's competitors "are looking to break down the demarcation lines because we all have to compete with Nissan," and wondering whether Nissan was "allowed" into the north-east, "not to produce employment . . . but to help get the car workers into line" (Oliver and Wilkinson, 1992, p. 112). Competition from Nissan UK and Japanese manufacturers has been used to justify extensive changes in GM's UK facilities, including management insistence on no-strike clauses (which unions successfully resisted), and a Nissan-style flexibility agreement in its Bedford plant (which it won only after closure threats).

Japanese emulation at Ford – quality circles, flexible working (reducing the number of shopfloor job classifications from 550 to 52 and allowing some flexibility across skills: for example, between production and maintenance) and team working – has also been both extensive and controversial. These changes contributed to a national strike at Ford UK in 1988, which, because of the strategy of regional integration of production, combined with just-in-time production, had immediate repercussions in layoffs and the disruption of production in Ford operations throughout Europe. In the second week of the strike, management sweetened the financial terms a little and, more importantly, conceded some critical issues on the hotly contested front of Japanese-style organization and work practices. Ford UK accepted a "non-imposition" clause which guaranteed that reforms in work practices would be subject to local agreement, effectively abandoning the right to introduce new work practices by management prerogative that the company had won in the 1985 agreement. As Oliver and Wilkinson note, "Ironically, it was Japanese-style production integration that gave workers the ability to hit Ford so hard in their resistance to Japanese-style work practices" (1992, p. 113).

range of labor-inclusion and exclusion models, pursued country-specific models and policy aims, most critically in constructing systems of production and governing the economy. In short, taken together, national policy sovereignty (especially with reference to economic policy) and class anchored politics. This chapter suggests that neither of these very basic elements of politics can any longer be taken for granted.

International competition, the application of computer-based technologies and the diffusion of new forms of work organization intensify the pressure on managers to find the right production and marketing strategy, from an expanding menu of scale and scope and organizational options. Given these processes of globalization, any national model, whether Italian industrial districts, Japanese lean production, or the German high-skill, high-wage, high-responsibility social market economy, presents rigidities in the face of cross-border pressures, whether in the form of FDI or a more inchoate emulation of apparently successful, often sector-specific, options.

These processes of globalization and technological and organizational innovation create challenges for national systems of production and for local and sectoral economies. Each model experiences tendencies toward cross-national hybridization, as cross-border influences infuse nationally specific industrial cultures, industrial relations systems, and the range of institutions and practices that constitute a system of production. Thus, one signal feature of this post-Fordist world of perpetual innovation and volatility is the fluid dialectical interplay of national institutional embeddedness and the disembeddedness of specific technologies, organizational routines, and local industrial relations systems.

In Europe, this process is exacerbated by the tendency toward EU regionalization, which makes community policy in critical areas superordinate to national policy and, at the same time, invites powerful multinationals to develop regional strategies, as in automobile production, that consign operations in one country to a particular niche within an international division of labor. Moreover, as noted above, for those countries that join the euro club, the European Central Bank assumes critical economic policy powers that reduce the sphere of maneuver of governments at the level of the nation-state and accelerate the tendency toward "an institutional monoculture of deregulated markets and hierarchies" (Crouch and Streeck, 1997, p. 13; Grant, 1998) that reduces national diversity.

It is important to note that this context provides a perfect opening for the UK government to make the most of the autonomous powers over economic and monetary policy that it retains, while exercising its "wait and see" option on the single currency. If and when the UK accepts the euro, it will sacrifice its capacity to cushion the effects of economic downturns or sectoral or regional declines in employment or competitiveness by adjusting interest rates and exchange rates. It is also likely that countries will be pressured to accept tax harmonization.

Before any coordination of direct taxation sets in, the UK has the opportunity to make the most of relatively low corporate and employment taxes to attract foreign investment, which it could do quite successfully without retaining the "most restrictive trade union laws anywhere in the western world" (Blair, 1997). At the same time, New Labour might profitably consider introducing more "anthropocentric" and collaborative labor market and industrial relations policies in order to modernize the UK model and achieve a higher measure of quality-competitive production. Indeed, the pre-euro experiences of alternative approaches to post-Fordist flexibility make a strong case for the competitive advantages of a more diversified national model of production. In short, the UK has ample opportunity to exercise national policy-making influence now and to enjoy the benefits of new thinking and modernization in industrial policy, labor market policy, and industrial relations policy before those opportunities are narrowed by EMU developments later.

Moving to class-based politics, the second critical constitutive element of the center-left project, what inferences can be drawn about how the organization of production structures politics in this era of hybrid post-Fordist production systems and sharply differentiated experiences of labor? It is important to recall that Fordism as a production system – characterized by Taylorist work organization, assembly-line production, and price-competitive scale economies – was linked symbiotically to a broader social and economic system of the Keynesian welfare state and the distributive bargains and social democratic politics of the postwar settlement. Non-market coordinating mechanisms, from incomes policies to public ownership of industries, reinforced the architecture of Fordist production, which was grounded in mass production of standardized goods for mass consumption. At the same time, in practice – and even more so, in principle – the workforce that experienced the stultifying rigidities of assembly-line mass production acquired the central role of political agency. Politics, therefore, and not just production, was organized by a Fordist scenario, as the immediacy and pungency of similar work experiences on the line created solidarities, reinforced organizationally and culturally by powerful trade unions, then underwritten and legitimized by party rhetoric and public policy.[9] By contrast, post-Fordism does not carry with it any comparable capacity for reorganizing politics on a new institutional basis.

It seems reasonable to suppose that the forced flexibility of post-Fordist production in the UK, the degradation of union power and privileges, and the decollectivization of industrial relations systems and conditions of employment, all reinforced by the ongoing processes of Japanization of British industry, fundamentally change the equation.

Workplace solidarities are more episodic and local, and the means for collective class agency have become sharply attenuated. Do the fluidity and variety of production systems help explain the uncharacteristic volatility in British party politics? What happens to center-left politics as class loses its autonomous capacity to organize politics, and as other attachments shape the daily experiences of individuals and influence political agendas?

Thus far both social democracy and alternative political projects have been defined largely by their connections to abiding collective interests, defined by production, expressed in distributive conflicts, animated and organized through powerful collective institutions. This distinguishing principle of politics is far harder to recognize in the UK today. In chapter 10 we will consider progressive alternatives to the UK's rather bleak post-Fordist landscape (challenge 1) and raise basic questions about the capacity of political agency to reconnect interests with a center-left project (challenge 5). As we will see in part III, once the frame of reference is widened to focus on the experiences of women and ethnic minorities, the challenges to reconnect politics and interests become even greater, but at the same time, new prospects for political mobilization emerge.

Part III
The Unmaking of the English Working Class

5

Women, Work, and Social Policy

If one could ever properly write about the making of *the* English working class, as E. P. Thompson did so brilliantly for the period between 1780 and 1832, when transformed productive relations inspired insurgency and growing political cohesion (Thompson, 1966), the time has surely passed. Very likely the process of class formation has been irretrievably reversed.

In empirical terms, as we have seen, hard-edged labor market and industrial relations policies have strengthened the tendencies of the UK's post-Fordist model of work organization to fragment the experiences of working people, disaggregate interests, and erode class-wide agency. In the face of concerted domestic political designs and powerfully reinforcing global processes, forced flexibility and decollectivized industrial relations chip away at class agency. Workers are fragmenting back into what Thompson observed before the struggle was successfully made: a loosely tied "bundle of discrete phenomena" (1966, p. 9). Of course, a second, more obvious point about the title of Thompson's classic should be noted: in this global era, amid the growing recognition of a multiethnic, multicultural society in the UK, it almost goes without saying that all working people, even within the territory of England, cannot be described any longer as English.[1]

More importantly, as should become clear by the end of this part of the book, the disparate patterns displayed in the work experiences of women and of ethnic minorities – as distinct from those of white men – provide powerful evidence that the prospects of unified class agency are few. Looked at from the side of production, it is not clear what – if anything – can bind the ever-loosening bundle pieced together from the disconnected careers of working peoples and their quite incommensurate experiences, as well, of family, community, and cultural life more broadly. Indeed, this is where the greatest challenge facing a center-left project begins, and the art of politics enters: to construct some design of unity from such a disjointed pattern of experiences when there is no apparent countervailing or transcendent bond of sufficient intensity or durability.

Of course, there remains a great deal to admire in Thompson's *agent-centered* or *processual* approach[2] to the understanding of class formation: that classes are not analytical constructs or locations based on objective conditions (see Katznelson, 1986; Wright, 1997, pp. 492–6). Rather, "class happens" when some people, "as a result of common experiences (inherited or shared), feel and articulate the identity of their interests," usually against others whose interests are opposed (Thompson, 1966, p. 9). Thompson's historical studies remain a powerful reminder that class formation occurs at this crucial level of lived experience, as shared understandings of the social world and common needs and interests inspire bonds of trust and solidarity, and develop in people a *"disposition* to *behave* as a class"[3] (1965, p. 357).

Class and the Formation of Collective Interests and Dispositions

Thompson suggests that class "happens" as a consequence of common experiences, traditions, and values, and that the process of class formation forges an identity of interests and political dispositions. As an historical claim, a normative preference, and an implicit methodological framework, Thompson supposes that all workplace experiences, as well as the traditions, social experiences, and values that laborers take with them from home, contribute to solidarities understood in class terms. It is necessary, however, to stress the historical contingency of the claim: even if class and no other animating collective identity "happened" then, and all tributaries of social experience contributed only to one torrent of unified class insurgency, the same salutary conjunction of formative influences is not occurring today.

In the contemporary period, different kinds of experience (family and community) and varied traditions and values (religious, moral, cultural) inevitably contribute to quite distinctive interests and political agendas. Work cannot be separated from the specific ethnic or gendered influences upon – and interpretation of – the work experience, whether commonly understood by reference to class or other systems of collective identity such as race, ethnicity, or gender.[4] Moreover, institutionalized expressions of cultural marginality and chronically underrepresented influences in shaping political party, trade union, or public policy agendas are likely to take their toll. As a result, a mix of on-the-job and off-the-job experiences can reinforce the "disposition to behave" as part of a group constituted by reference to alternative attachments and collective designs. What does it take to forge the disposition to behave as a gender-based collective actor or as a minority ethnic community? How, concretely and interactively, do class and alternative collective identities combine and recombine in a perpetual process of interest formation? These are empirical questions inviting careful study and permitting only contingent protean answers.

In this part of the book, the scope of analysis extends beyond the traditional focus on manufacturing industry in its Fordist and post-Fordist configurations to a consideration of how the individual biographies and collective histories that frame the experience of work may be shaped by gender, race, and ethnicity. In trying to understand this fluid dynamic, I will assume that it is far more difficult for women or ethnic minority men, than for white men, to experience the unmediated formative power of "just plain work": that is, to treat as natural or automatic the translation of raw experience or group identity into interest, viewed solely in terms of class. Class happens, but race, ethnicity, and gender invariably happen as well. Whatever epistemological distinctions may be claimed – or differential strategic potential asserted – no process of collective formation occurs autonomously. They all happen in splendid and bewildering transmutation. This chapter looks at the fluid interplay of class and gender identity as it is shaped by changing patterns of female labor force participation, and the increasingly conflict-ridden connection between work, social policy, and family.

Women's Employment: Context, Patterns, and Implications

It is widely recognized that one of the most decisive changes in the labor market and in UK patterns of employment in the last quarter-century has been the increased participation of women in paid labor. Between 1971 and 1995, the number of women in the civilian labor force rose by 40 percent, from 8.6 million to 12.0 million, while the number of men in the workforce increased by a meager 2 percent. Accordingly, during this period women increased their share of the workforce from under 36 percent to 44 percent (Johnes and Taylor, 1996). Since the 1970s, one of the clearest and most significant trends in the UK labor market has been the narrowing gender gap in rates of economic activity (the percentage of persons of working age who either have or are seeking a job). In spring 1996, 71 percent of working-age women were economically active compared to 85 percent of men. To put this figure in perspective, from a gap in economic activity rates between men and women of 36.6 percent in 1971, according to government projections, by 2006 the gap is expected to narrow to 9 percent (Office for National Statistics, 1997b).

However significant in themselves, these data indicate annual employment snap-shots rather than careers at work. What does the pattern of labor force participation for women in the contemporary UK look like during the course of their whole working lives? While it is very difficult to pinpoint life-cycle participation rates for women, it seems safe to say that, of women of working age in the 1990s, three-quarters or more will at some time in their lives participate in paid labor, and that participation declines between the ages of 25 and 40, when some women concentrate their energies on child care. It should be noted also that there is a marked upward trend in the economic activity rates of women between the ages of 25 and 54, which has been explained by the tendency for women to have children at an older age and then return to paid work more quickly (Office for National Statistics, 1997b). Hence, given the trend line, for women presently in their twenties, one could predict that roughly 80 to 90 percent will be economically active at some point in their lives.

Most women in the UK work part time, often in jobs with fewer than sixteen hours of work per week and often with fewer than eight hours (while fewer than one in every fifteen men are employed part time). More than three-quarters of women working part time report that they do not want a full-time job,[5] yet more women than men (in raw numbers, not simply as a percentage) take on second jobs. In addition, women are far less likely to be self-employed than men: in 1996 there were roughly three self-employed men for every woman, although, as will be discussed below, the concept of self-employment is quite elastic, and among some ethnic minority groups female self-employment is very significant (Central Statistical Office, 1994; Nolan and Harvie, 1995; Duncan, 1996; Office for National Statistics, 1997b).

It should come as no surprise, moreover, that women's experiences of work in the contemporary UK, like those of men, have been shaped by the forced flexibility imposed on large sectors of the workforce as a consequence of the global pressures, governmental policies, and managerial preferences that have transformed the organization of production. These broader developments, however, have had a disparate impact on the work experience of women, due in large measure to the combined influences of several related processes: the growth of service sector employment at the expense of manufacturing (deindustrialization); the way global pressures for the introduction of new technologies have shaped women's work; and the resulting labor market segmentation in the distribution of jobs, their quality, and changes in the work experience.

Deindustrialization

A secular trend involving increased labor in service sectors at the expense of manufacturing may be observed in all mature economies.

Widely referred to as deindustrialization, the trend often carries with it an alarming assumption of declining competitiveness, and the fear of slow growth and rising unemployment. The mere fact of heightened employment growth in the service sector, however, does not necessarily imply structural imbalances or signal declining manufacturing. On the contrary, reduced employment in manufacturing, corresponding with rapid increases in productivity in agriculture, manufacturing, and extractive industries, is a commonplace feature of maturing economies.

Deindustrialization becomes a problem, however, as it has in the UK, when growth in the service sector occurs at the expense of industrial production, without strategic restructuring of the kind employed in the FRG prior to unification. Unification doubtless destabilized the German model, and the precipitous increase in unemployment since the 1993 recession underscores the constraints that global competition can impose on even the strongest national economies. Until unification, however, the FRG illustrated a relatively benign form of deindustrialization. Although service sector employment rose from approximately 40 percent to nearly 60 percent between 1960 and 1990 (Temple, 1994), Germany benefited from the sustainable productivity gains associated with effective quality-competitive products on the international market (diversified quality production) (Streeck, 1991). At the same time, collective negotiations with labor and extensive welfare state support helped ease the inevitable redistribution of employment. This process has been called "positive" deindustrialization (see Streeck, 1991; Nolan and Harvie, 1995; Streeck, 1997).

Although much scholarly controversy surrounds discussions of the UK's industrial trajectory, it seems safe to say that in the case of the UK declining manufacturing employment has been occasioned by lack of investment and competitiveness, and adverse developments in patterns of demand: domestic demand favoring overseas products, and manufacturing enterprises located in the UK facing increased difficulties in maintaining their market share of international demand ("negative" deindustrialization) (Nolan and Harvie, 1995). As this very brief comparison of the German and British processes and patterns of deindustrialization indicates, deindustrialization is as much about politics as economics: without effective collective institutions backed by training programs and comprehensive social policies, there is little to cushion the dislocating effects of a massive shake-out of labor from manufacturing industry.

The comparison makes equally clear that patterns of global competitiveness powerfully shape national experiences of deindustrialization. Clearly, Germany's highly competitive diversified quality production could sustain employment in key manufacturing sectors longer than most, and could for a time ameliorate the effects of a perilous decline in employment when it came (Streeck, 1991). Conversely, deindustrialization in the

UK tended to reinforce structural weaknesses. It helped consolidate the UK's international role as a relatively low-wage, low-value-added, low-technology producer (in a European frame of reference).

At the same time, the processes of industrial change reinforced the UK's position as a leading technological and organizational innovator in key services, including retailing and property-related services, all led by the City of London, and supported in this area by a world-class skill base and very propitious Thatcher-era macroeconomic policies. As one observer explained, "deregulation in both banking and foreign-exchange controls, encouraged consumption, travel and leisure services, while the deregulation of telecommunications thrust the City of London into the forefront of innovation and experimentation" (Sharp and Walker, 1994, p. 426). Areas of quite startling success and notable failure combined to fix in place a workforce that was highly divided in skills and prospects and, as will become clear, segmented along gender lines.

Unfortunately, the UK's success in retailing, distributive activities (hotels and catering), financial services, and other areas of competitive service sector specialization has not spilled over into industrial sectors. The UK's withdrawal from technologically innovative manufacturing means increasingly that capital equipment needed in the more robust service sectors must be purchased externally (or from foreign-owned companies with subsidiaries in the UK), so expansion of services has little multiplier effect on manufacturing industries. Although foreign investment in manufacturing has some ameliorative effect, there seems to be little reason to anticipate that the structural imbalance in the UK economy will soon right itself (Sharp and Walker, 1994). Broadly speaking, therefore, what has evolved in terms of the distribution of jobs, conditions of employment, and patterns of employment is likely to remain in place for some time.

Changes to date in the division of labor in the UK associated with deindustrialization have displayed quite a distinctive pattern: they have proceeded in clear phases, in an unbalanced manner, at a faster pace than elsewhere, and with particular repercussions for female employment (see Temple, 1994). The growth in service employment occurred in two phases, roughly corresponding to the ebb and flow not in aggregate levels of social expenditure (since real spending on welfare programs as a percentage of GDP was surprisingly impervious to change, even during the Thatcher years) (Pierson, 1994), but in the institution building of the welfare state. In the first expansionary period, from 1948 to 1973, service sector growth characteristically occurred in the non-commodified public sector (health, education, and public administration). After 1973, and more decisively after 1979, the pattern reversed (except for steady increases in health workers), with public sector employment reaching its high point in 1979 and declining by roughly one-third by 1996.

Since 1979, the shift into services in the UK has been significantly greater than in Germany, Japan, or the United States (and somewhat greater than in France): in fact, the rate of decline in manufacturing employment has been more pronounced in the UK than anywhere else in EU Europe, shrinking from over seven million to approximately four million jobs since 1979 (Nolan and Harvie, 1995). Moreover, during this second period, the bulk of service sector growth has come in the private sector, with the largest increases in banking and finance. Substantial gains have also occurred in distributive activities (hotels and catering), management consultants and business services, cultural and recreational activities, and sanitation services (Temple, 1994).

Service sector employment and new technologies

Most significant here, the rapid growth of the female labor market has proceeded hand in glove with a corresponding growth in service sector employment – a pattern that seems likely to continue and, quite possibly, deepen. As is widely reported, women are disproportionately represented in service sector employment. Therefore, the sectoral changes in patterns of employment associated with deindustrialization raise particularly salient questions about women's employment.

The growth in casual or non-standard forms of employment (part-time working, new patterns of shiftworking, homeworking, teleworking, and so forth) is widespread: it is occurring across industrial sectors throughout Europe and the rest of the world, and it affects both men and women. There is a broad consensus that the shift from manufacturing to service sector jobs increases non-standard forms of employment, with part-time work a particularly salient characteristic both of service sector employment and of female-dominated occupations (McFate, 1995; Webster, 1996). In addition, it is very clear that the proliferation of part-time and other forms of casual or non-standard employment has a disparate impact on women's employment: 85 percent of part-time workers in the UK are women and 45 percent of all women who are engaged in paid labor work part time (Office for National Statistics, 1997b). Approximately 40 percent of those who work part time work fewer than sixteen hours a week and enjoy none of the protections of standard employees: they have no statutory right to payments when laid off and have no right to appeal against unfair dismissal. This trend toward less secure and protected employment is deepening, since 70 percent of all new part-time employment opportunities involve casual jobs of sixteen hours or fewer (Hutton, 1995).

Since such a high proportion of the expanding employment opportunities for women are in the service sector, it is worth looking more closely at the quality and conditions of employment in these jobs. Needless to say, the quality of work varies enormously, with substantial differences in conditions of employment and pay. A quick look at what may be the two polar opposites – retailing and financial services – helps provide some hint of the range of women's employment, illustrating both the variety and commonality in work experiences. It will also identify some interesting developments linked to the introduction of new information and communication technologies.

The retail sector   In retailing, where low-end or entry-level jobs are staffed almost entirely by women, the large chain stores have introduced a very wide range of part-time and "zero hours" contractual arrangements, with some form of part-time work covering more than two-thirds of this labor force. Perhaps more than in any other sector, technological innovations have been used to reconstitute, break up, and casualize low-end retailing jobs. Management in leading British retailers routinely use electronic "point of sales" systems, combined with information technologies that track sales patterns and customer profiles and computerized "scheduling engines" to create elaborately subdivided staffing rotations. With an attention to detail and planning that almost defies belief, staffing requirements and scheduling are often broken down on a person-by-person basis to fifteen-minute intervals over a one-week or two-week period, with the result that small efficiencies create the impetus for a massive balkanization of positions.

This is how the tendency for casualized, insecure employment, driven by automation, looks in one division of a major retailing group, with 279 DIY stores and 15,000 employees: 55 percent of employees are part time (and 70 percent of the part-timers are women); of the part-timers, 16 percent work Saturdays only; 14 percent work Sundays; and for the remaining 70 percent, the work schedule can vary daily or weekly depending on local staffing needs, with some employees working mornings, some afternoons, and some a mixture of shifts (Webster, 1996). It is perhaps not surprising that this kind of forced numerical and functional flexibility is imposed disproportionately and so crudely on women in low-end employment in retailing. How have women fared, by contrast, in the ostensibly more rarefied environment of financial services?

Financial services   It turns out that financial services are a good laboratory case for observing evolving patterns of gender-based job segregation. Two forms of job segregation are often introduced to explain why women receive lower pay: either women are sorted out of jobs requiring high education, skills and responsibilities, or alternatively "good" jobs can become "feminized." When women come to occupy them, they tend to become reclassified as requiring lower skills and are assigned lower pay grades, independent of job content or responsibility, and conversely, jobs tend to be reclassified upwards when men perform them. Research has shown that, while both tendencies apply, the effect of feminization predominates in British financial services.[6] For example, in building societies that had no management training programs, sub-branches were often run by senior women cashiers, receiving relatively low pay. However, where in-house training schemes were introduced, men in junior management positions assumed these responsibilities and received correspondingly higher pay (Craig et al., 1985).

More generally, studies have shown that, even after a complaint against Barclays Bank brought to the Equal Opportunities Commission in 1983 forced changes in the recruitment structure to reduce vertical gender segregation, progress by women into managerial grades has been limited. Interestingly, despite the increasing reliance of both clearing banks and building societies on the recruitment of female labor, the substantial upgrading of women's employment in the financial sector and real changes in women's opportunities for advancement through "short career clerical hierarchies" has not frontally challenged labor market segmentation. As one study noted, gains to women in the managerial ranks of the financial services sector, which have "developed as a consequence of technical and labour market changes do not represent the taking over of 'men's jobs' by women, rather, they are new jobs" (Crompton and Sanderson, 1994, p. 294). In short, patterns of job segregation, with some modification, remain in the financial sector. Moreover, although non-standard employment is less common than in retailing and many other services, the "information revolution" has rendered part-time and temporary work more prevalent in financial services than before. As high street branches are closed, and retail banking is reorganized by the use of automated teller machines and centralized processing centers, the use of largely part-time and casual workers to process credit card accounts and service customers is growing rapidly (Webster, 1996).

Clearly, conditions of employment for women in the financial services sector do not mirror the more dreary circumstances of low-end, casual labor that is typical of retailing. Indeed, the point should not be lost that, for women who are core, full-time workers, opportunities for advancement into middle-level career clerical grades, if not upper management, spurred by the introduction of new technologies, are plentiful. However, a crucial gendered dimension of innovation should also be noted. Unlike the most exalted cases of male manufacturing discussed in chapter 4, such as Swedish automobile assembly or German machine tools, in both financial and retail services the introduction of new technologies holds little chance for women to find improved work satisfaction or high-skilled, high-wage employment. On the contrary, innovation implies greater job fragmentation, casualization, and loss of protection and security for the vast majority of the growing army of women in service sector employment.

The comparative context

Finally, a useful context for understanding women's employment experiences in the UK can be provided by some international comparisons. A comparative study of female labor force participation and wage rates in central and eastern European countries in the late 1980s to those of selected OECD countries provides one interesting perspective. At approximately 62 percent, the female participation rate in the UK (second only to Sweden in Western Europe) approached the traditionally high participation rates of the communist-party states to the east. However, although average female earnings as a percentage of male earnings were on average higher in western than in eastern or central European countries, the greatest differential between male and female earnings, East or West, was found in the UK (Sohinger and Rubinfeld, 1993).

Another useful context for understanding women's labor market participation in the UK can be provided by locating the differential between male and female wage rates within a broader comparative pattern of changes in wage inequality. Richard B. Freeman and Lawrence F. Katz have shown that, for the period from 1979 to 1990, the United States and the United Kingdom displayed some notable similarities in patterns of wage inequality (measured in terms of a log of the ratio of earnings in the top decile of the workforce compared to the bottom decile). A comparison of eight OECD countries indicates that only the US and the UK experienced double-digit increases in wage inequality, with the UK far outpacing its North American counterpart (0.28 compared to 0.17 for the UK and the US, respectively). Moreover, not simply the magnitude, but two important additional characteristics about the wage changes distinguish the British and American cases. First, on the positive side for the UK, real earnings rose during the 1979 to 1990 period for workers across the board, so increased inequality notwithstanding, the real wages of workers in the lowest decile rose, while real wages declined markedly for workers at the bottom of the earnings distribution in the US. Secondly, and far less auspiciously for the UK, although in the United States wage differentials between women and men narrowed despite the general pattern of growing inequality, the female-to-male earnings ratio widened sharply in the UK. In fact, gender wage differentials narrowed or remained fairly stable nearly everywhere else among the OECD countries during this period, with the exception of Japan (Freeman and Katz, 1994).

Finally, a 1997 survey from Eurostat, the statistical arm of the European Union, confirms that in several EU countries women still get paid substantially less than men, measured in hourly earnings, even when they have comparable education and work in the same industry and occupation. However, the differential is greatest in the UK, where it is just below

25 percent. Moreover, when the overall mix of jobs and the effects of sex segregation in the labor market are taken into account, including both full- and part-time workers, the gap increases to 36 percent – and gender pay inequality in the UK remains the worst in the European Union. To complete the picture, when women are able to move up the job ladder, patterns of inequality actually deepen. Women and men performing lower-paid service jobs, such as shop assistants or clerks, come closer to parity than those who have moved into the better-compensated and more prestigious positions: women in management positions in the UK receive only two-thirds the pay of their male counterparts (Bien, 1997).

Where politics meets markets   The organization of production as well as broader social, political, and policy directions have created serious impediments for women both in and outside the workplace. Taken together, labor market policy and the persistent drumbeat of the enterprise culture, which encouraged forced flexibility in work assignments, hastened the proliferation of the less favorable service sector jobs that have largely shaped the pattern of female employment in the UK. In addition, as recent research has shown, intensified employment restructuring in the NHS, the UK's largest employer, has held wages down, intensified work, and reinforced women's labor market subordination – in part because "male and female employees refuse to . . . cross traditional gender lines" (Kahn, 1997, p. 22). APS is hardly the issue for women, who continue to face an uphill battle to achieve secure, well-compensated, full-time employment, much less equality with men in the labor force.

Both the Thatcher and Major governments made clear that numerical and functional flexibility for management, resulting in the creation of a growing permanent cadre of part-time and casual workers with lower wages and vastly reduced benefits packages, would take priority over efforts to equalize the job quality and wage levels of women. The pay differentials compounded the effects of limited pension rights and employment protection as well as the reduced status and opportunities for advancement associated with part-time jobs. For the sizable proportion of British women occupying low-paying and insecure jobs, especially those in mother-only families, there is a palpable connection between labor force participation and their experience of the welfare state. As should become clear, however, the close connection between work and social policy, and the incessant pressures that many women (and some men) experience in trying to reconcile and coordinate employment and family responsibilities, is in no way limited exclusively to those in lower-paid or non-standard or insecure jobs. To understand the consequences of social policy on women's work and lives in the UK, and its potential importance for identity and interest formation, it is necessary first to note some of the defining characteristics of the welfare state in the UK, and to locate it broadly in a comparative perspective.

The Work–Welfare–Family Nexus

Students of the welfare state have noted that policy goals and instruments can be as important as spending levels. Are benefits means-tested or universal? Are provisions conceived as social assistance designed to meet the temporary needs of individuals, or are they intended to redistribute resources between the more and the less prosperous in society as part of a strategy of "class abatement" (Marshall, 1950), or as part of a more robust social democratic strategy to decommodify the provision of goods and services such as housing and health care (Esping-Andersen, 1990)? Does the state directly provide services or offer cash benefits that can be used to purchase services from private providers?

Welfare and breadwinner regimes

With some exceptions (notably in the provision of health care), from its inception following the 1942 Beveridge Report (Government, 1942), social provision in the UK has fit the model of a "residual" welfare state (Titmuss, 1958). Although not a pure case due to the historic universalism of the Beveridge plan, the UK also shares many of the features of a "liberal" welfare regime (Esping-Andersen, 1990). The welfare state in the UK offers relatively few comprehensive services, relies more on subsidies for private provision than on direct state provision of services, and stresses means-tested assistance and modest social insurance programs, with increasingly strict eligibility rules, modest benefits and acceptance often stigmatized. The sanctions associated with New Labour's New Deal, the powerful assertions that rights must be linked to responsibilities and the emphasis on means-tested benefits deepen the liberal orientation of the welfare state in the UK.

The *liberal* orientation of the welfare state, which is found in its purest form in the United States, may be distinguished from two other welfare state regime types identified by Esping-Andersen. The *social democratic* welfare regimes found in Scandinavian countries such as Sweden and Denmark provide far more generous, comprehensive, redistributive social policies, intended to promote equality of outcomes and, wherever possible, substitute the social rights of citizenship for market forces. From the perspective of the institutional tools and policy aims that broadly characterize a welfare regime, the *corporatist-statist* welfare regime, which is found in countries such as France, Germany, and Italy, may be considered a moderate alternative to its liberal or social democratic counterparts. The corporatist-statist welfare regimes are prepared to displace market forces in order to sustain social rights, but are designed nonetheless to preserve the differentials associated with class and occupational status. As a consequence, social provisions, while more generous, comprehensive, and universal than in the liberal model, have quite limited redistributive consequences (Esping-Andersen, 1990).

Analyzed from the perspective of the gendered implications of social policy, however, this erstwhile moderate regime becomes the outlier. Since social policy is strongly influenced by the Church, preservation of the traditional male-breadwinner family model is an important defining characteristic of the corporatist-statist welfare regime. As a result, social policy tends to privilege women's family roles (as mother and later as widow) and, for the purposes of social entitlements, treats women primarily as dependent wives. In Germany, for example, as one recent study of gender and European social policies emphasizes, the purpose of family benefits and supplementary benefits has been "to enable women – married ones – to stay at home as housewives and mothers, as well as to acknowledge both the importance of women's work at home and the need to raise the value of such nonwage labor" (Ostner and Lewis, 1995, p. 187).

The role of Germany in trying to derail EU efforts to foster greater workplace equality between men and women provides a telling illustration of the correlation between welfare regime type and specific gender orientations of social policy. Germany, the founding member of the corporatist-statist welfare regime, has resisted EU initiatives concerning equal pay and equal treatment at work for men and women, complying with directives only reluctantly. It should come as no surprise, therefore, that women's labor force participation in Germany, a corporatist-statist *strong male breadwinner* country, is chronically low in comparative terms.

Some other countries, including the UK as we shall see, present interesting mixed cases in which institutionalized policies may be inconsistent or at cross-purposes with the aims and cultural values of the welfare state. The gendered "breadwinner" categorizations of Ostner and Lewis and the welfare state regime designations of Esping-Andersen do not match these cases as well as they do the case of Germany.[7] This point is well illustrated by France, where the tendency of state policy to promote mothering as well as active participation in paid labor leads to its designation as a *moderate male breadwinner* country (Ostner and Lewis, 1995) with an inconsistent legacy of employment policies and cultural expectations. In the 1970s and 1980s France introduced a host of legislative initiatives to advance gender equality in employment and even to encourage women to improve skills in science education and move into high-technology industry, but at the same time, due in part to state policy, part-time work in France has become "a feminized ghetto" (Jenson, 1988). A perfect indication of France's mixed picture on gender and social policy, it focuses policy on providing women with the means either to stay at home as primary care providers, with little economic hardship, or to remain in the workforce. In order to ensure that low-income mothers enjoy the same opportunities as mothers with high incomes, France provides more low-cost, licensed, and subsidized child care than any other western country (Bakker, 1988).

Analysis of labor force participation rates for women under the age of sixty with children less than eighteen years old, grouped by welfare state regime type, indicates a distinctive pattern: an average of 52.7 percent for the corporatist-statist regimes, Germany, France and Italy (46.2 percent if France is excluded), compared to an 87.8 percent average in a set of countries with social-democratic welfare regimes (Denmark and Sweden) and 61.9 percent for the US and the UK, representing the liberal welfare regime (see Kamerman, 1996). It seems evident that employment rates for mothers tend to be low in countries whose welfare regimes fit Esping-Andersen's corporatist-statist model; conversely, labor force participation for women with children is very high in social democratic welfare regimes. In fact, Ostner and Lewis (1995) categorize these countries as *weak male breadwinner* cases, since social policy has tended to define women primarily as wage workers, albeit predominantly part-time workers, rather than as wives and mothers. Interestingly, in the French case, the breadwinner and welfare regime models diverge to a degree, with activist public policy supporting both mothering and work, although with the paid work option receiving mixed signals with reference to equality of opportunities and conditions of employment.

The British welfare state: gendered implications

How should one assess the gender implications of contemporary British social policy? It has long been the stock-in-trade of feminist commentaries on the welfare state to argue that the British system of social security[8] normatively embraces a view of women as wives and mothers, reinforced by policies that foster women's economic dependency on husbands or, failing that, on the state (Wilson, 1977; Dale and Foster, 1986; Sassoon, 1992). Critical observers of social policy point first to the 1942 Beveridge Report, which provided the initial blueprint for the UK welfare state (Government, 1942). By offering married women the option to decline all insurance contributions except for the industrial injuries scheme, the highly influential Beveridge Report contributed powerfully to the notion that women's participation in the labor market was incidental to their "more important" unpaid work at home. Contemporary critics argued that the report treated women as "a class of pin money worker" (Dale and Foster, 1986).

In addition, recent scholarship confirms the formative significance of Beveridge's assumptions of female domesticity, women's dependence on the male wage as the "family" wage, and their characterization as dependants for the purposes of assigning social security rights and entitlements.

Contemporary feminist scholarship acknowledges, however, that in some ways Beveridge was ahead of his time regarding women: he insisted that marriage be considered a "partnership" rather than a classically patriarchal relationship (Wilson, 1977; J. Lewis, 1993) and that inadequacies of this male breadwinner system warranted compensatory remedies from the state (Gordon, 1990). In general, however, the Beveridge Report has been associated far more with inspiring invidious gender-based distinctions in British social policy than with inviting forward-looking reappraisals of women's role in society.

In fact, from its origins in the 1940s at least until the 1980s, despite relatively early changes that brought women into the national insurance scheme on an equal footing with men, Beveridge-era family wage assumptions continued to shape policy. For example, limits on a married or cohabiting woman's right to claim benefits on her own persisted for decades. Until the 1986 Social Security Act, the household was treated as a single unit for the assessment of supplementary benefits, and the award was payable to the man of the house rather than his married or cohabiting partner. Similarly, the invalid care allowance, introduced in the 1970s for those who looked after the infirm or elderly, was made available to cohabiting or married women "carers" only in 1986 after legal challenges were brought to the European Community (Lovenduski and Randall, 1993).

Work, policy, and family life

Feminist scholarship has looked critically and insightfully at the crucial nexus of work, policy, and family life. Especially important for the analysis here, some sharply etched critiques of social policy during the 1980s identified the connections between industrial and social policy, and pinpointed their central role in advancing the broader political agendas of the enterprise culture and market liberalization.

The Thatcher legacy revisited   As industrial relations policy encouraged managerial flexibility in work assignments and increased the proportion of women in less secure, poorly compensated, part-time work, the often precarious financial position of female heads of household worsened. In some cases, tighter eligibility criteria and reduced state provision for the care of family members forced women to accept part-time jobs or to leave paid labor altogether. "The disabling stance of the state has involved both a direct attack on women's rights to paid work and an indirect, perhaps more damaging, assault on their ability to perform wage labour through the selective withdrawal of services," observed economists Jane Humphries and Jill Rubery at the height of Thatcherism in the late 1980s. "Both attacks are consistent with the government's aim to reduce the role of the state and make individuals and families more self-reliant, and with the practical corollaries of this grand design: privatization, cuts in government spending and the liberalization of the market, including the labor market" (1988, p. 92).

With regard to European policies that affect the conditions of women's employment, the Thatcher government continued the discouraging record of its Labour predecessor, which produced the largest number of derogations and exceptions to the 1976 Equal Treatment Directive of any Community member. During the Thatcher years, the government stoutly challenged virtually all EU proposals to improve conditions of employment for women.[9] These included two draft directives issued in 1983, one concerning parental leave and the other part-time workers. Similarly, the government strongly resisted a 1988 draft directive concerning sex discrimination that would have placed a greater burden on employers to demonstrate that there had been no discriminatory practices. With employment policy a central element of government policy and the commitment to flexibility the cornerstone of employment policy, with deeper ideological ramifications for Thatcherism, it is easy to understand the depth of government resistance to EU initiatives.

It also comes as no surprise that domestic initiatives to improve employment opportunities and the work experience for women were mainly private sector initiatives driven by labor market pressures. During the boom of 1985–8, some employers implemented their own initiatives. For example, Boots and Dixons introduced nurseries at work, but these were mainly targeted at managers and justified by the need to attract and retain the most highly qualified personnel. With regard to government-sponsored plans, the initiatives of the Thatcher years were limited to programs like the 1984 "Women into Science and Technology" (WISE), which was far less serious or effective than comparable programs in France and Germany. The Thatcher government introduced no broad domestic legislation to ameliorate the conditions of female employment and made few efforts to improve the weak record of compliance with the "notoriously ineffective" British Sex Discrimination Act of 1975 (Chamberlayne, 1993, p. 177).

Despite an unambiguous record on the employment front, Thatcher's alleged "anti-feminist stance" remains a matter of some contention, however, even among feminists (Jessop et al., 1988). Interpretations differ in part because of the inconsistent rhetoric of Thatcher herself, as well as her ministers, and the tendency for the more traditional and "natalist" pronouncements to receive no legislative or policy follow-up. For example, the stridently pro-family and anti-wage labor views expressed by the Family Policy Group formed by the cabinet just before the 1983 election, which encouraged young mothers to stay home and give their all to the "caring" responsibilities, never saw the light of day during the campaign (Lovenduski and Randall, 1993). Accordingly, as

Michèle Barrett and Mary McIntosh argue, the position espoused by "Thatcherism" regarding the role of women in paid employment and in the family was "in many ways far more contradictory than the support for a stereotypical nuclear family embedded in the Beveridge Report and the host of welfare policies and reforms developed in the post-war decades" (1982, p. 13). Moreover, posturing aside, the participation of women in paid labor, the vanguard of forced flexibility, rose steadily throughout the 1980s. It is thus very difficult to disentangle the putative consequences of pro-family and anti-feminist orientations from the neoliberal policy agenda that clearly animated Thatcherism (see Gardiner, 1985).

In general, critics of the gendered dimension of the social security system in the UK before, during, and after the Thatcher era argue quite persuasively that, through a mix of normative expectations and benefit rules, social welfare policies define the male role primarily in terms of paid work and the female role mainly by reference to the domestic realm. It is important to add that this framework persists despite overwhelming evidence that the vast majority of women in the UK are permanently involved in paid labor, except for a short stay-at-home interval when children are very young (Wilson, 1977; Sassoon, 1992). Affirming this analysis and placing the British case in comparative perspective, Ostner and Lewis (1995) locate the UK firmly in the *strong male bread-winner* category.

There is reason to suspect, however, that the story is somewhat more complicated. Viewing this bleak gendered policy landscape in comparative terms, two features especially warrant closer attention: the changing labor force participation of women; and family policy, including child care. Taken together, analysis of developments in these two realms contributes to a useful complication of the male breadwinner argument and sharpens our understanding of the work–welfare–family nexus in the UK.[10]

Labor force participation

For a start, it is important to emphasize that women's participation in paid labor in the UK tells an interesting and, in a sense, inconsistent story. Female labor force participation rates are high (far higher than in other strong male breadwinner countries). At the same time, the labor force participation rates for married mothers, at approximately 60 percent, are also high in comparative terms, and rise to 67 percent after thirty-five, when children are more likely to be in school, and to over 70 percent once the youngest child is ten years old (Sassoon, 1992; McFate, 1995). By these measures, the UK departs markedly from the strong breadwinner model: the expectation of a dual role, with active participation in paid labor, extends to the vast majority of women. That said, the character of female employment – its location in the division of labor, its pay scale in comparison to men, and the very sizable proportion of non-standard work (part-time jobs, temporary work, or self-employment) – demonstrates the perseverance of a gender regime. By these measures the conditions that women face in paid employment seem far less favorable in comparative terms: gender inequality in earnings has widened and the percentage of all part-time employees who are female remains extremely high (second only to Germany within a comparison group of eight North American and European countries) (McFate, 1995).

Family policy

It is at the juncture of employment policy and family policy that the work–welfare–family nexus, and the critical choices and life experiences that women face, are most clearly revealed. On the matter of child care, as Joni Lovenduski and Vicky Randall observe, "Britain has an almost inexplicably poor record of public provision" (1993, p. 50). Unfortunately, this observation is confirmed by comparative analysis. By contrast to countries such as Sweden and France, which provide significant public child care to the youngest children (aged three years and below) in order to facilitate a dual role for women throughout their working life, public provision for child care in the UK is mainly limited to pre-school children of four years or older. In addition, publicly funded places are limited to about 35 percent of all children in that age group (compared to roughly 95 percent in France and Belgium, and 85 percent in Italy), and the child care that is provided is often part time (mornings or afternoons) (Duncan, 1996). Although European comparisons do not indicate a clear correlation between women's labor force participation and levels of public child care provision, the British case is the most anomalous – with extremely high labor force participation and extremely low child care provision.

Work and state policies: anomalies, inconsistencies, mounting pressures

In part, the paucity of child care provision can be explained by the general features of the welfare regime, since it can be expected that corporatist-statist regimes will provide more extensive child care to support full-time mothering, and liberal regimes will be more likely to target child care provision, like other non-contributory programs, at stigmatized groups of mothers who experience particular neediness (Duncan, 1996). It is also illuminating, however, to recognize the specificity of the UK's gender regime by placing these developments in family policy clearly within a broader context of welfare state retrenchment, forced flexibility and contracting-out or privatization. Although welfare retrenchment during the Thatcher years was not as dramatic as one might infer from the rhetoric (Pierson, 1994), viewed with reference to the disparate gender-specific outcomes of policy, the cuts in benefit levels and relatively subtle changes in specific social policies may seem more significant.

Pension reforms   For example, the pension reforms contained in the Social Security Act of 1986 sharply reduced the state's contribution to the State Earnings-Related Pension Scheme (SERPS) and, in yet another example of policy in the service of managerial flexibility (and privatization), added flexibility to the way companies could contribute to pension schemes, and provided incentives for employees to contract out of SERPS. Since SERPS provided relatively generous pension support for low-wage workers and those with interrupted work careers, it was a particularly important pension program for women. Taken together, the sharp decline in SERPS benefits, the decremental winding down of the policy, and the tilt toward private sector pensions and personal (as distinct from occupational) pension schemes therefore had particularly adverse effects on women (Chamberlayne, 1993; Pierson, 1994).

Community care   The evolutionary individuation and privatization of pensions, like the decollectivization of industrial relations, follow the omnipresent rhetoric of the enterprise culture, flexibility, and individual responsibility that framed much of public policy throughout the 1980s and 1990s. Just as women have experienced more than their share of the forced flexibility in employment policy and the organization of production during this period, so too have women's lives been disproportionately affected by the rhetoric of "community care" and the material limits placed on state provision for the elderly or for children. Public appeals that care be provided by neighbors and volunteers (kith as well as kin) invariably take for granted women's caring role. Since, for the most part, men will not satisfy these functions in equal measure, particularly outside the immediate household unit, the withdrawal of state provisions or decline in support from the state turns the image of women as "natural" care givers into a self-fulfilling prophecy. As one observer put it, "Women's lives are more directly dependent on and determined by the welfare state than men's through their care of people" (Bagilhole, 1996, p. 39). This is nowhere more clear than with reference to child care policies, since, perhaps more than any other policy, they articulate the work–welfare–family nexus.

Child care policies   Between 1979 and 1985, many local authorities actually reduced the number of places in their nurseries, even as female employment rose. In 1988 a report for the Child Care Network of the

European Commission, detailing the grave inadequacy of public day care provision in the UK, helped inspire grass-roots campaigns, provoke parliamentary questions, and reveal deep-seated government attitudes. "Our view is that it is for the parents who go out to work to decide how best to care for their children," replied a government minister to a question about the report, which showed the UK lagging far behind other EU countries in the provision of child care. "If they want or need help in this task they should make the appropriate arrangements and meet the costs" (quoted in J. Lewis, 1993). Throughout the Major government, this line of reasoning held the day: discussion of increasing child care provision focused on private rather than public initiatives, despite the rapid growth of child care campaigns in the 1980s and the increased salience of proposals to expand child care in the 1992 general election. Nor are fundamental changes to be expected as a consequence of the change in government, despite proposals that locate child care in the broader context of economic policy, offer generous tax credits (available only for registered child care), and aim to increase the supply of child care provision (Oppenheim, 1998). It remains to be seen if subsidies will generate a supply of quality child care sufficient to meet a burgeoning demand and whether the tax credits will make child care affordable across the board. New Labour's fiscal prudence and commitment to informal care by family members as the "mainstay of social support" limit any realistic expectations of fundamental changes in direct state provision of child care for the short-term future (Mandelson and Liddle, 1996, p. 129).

Policy and rhetoric trap women in a set of conundrums when it comes to balancing responsibilities for child care and the expectations of employment. It is difficult to reconcile the growing participation of women in paid labor with the persistent inadequacy of child care provision. Other European governments do a reasonable job of matching policies and deep-seated cultural values about women's role in society, albeit in quite different ways: in France by enabling women to choose paid or unpaid work; in Germany by emphasizing the domestic and nurturing role of women, and providing an extensive set of paid maternity leaves, flat-rate and means-tested benefits, and a comparatively generous parental leave program funded by old age insurance (Ostner, 1993); and in Sweden by assuming that women will be engaged in paid work, and providing extensive child care and parental leaves that reduce the burden on working mothers. Despite attention by New Labour to the problem of child care, the UK's rhetoric and policy lack comparable coherence.

Implications for interests and political agendas   These inconsistencies at the point of connection between employment experiences and public policies place a particular burden on parents, and most particularly on mothers. To be sure, the dual demands of child care and work place intractable pressures on women everywhere in Europe, even where the state provision of day care is far greater, as in Sweden or France. But the tensions in the UK are magnified by the existence of the widest gap between child care supply and the demands imposed, first, by the very high percentage of women who are active in the labor market, and secondly, by their relatively low wage rates.[11] Whereas elsewhere the supply of child care is far more collectivized, UK policy and practice individuate provision, with women (and men) often left to cobble together informal care arrangements either for pay or by relying on the voluntary assistance of neighbors and family. By proposing helpful but insufficient remedies as if they were radical breakthroughs, government only exacerbates these tensions between work and family responsibilities, which are probably greater in the UK than anywhere else in EU Europe (J. Lewis, 1993, p. 5).

Particularly in the UK, this conflict-driven and dysfunctional connection between work, social policy, and family is shaped by the wholesale denial of a defining feature of contemporary social life. As Anne Showstack Sassoon aptly observes, "although women are in the labour force on this massive scale, society as a whole has not really accepted this fact of life: the domestic sphere, the world of work, the welfare state are all organized as if women were continuing a traditional role." The fact that this presupposition no longer matches the practical realities of women's everyday life has profound consequences: in immediate and palpable ways it frames the choices women make, as Sassoon puts it, "in which the need and desire to *combine* having children and to remain in the labour force structures their lives" (1992, p. 160).

Exacerbated by mixed signals and incoherent policy, the tensions that women everywhere experience between work and family responsibilities are acutely faced by British women, and reconciled not through public policy, and not thus far collectively, but in their individual and family biographies. It is not so much that class happens or that gender happens, but that everyday life happens for women in a manner that exposes all the cross-cutting pressures of work and family, and inspires a set of concrete interests for a more coherent approach to child (and elder) care, employment, and family policy, where flexibility has taken on a whole new meaning. Can these "shared congeries" of interests and social experiences provide the impetus for women to forge a collective political disposition in service of a more positive vision of flexibility? What are the political implications of this alternative version of flexibility – a flexibility that would allow women (and men) to shape work and family responsibilities in a way more satisfying and less pressured than that imposed by today's circumstances? Can this alternative vision of flexibility be accommodated within the existing organization of production in the UK – and within the political agenda of a revitalized social democracy?

Before returning to these questions in chapter 10 (challenge 2) and considering the mobilizing potential of "wage earner feminism," we first consider how some of these same processes of deindustrialization and forced flexibility shape the experiences of ethnic minorities in the UK.

6

Ethnic Minority Groups: Employment and Settlement Patterns

Demand structures initially shaped the role of immigrant labor, and changing economic circumstances, including deindustrialization, subsequently channeled particular groups of ethnic minority workers into a variety of economic niches. The evidence is clear throughout this dynamic that the experiences of different ethnic communities vary in important ways as distinctive patterns in economic circumstances, political and cultural attitudes, and social organization shape employment patterns at every turn. This chapter first describes some basic characteristics of the ethnic minority communities. It then considers employment patterns and economic opportunities, followed by housing policies and settlement patterns. It concludes with a brief comment on the gendered and ethnic dimensions of the "unmaking" of the working class in the UK and some questions about the implications for identity and interest formation.

Throughout the postwar period, the pattern of immigration and ethnic minority settlement proceeded in a context set by two cross-cutting pressures: the labor demand for New Commonwealth[1] immigrants on the one hand, and the hostility directed against ethnic minority residents, combined with restrictive immigration and nationality legislation (to be discussed in chapter 8), on the other hand. To begin with the basics, official Labour Force Survey estimates place the ethnic minority population at around 3.3 million or just under 6 percent of the British population. Among ethnic minorities, the Indian group comprises the largest ethnic minority (27 percent), Pakistanis and Bangladeshis represent about 23 percent; and African-Caribbeans comprise 23 percent.[2] Despite the political salience of the issue, it should be noted that international migration into the UK remains low. In 1995 there were approximately 55,000 acceptances for settlement in the UK – a typical figure for the last two decades. Approximately three-fifths were marriage partners and another one-sixth were children; nearly half of those accepted were from Asia and around one-fifth from Africa (Office for National Statistics, 1997b, p. 35).

It should be noted, further, that due to past immigration and fertility patterns,[3] the ethnic minority population in the UK is considerably younger than the white population: more than one-third of all ethnic minorities are younger than 16, nearly half are under 25, and more than four-fifths are under the age of 45. By contrast, only about one-fifth of whites are under 16, fewer than one-third under 25, and three-fifths under 45. Accordingly, there is a growing disjuncture between the political issues of citizenship and nationality, with their associations to empire and decolonization, and the experience of members of ethnic minority groups, which is increasingly that of a homegrown population, rather than an immigrant group. Among those under 25, 92 percent of people of Indian descent, 76 percent of people of Pakistani/Bangladeshi descent and 80 percent of black people were born in the UK (Office for National Statistics, Social Survey Division, 1997).

These data should help put in perspective the experiences and political implications of ethnic minorities in the UK: the scale of ethnic minority groups is quite limited, the membership is ethnically and culturally diverse, and it is increasingly young. Despite preoccupations with immigration and nationality, and a persistent tendency in popular usage to refer to ethnic minorities as "immigrants," the immigrant experience is rapidly receding, although, as we shall see, its legacy remains a potent force.

Employment Patterns

In the post-Second World War period, the UK drew on immigrants from former colonies in Africa, the Caribbean, and the Indian subcontinent to fill severe labor shortages, especially in unskilled and semi-skilled jobs at the lower end of the labor market. These included service sectors like transport and other employment venues where wages were low and labor often involved shiftwork at night: for example, in metal manufacturing and textiles. The demand came from several sources. Postwar reconstruction increased the demand for labor in construction, the building trades, and related services. In addition, industrial restructuring meant that a new workforce was needed in the less skilled positions to replace workers who were moving up the labor ladder into higher-skilled and better-paying jobs in expanding capital-intensive and high-value-added industries such as automobile manufacturing. At the same time, expansion of the service sector in the newly institutionalizing welfare state created a tremendous source of demand: for example, for nurses and other health care workers in the NHS. Finally, the drive to substitute labor for capital investment in declining industries (such as textiles) provided an additional source of demand.

This pattern of labor shortage created vacancies that could be met only by immigration, which flowed from the New Commonwealth in fairly substantial numbers during the 1950s and until controls were introduced in 1962. The net migration from the New Commonwealth to the UK between 1953 and 1962 has been estimated at nearly half a million.[4] To be sure, "push" factors – poverty, unemployment, insufficient opportunities, expanding population – existed in the West Indies and South Asia, encouraging emigration. It seems clear, however, that during this peak period, and through the 1960s, migration was closely connected to job vacancies, in some cases enhanced by specific recruitment efforts. For example, textile concerns advertised in the Indian press, London Transport opened a recruiting office in Barbados, and Caribbean women were drawn to employment in the NHS through direct recruitment and subsidies from their home governments (Layton-Henry, 1984, pp. 16–29; Bryan et al., 1985). The extent of labor demand during the postwar period and the New Commonwealth origins of the workforce "pulled" by this demand were significant enough to "give rise to the ethnic profile of modern Britain," as one observer put it, adding that "in popular parlance, and much political discourse, the term 'immigration' is now associated almost exclusively with the immigration to Britain of people whose origins lay in these countries" (Mason, 1995, p. 24).

Research confirms broad patterns of continuity in the employment experiences of citizens of New Commonwealth descent, but also significant changes and variations. Despite the often overlooked presence of a sizable cohort of middle-class blacks in the UK (Daye, 1994), people from ethnic minority communities have been overrepresented in semi-skilled and unskilled jobs, and have persistently experienced higher rates of unemployment than their white counterparts. In addition, settlement patterns have remained fairly static, with much of the ethnic minority population remaining clustered around initial settlement areas: for example, certain boroughs in London (Hackney, Newham, Brent), and cities such as Bradford, Leicester, and Birmingham. Despite these continuities, since the 1970s the twin processes of labor market restructuring and deindustrialization have brought some important changes and refinements within the general pattern.

One of the most noteworthy developments is the increasing diversity of employment experiences across different ethnic minority groups, which is the result of a complex interplay of market forces driven by deindustrialization and differences in the cultural and organizational resources of particular ethnic communities. The story of ethnic minority employment is becoming more complicated as the experiences of members of different groups continue to diverge. We will consider male and female labor market experiences, in turn.

Male employment patterns among ethnic minorities

Contemporary research has demonstrated that variations among the minority communities among men may be as great as the variation between the black and Asian population as a whole and the white majority population (I. Gordon, 1995), and that the employment experience of men in some ethnic minority groups is, in fact, approaching that of white men. For example, among men of African Asian, Chinese, and Indian descent, the proportional representation in the managerial and professional ranks is actually higher than for white men (although they are much less likely to be senior managers in large firms). There is also strong evidence of a bipolar distribution in the labor market for some groups. Men with Indian origins are found disproportionately both at the top managerial and professional end and in the unskilled manual categories, suggesting limited points of access and subsequent mobility (Mason, 1995).[5] This pattern of employment indicates strongly that economic restructuring has intensified processes of polarization among the South Asian communities, as it has in the population more generally (Robinson, 1990).

In addition, the high rate of entrepreneurship among Britons of South Asian and, especially, Indian descent has attracted a great deal of attention and generated a plethora of debate. It is very clear that the rate of self-employment within these groups has been very high, with tremendous growth in the 1970s and 1980s: 23 percent for those of Pakistani/Bangladeshi descent and a quite remarkable 27 percent for those of Indian descent for the period from 1987 to 1989 (Luthra, 1997). Interpretations differ considerably, however. Some emphasize Thatcher's enterprise culture, but there is little evidence of institutional support for ethnic minority entrepreneurs; others suggest a more reluctant entrepreneurship, spurred by redundancy and the decline of the inner city, which created a ready supply of cheap shops, including lock-up shops, and shops with accommodations above them (Luthra, 1997). Still others emphasize cultural and organizational differences, contrasting the greater insularity and ethic of self-sufficiency exhibited in Muslim communities of Pakistani descent, contrasted with the more expansive, outward-looking approach of South Asians of Indian descent (Nana, 1997).

Another interesting development is that the gap in self-employment rates between those of Pakistani or Bangladeshi descent and those of Indian descent appears to have narrowed or closed altogether in recent years, although the Indian community has shown greater entrepreneurship than other South Asian groups in expanding the range of business ventures to metals, vehicle parts, commodity trading, chemicals, and hotels (Luthra, 1997). Explanations and interpretations differ, but there is no denying the significance or scale of entrepreneurship within specified ethnic minority groups. As one observer who compared the experiences of ethnic minorities in the UK, France, Germany, and the Netherlands observed, "South Asian migrants to Britain represent the one substantial example of entrepreneurial 'success' among European minorities to set alongside the well-documented cases of the Japanese, Chinese, Cubans, and Koreans in the United States" (I. Gordon, 1995, pp. 536–7).

In general, the employment picture for men of African-Caribbean and Bangladeshi descent is far less encouraging. The latter group, in particular, is concentrated in the lower end of the labor market, with 65 percent in semi-skilled manual occupations (such as the textile and footwear sectors) or poorly paid service sector employment, including much shift-work (such as hotels and catering). If Britons of Indian descent have enjoyed the greatest mobility into business and professional careers, those of Bangladeshi descent are at the other end of the spectrum. The latest arrivals, they face a set of acute problems: recent migration from a predominantly peasant economy means that they enter the UK with few marketable skills in an industrial urban economy; their proficiency in English is low; and they are the object of outright discrimination (Robinson, 1990).

Men of African-Caribbean descent are disproportionately represented in services (such as transport and communication), are the most likely of any group to be involved in shift work, and are well represented in construction (Mason, 1995). They are disproportionately represented in the metal and processing trades, and therefore, in areas like Birmingham and elsewhere in the West Midlands, they are exposed to some of the sharpest effects of economic restructuring and deindustrialization. Their exceptionally high rates of unemployment in the 1980s, for example, mirrored – but at a much higher level – the declining economic opportunities that all workers faced. Although observers differ in the selection and emphasis they place on explanatory variables, it seems likely that processes of growing ethnic concentration in declining urban areas and industries are producing a pattern of "incipient ghettoization" (Cross, 1992). In addition, men of Pakistani, Bangladeshi, and Black-African origin experience higher rates of part-time employment than do white men (Mason, 1995).

Female employment patterns among ethnic minorities

The employment pattern for ethnic minority women seems at first to display a picture with less variation than that of ethnic minority men, at least when limited to aggregate data: for women from all ethnic groups, the largest concentrations are located in the "other non-manual" category (42 percent of Pakistani, 47 percent of Indian, and 54 percent of African-Caribbean), followed by "semi-skilled manual" (45 percent Pakistani, 34 percent Indian, and 25 percent African-Caribbean), and exhibiting only limited representation across all other job levels.

The female labor participation from every ethnic minority group indicates a marked concentration in the service sector and thus displays in a particularly acute form the characteristic pattern of female labor market participation in a British economy structured by deindustrialization. There is some variation in concentrations of employment among ethnic minority women, however. Women of African-Caribbean descent are especially concentrated in the hospital and health care sectors, while women of Indian descent are represented heavily in hotels and catering services and low-end manufacturing industry. Women with West Indian and Guyanese origins are strongly overrepresented in a range of relatively low-paid service work, including health care provision (approximately three-fifths of all those reporting economic activity). It is important to add, however, that the gap in conditions and type of employment between ethnic minority and white women is far less than that between ethnic minority men and white men (G. Lewis, 1993).

One of the most interesting and consistent findings about patterns of labor market participation by ethnic minority women, nevertheless, shows a marked divergence from the experience of white women with reference to part-time employment. Approximately half of white women work full time, but more than two-thirds of ethnic minority women work full time, with little variety in the rate of part-time work among women from different ethnic minority groups (Mason, 1995; Phizacklea and Wolkowitz, 1995; Webster, 1996). Accordingly, the difficulties posed by the pressure to balance domestic responsibilities and paid employment are often greater for ethnic minority women than for white women, since the balance between home and work spheres must be achieved more commonly within the demands imposed by full-time employment, with little left over in very tight family budgets to ease the way with paid child care assistance. In a pattern common among hospital workers, some ethnic minority women – according to one study in the mid-1980s, approximately one-fifth of West Indian women – have managed these pressures by working full-time hours on a shift basis (G. Lewis, 1993).

Since the health care sector remains the area of greatest labor market concentration for black women, especially those with origins in the West Indies and Guyana, the history of their treatment in the NHS warrants special attention. The story gives concrete expression to the general observation that immigration followed sector-specific and job-specific labor demand, and that women's participation in the labor market is often linked to the caring professions; it vividly illuminates the role of black immigrant women in the economy and how the legacy of immigration shapes labor decades later; and it places in sharp relief the experience that black women have of the welfare state as employer.

Beginning in the 1950s, Caribbean women were directly recruited to fill the burgeoning need for hospital staff. Particularly since nursing is a highly regarded occupation throughout the Caribbean, opportunities in the NHS were considered quite attractive and recruits typically came to the UK with the expectation of training to become State Registered Nurses (SRNs). Almost invariably – even when they came with the necessary qualifications and exam certificates – they were slotted into the less demanding and prestigious track for State Enrolled Nurses (SENs), often reporting that their initial placement was determined by a quick sorting based on racial stereotyping. In fact, many nursing recruits were permanently relegated to the hospital laundries and kitchens, or worked as cleaners, "tea ladies," or orderlies. Even among those few that persevered against the odds and were able to make their way into the nursing ranks, reports abound of indignities directed at them from patients, suspicious disciplinary action, pressures to conform, and disparate chances for advancement into managerial roles (Bryan et al., 1985, pp. 38–50).

Problems of interpretation: self-employment, homeworking, part-time work

Although experiences certainly vary and some distinctive employment patterns among women from different ethnic groups can be observed, research in the area of female ethnic minority employment in the UK is frequently inconclusive. It is often based on aggregate survey data that are difficult to interpret, or on more ethnographic accounts that are compelling, but not well suited to generalization. Much in the patterns of labor market participation by ethnic minority women has not been – and probably cannot be – authoritatively analyzed, and much remains elusive. This much can be said with confidence, however: the aggregate labor force participation data, which show relatively little variation across ethnic minority groups, tell only part of the story. Some of the most revealing complexities emerge outside paid labor, in patterns of self-employment and homeworking, and in other non-standard forms of employment. In these areas, interestingly, the fragmentary evidence is often more significant for the important questions it raises, rather than for the patterns it identifies.

For example, it is difficult to interpret the role of women in small family-run entrepreneurial ventures, although data suggest some very interesting developments. In the 1980s, there was a substantial increase in self-employment among women of Pakistani and Bangladeshi descent, from an average of 11.1 percent for the period between 1979 and 1983, to 18.1 percent for the period from 1987 to 1989; at 11.1 percent, the level of self-employment for women of Indian descent was also noteworthy (compared to 7.3 percent for white women).[6] In addition, during this period the percentage of self-employed women who are ethnic minorities and who employ others compares favorably to the figures for ethnic minority men, and is considerably higher for women than for men among those of West Indian and Guyanese descent (Luthra, 1997, pp. 366–79).

Although the high and increasing rates of self-employment among women of Indian and Pakistani or Bangladeshi origins intuitively suggest enhanced economic circumstances, even potential independence, inferences should be drawn with considerable care. Annie Phizacklea's research in the clothing industry suggests that the respondent's declaration that she is self-employed can be misleading. Many of the clothing workers, in fact, work under supervision on the premises of a company that, in effect, serves as sole employer, but refuses to accept the legal and fiscal responsibilities. These workers are "self-employed" in a technical sense, but actually experience the conditions of employment of unprotected laborers (Phizacklea, 1990).

Phizacklea and her colleague, Carol Wolkowitz, found a similar pattern in the overreporting of self-employed status in their study of homeworking in Coventry (Phizacklea and Wolkowitz, 1995).[7] Many women, including ethnic minorities, describe themselves as self-employed although their circumstances, in some important ways, more closely approximate those of nineteenth-century outworkers during the transitional stages of the industrial revolution, as described by E. P. Thompson, than those of the high-street shopkeeper implied by the term "self-employed." They do not control the quantity of work they are given, the schedule for its completion, or to whom it is sold. The significance of these qualifications for the real meaning of self-employment for women of Indian and Pakistani or Bangladeshi descent, particularly in the clothing industry and in the West Midlands, should not be underestimated. Asian women (and particularly Indian women) are quite substantially overrepresented in the clothing industry, and the West Midlands is an area of dense ethnic minority settlement. Moreover, homeworking is quite widespread: research indicates that in the West Midlands, for each person working in a factory, there are likely to be two unregistered homeworkers, who are quite likely to be Asian women.

In fact, alongside self-employment, homeworking presents another area of female employment where, especially with reference to ethnic minority women, findings must be treated with caution. Reliable data are very hard to find, since many of those working at home are recorded as economically inactive. In addition, the frequency and distribution of homeworking in different ethnic groups, what brings a woman to take up this form of employment, and understandings concerning the conditions of employment all remain elusive (see Mason, 1995, pp. 43–63). Although one should generalize with caution, according to the Coventry study it seems clear that there is a "racialized" division of labor in contemporary homeworking. White women with homeworking jobs are distributed across a range of better-paid clerical jobs (for example, bookkeeping or telephone-based work for a software development firm) or manual work across a range of industries. In contrast, none of the Asian women in the sample has acquired clerical work, and the vast majority work in the lower-paying manual sewing and assembly jobs in the clothing industry.

The study indicates a strong similarity in the situations of the white and Asian homeworkers: very low pay, no employee benefits or rights or compensation for work-related expenses, long hours, work-related health problems, and a positive choice to care for their own children. The differences of degree, however, are significant, with the pay levels of the Asian workers sufficiently lower that they are obliged to work far longer hours, suffer greater irregularity with reference to the demand for their work, and live on lower incomes (with greater reliance on welfare benefits). The Coventry study confirms the broader national picture of homeworking, in which ethnic minority women (and especially women of Asian descent) are concentrated in a narrow range of jobs, vastly over-represented in the clothing industry, and excluded from the better-paid and, in some cases, substantially more engaging clerical jobs, in which recruitment of kin and friends tends to exclude ethnic minorities (Phizacklea and Wolkowitz, 1995).

On one important issue, however – the question of whether women choose to work at home, and if so, why – the Coventry study raises interesting questions about explanations and expectations that emerge from previous literature. Although half the clerical workers and two-thirds of the manual homeworkers among white women in the sample report a preference to work at home, only 10 percent of women of Asian descent report the same preference. This contrasts markedly with the common understanding, such as that reported in a study of West Yorkshire homeworkers a decade earlier, in which both white and Pakistani homeworkers almost uniformly mentioned the need to take care of their children. Moreover, Pakistani homeworkers routinely reported that their husbands would not "permit" or "allow" them to take employment outside the house. It is interesting to note that too much may be made of cultural differences on this point: white women reported that their husbands "preferred" them to work at home, which might reflect, in terms of practical influences on their proclivities to work outside the home, a distinction without a difference[8] (Allen and Wolkowitz, 1987). Is the widespread view that women of Asian descent work at home as a consequence of patriarchal pressures and culturally specified responsibilities for home child care little more than a stereotype? Or have economic pressures and broader changes in the social role for women mitigated the force of the husband's preferences in recent years (or modified those preferences)? More research will be needed before it is possible to answer these questions with confidence.

Unemployment patterns

Of course, among the most telling information about labor market position is information on unemployment. Data based on the 1991 Census indicated that unemployment for ethnic minority women is approximately twice that of white men. The comparisons were even more discouraging for ethnic minority women, at about two-and-a-half times the rate experienced by white women. Moreover, unemployment rates differed markedly for women from different ethnic minority groups. Among those of Indian descent, the group that has probably experienced the greatest improvements, the unemployment rate was approximately twice that of white women, while for women of African-Caribbean descent the unemployment rate was about two-and-a-half times that of white women. For women of Pakistani and Bangladeshi heritage, the unemployment rates were extremely high: nearly 30 percent for the former and nearly 35 percent for the latter – compared to 6.3 percent for white women (Mason, 1995).

It is important to add that this trend in unemployment continues despite evidence that minority youths, especially women, stay in school longer than white students, and that a higher proportion of African-Caribbean women (37 percent) successfully complete the course work necessary for university admission (A levels) than do their white counterparts (31 percent). Two reports published by the Equal Opportunities Commission in 1994 confirm that ethnic minority women with a full complement of skills and experience are twice as likely as white women to face unemployment, and when employed are likely to work more hours for lower pay under poorer conditions (see Phizacklea and Wolkowitz, 1995, p. 60). Although considerable debate surrounds the causal explanations of the unemployment and disadvantageous labor market position facing ethnic minority women as well as men, it seems reasonable to conclude that, through the 1990s, "many of the better educated minority ethnic people were denied employment on the basis of their background, and that people of Pakistani and Bangladeshi origin constituted a highly disadvantaged underclass" (Forbes, 1994, p. 199).

Settlement, Housing Policy, and the State

As will be discussed in part IV, both a general sense of exclusion by the state and particular issues about the politics and representation of communities, actual and imagined, have played a significant role in identity and interest formation for the UK's ethnic minorities. For these reasons, issues associated with housing, perhaps more than any other area of social policy, resonate very deeply among ethnic minority groups, provoking debate and even resistance.

From the start, housing policy influenced the settlement patterns of early migrants, most of whom did not qualify for public housing, and contributed to their residential clustering. To simplify a much more complex pattern, migrants faced a triumvirate of urban gatekeepers – private landlords, real estate agents, and local authority housing officials – who colluded in discriminatory practices that helped channel members of different ethnic groups into specific settlement concentrations. In broad terms, African-Caribbean migrants tended to rent from those private landlords who were willing, often placing entire families in one- or two-room accommodations. South Asians, by contrast, were more likely to pool resources among extended families and buy cheap, large, run-down inner city houses. Each of these arrangements, in different ways, established disadvantages with long-term consequences. Renters lost the advantages of equity building, an increasing proportion of personal wealth in the UK during the postwar period, and a rare opportunity to leverage meager initial capital into a sizable asset. Alternatively, the purchase of poor, run-down housing created a tendency toward what in the United States is called redlining – ghetto areas cut off from financing for new purchase or repairs, and generally left to growing dilapidation and withdrawal of services. In the 1950s and 1960s, housing shortages in expanding urban slum areas, and resentment directed at overcrowded and deteriorating communities with high ethnic minority concentrations, became a flash point for anti-immigrant hostility, resulting in increasingly restrictive immigration controls and the notoriously racist (and victorious) Conservative election campaign in Smethwick in 1964, discussed below in part IV (Mason, 1995, pp. 80–3).

From the 1970s onward, ethnic minorities have faced the challenges of a succession of social policy orientations focused on settlement issues and the development of ethnic minority communities, a detailed analysis of which lies outside the framework of this study (see Mason, 1995, pp. 80–92; Law, 1996, pp. 81–112; Luthra, 1997, pp. 305–41). There are a few key points worth noting, however. First, over time, ethnic minorities gained access to public housing, but incorporation did not substantially reduce marginalization: there is considerable evidence of discriminatory practices, cultural insensitivities, and allocation of "points" to qualify for housing according to rules that have disparate impacts on ethnic minorities. As a result of these practices, ethnic minority tenants were more likely to be housed in older, less attractive properties, on less popular estates, with fewer amenities. In addition, there is strong evidence that gendered inequalities have contributed to the housing sorting process, as female heads of household of African-Caribbean origin were allocated the poorest-quality units, disproportionately in high-rise slums, and were subject to high rates of racial harassment. This distribution of housing, of course, positioned members of ethnic minority groups very poorly to make the most of the opportunities offered by Thatcher's "sale of the century": the much-heralded initiative to offer council accommodations for sale to residents at very substantial discounts. Most of the units in which ethnic minorities resided were in relatively poor condition and held few prospects for resale.

Secondly, there is a broad pattern of continuity in housing tenure among ethnic minority groups from the period of early postwar migration to the present, complicated by a tendency for economic pressures to prevail over cultural or ethnic considerations. In the 1990s, whites and ethnic minorities lived in council housing in roughly the same proportions (approximately one-fifth of all households). However, distinctions within the major ethnic minority groups mirror initial housing tenure patterns: persons of South Asian descent, whose antecedents typically began as homeowners, are underrepresented, and those of African and Caribbean descent, who began as private renters, typically remain renters, but now are significantly overrepresented in council housing (as are households of Bangladeshi descent). Particularly since the sell-off of the more attractive middle-class properties by the mid-1980s, this distribution of ethnic minority groups can be seen to have powerful economic causation. It would appear that a keen aspiration for home ownership contributes to a growing reluctance on the part of Chinese, Indian, and Pakistani households to apply for local authority housing, which is viewed increasingly as a residual "underclass" sector, rife with racial violence. But an explanation of housing tenure patterns based on ethnic or cultural preferences or aspirations breaks down in the face of intensified housing need, as we find that nearly two-fifths of all Bangladeshis live in council housing – a proportion comparable to black and nearly four times that of Pakistanis – despite the broadly similar cultural backgrounds of Pakistanis and Bangladeshis (Law, 1996).

Finally, we come to one of the most controversial and potentially significant aspects of ethnic minority settlement patterns and housing policy: despite concerted efforts to foster the geographic dispersal of ethnic minority populations by national and local government in the aftermath of the Notting Hill and Nottingham riots of 1958, there remains a high degree of concentration in the residential location of the

UK's black citizens (see James, 1993, pp. 261–2; Mason, 1995, pp. 89–92). Inevitably, UK academics and policy makers have long considered – and disagreed about – the applicability of comparisons with settlement patterns in the United States, processes of residential segregation and inner city ghettoization, and the deleterious "concentration effects" of degraded, largely black communities identified by William Julius Wilson (Wilson, 1987). To use the more neutral term, clustering seems to reinforce, at a minimum, labor market and housing disadvantage, but it may also provide the basis for collective identity formation and collective organization, whether through the "new municipal left" of the mid-1980s or the emergence since the late 1980s of black-led housing associations.

In sum, like the complicated interplay of work, family, and social policy discussed in chapter 5, the interactive effects of work experiences, housing policy, and settlement patterns capture a critical set of pressures on ethnic minorities in the UK – and identify an important political agenda and opportunity for significant ameliorative policy.

Conclusion: Identity and Interest Formation

In chapter 4, the story of the transition from Fordist to post-Fordist production systems underscored the decollectivization of production in all its aspects, including conditions of employment, systems of industrial relations, and organizational capacities to advance solidaristic working-class agency. In this part of the book, when the frame of reference shifted to the work experiences of women and of ethnic minorities in the UK, it became clear that these systemic processes proceeded with a vengeance. The combined force of domestic policy agendas and deindustrialization, magnified by a set of specific gender and ethnic labor market considerations, produced a picture of extremely disaggregated and often discouraging experiences.

Here we find women exhibiting extremely high rates of economic activity, often in part-time and non-standard work, and pressured more than anywhere else in EU Europe by the inadequate public provision of child care. There we see the distinctive employment trajectories of different ethnic groups. One can observe large numbers of professionals, managers, and entrepreneurs of Indian descent, but also a bimodal distribution of opportunities for men of Indian and Chinese descent at each end of the employment spectrum, suggesting limited points of entry into the labor market and minimal mobility. Looking, for example, at the West Midlands, it is easy to observe the incipient ghettoization of men of African-Caribbean descent and, turning to London, we see in Tower Hamlets a growing Bangladeshi underclass thus far trapped in grave poverty. We see remarkable (although somewhat ambiguous) rates of entrepreneurship among women of Pakistani and Bangladeshi descent, a sizable proportion of West Indian and Guyanese women locked into relatively limited roles as SENs or laundry workers or orderlies in the NHS, and a very high percentage of South Asian women occupied as manual homeworkers in the textile trades.

Women and ethnic minorities experience the broad formative processes of post-Fordism, forced flexibility and deindustrialization in particularly acute forms. One sees an enormous range of experiences of work, a blend of ethnic and gender sorting and differential opportunities, constituting complex and revealing patterns. Sifting through research about the economic activity of women and ethnic minorities, both the depressing and inspiring can be found in abundance. It is impossible, however, to locate "the working class" in this picture, with its unifying agency majestically shaped by common experiences, as E. P. Thompson posits for a much earlier era.

Why is the unity of purpose and the muscular capacity for broad-based insurgent collective action that Thompson saw in his working class absent today? Thus far, the discussions of "male manufacturing labor" in its Fordist and post-Fordist incarnations, as well as the treatment here of female and ethnic minority experiences of work, lay a critical groundwork by detailing the centrifugal and decollectivizing tendencies of production, but that is only part of the story. Another critical portion of the answer involves more complicated transformations in identities, which fragment political agency and create powerful normative divisions in a way that presents tremendous challenges to government. We take up this subject in part IV under the rubric of "modular politics."

Part IV
Modular Politics

7

Modularity, Identities, and Cultural Repertoires

In *Conditions of Liberty: civil society and its rivals*, Ernest Gellner (1994) presents a wonderfully playful conceit that helps deepen our understanding of the volatility of contemporary politics, the transitory character of allegiances, and the fluidity of identity formation. He begins simply enough by contrasting modular furniture to ordinary furniture. Gellner explains that modular furniture "comes in bits that are agglutinative." Initially you purchase one piece that can function on its own, but when preferences or circumstances change, you can tack on another piece to what is already there, and "the whole thing will still have a coherence, aesthetically and technically." Further, you can combine and recombine the bits at will. The contrast with ordinary furniture is clear. "[W]ith the old kind, if you want coherence you have to buy it all at once, in one go, which means that you have to make a kind of irrevocable commitment, or at any rate a commitment which it will be rather costly to revoke," observes Gellner. "If you add a new bit of non-modular furniture to an old bit, you may end up with an eclectic, incoherent mess. It is very difficult to adapt or modify traditional furniture and achieve coherence: success requires the "careful and possibly arduous search for new stylistically compatible items" (1994, p. 97). Alternatively, one can live with incoherence or make the costly choice to throw out the old and start again.

For Gellner, modularity is an equally distinguishing attribute of liberal democracies, where obligations freely made can be quite effortlessly broken. Civil society is constituted by institutions that are strong enough to counterbalance central authority, but above all, membership is voluntary and can be nullified simply enough, without ritual or penalty. "You can join (say) the Labour Party without slaughtering a sheep, in fact you would hardly be allowed to do such a thing," he wryly observed, "and you can leave it without incurring the death penalty for apostasy" (1994, p. 103). Institutional affiliations and group attachments come and go: they are revocable, situational, and subject to constant combination and recombination. The concept of *modular politics*[1] helps provide a framework for understanding the increasingly fluid and situational interplay of collective identities as well as the political significance of alternative ways of representing identities and cultures. In addition, the concept offers an interesting way to analyze some critical normative dimensions of politics in the UK, including conceptions of nation and community.

Collective Identities

I will use the term, first, to refer to *modularity in collective identities*. By referring to identities as modular, I mean, as Eric Hobsbawm put it, that "in real life identities, like garments, are interchangeable or wearable in combination rather than unique and, as it were, stuck to the body" (1996, p. 41). Although the term "identity politics" usually suggests that one identity determines or dominates politics (see Hobsbawm, 1996), modular politics implies multiple identities, fluidly combined and ordered without fixed priority, perpetually recombined and modified.[2] The extensive debate over the concept of identity politics, on the one hand, and recent empirical work on identity formation in the UK, on the other hand, provide an important context for our conceptualization of modularity with respect to collective identities.

Identity politics and class politics

In recent decades, discussion of non-class collective identities has mushroomed, as have preoccupations with identity politics. One camp advancing identity politics, and featuring those influenced by postmodern theory, has claimed that the diversity of lived experience and the terrifying failure rate of progressive political projects render Enlightenment expectations meaningless or obsolete; along with other providential "grand narratives" that sustain political beliefs, they reject class politics and the transformative project it represents (see Wolin, 1988; Norris, 1990). In place of class politics, they privilege the more immediate attachments of gender, sexuality, race, and other "subject-positions" built on the "ruins of the old universal values of modernity" (Aronowitz, 1992, p. 12).

Others, relying on more grounded historical and sociological analysis, suggest that racial, ethnic, or cultural identities have gained a kind of compensatory salience as traditional sources of identity – nation, class, family, community – rupture or dissolve. Daniel Bell was among the first to make this argument, a quarter of a century ago, when he observed, "The breakup of the traditional authority structures and the previous affective social units – historically nation and class . . . make the ethnic attachment more salient" (1975, p. 171).[3] Eric Hobsbawm locates the same phenomenon in the "extraordinary dissolution of traditional social norms, textures, and values" and the destruction of "communities in the sociological sense" from the late 1960s to the 1980s, which "left so many of the inhabitants of the developed world orphaned and bereft" (1996, p. 428). In a similar vein, Stuart Hall has argued that people seek attachments – a sense of "belonging to" a group – to offset the dislocating effects of the processes of globalization. These contribute to the fragmentation of the "cultural landscapes of class, gender, sexuality, ethnicity, race and nationality which gave us firm locations as social individuals" (Hall, 1992, p. 275).

In common usage, the term "identity politics" usually suggests that identities located in gender, race, nation, and ethnicity are separate and distinct from class and, moreover, that they "trump" class and dominate politics. The approach here will be quite different: to assume the interactive effects of gender, ethnicity, and workplace experiences, to elucidate the multiple paradoxes of active agency and habituation that condition ideological dispositions and political agendas that flow from collective identities, and where possible to provide, at least illustratively, concrete analyses of identity formation and change (see James, 1993, p. 232). Throughout the discussion that follows, I emphasize the political implications of identity formation. How do the beliefs, cultural orientations, collective memories and, especially, lived experiences of members of a group shape political values, normative orientations and, ultimately, interests and political concerns? How is politics – from the community level to the UK level – influenced by the strategic appeal to and representation of identities?

Complications in identity formation

Before investigating the politics of plural, modular identities, it is useful to review two critical scholarly insights that have influenced my use of the concept.[4] First, although it is widely agreed that identities are constructed, the formation of collective identities, nevertheless, involves a paradoxical appeal with essentialist overtones. Stuart Hall observes in reference to our identities that we "think of them as if they are part of our essential natures" (1992, p. 291). Orlando Patterson emphasizes that identity formation involves a complicated interplay of a voluntary display of commitment to a group identity, and a belief, at the same time, that there is no choice (see Hobsbawm, 1996, p. 40):

> It is imperative that he or she always believes that a choice is being made; otherwise the commitment is meaningless. We cannot commit ourselves if we have no choice in the matter. And yet, at the same time, it is a choice predicated on the strongly held, intensely conceived belief that the individual has absolutely no choice but to belong to that specific group. (Patterson, 1983, pp. 28–9)[5]

Individuals feel they have no choice, that their identities are inevitably determined by "who they are" – by their essential natures.

Secondly, this paradox between choice and inevitability helps explain a further puzzling characteristic of group identities. It explains why identities are so passionately held (they feel like a part of us) and yet remain situational, context-dependent, relational, and subject to pragmatic and strategic manipulation (to choose an identity does not mean that an alternative identity cannot be added in modular fashion or substituted). The notion of "adopted" situational identities is being taken very seriously even in authoritative survey research on political and social attitudes in the UK (Dowds and Young, 1996). Perhaps more significantly, the context-dependent character of identities is manifested in how individuals actually classify themselves in multiethnic, multiracial contexts. For example, when participating in a multiethnic theater group in Oldham, a town near Manchester in the north-west of England, the members of the group (Peshkar), who are predominately of South Asian descent, employ great flexibility in labeling themselves and others. A participant observer in the theater group captured the situational dynamic – the modular self-ascription of identities – with great clarity.

> [M]y fellow Peshkar members identified themselves in a number of ways: as Asians, British, black, white, by area of origin (India, Bangladesh, Pakistan, England), by subregion within the area of origin (Punjab, Kashmir, Bengal), by religion (Hindu, Muslim, Sikh), or language (Punjabi, Bangla, Hindi-Urdu English, Marathi). (Lyon, 1997, p. 187)

In the theater group, alternative identity labels were employed to ease tension and build cohesiveness. This situationally driven process of incorporation and exclusion through the use of "labels-as-identities" has wider application, however, and holds considerable political significance. Ethnic minorities themselves may elect to advance specific alliances ("black" or "Asian") by submerging differences in ethnicity, religion, or national origins; politicians or city administrators may try to construct a more manageable identity (by labeling a group by reference to national origins rather than religion or ethnicity) and thereby try to influence the way interlocutors in an ethnic minority community mobilize politically (Modood, 1997).

Political-cultural Repertoires

Following Sidney Tarrow (1994),[6] I will now use the concept of modularity in a second application, referring to *modularity in political-cultural repertoires*. In his studies of collective action, Tarrow uses the concept of modularity to refer to the capacity of social actors to use particular "repertoires of collective action" in different locations and political milieux against different adversaries. In this chapter, I wish to draw attention to the political and normative significance of alternative narratives about nation and community, and to consider the political repercussions of the cultural representation of identity groups and normatively loaded political concepts, such as nation and community. It will therefore be useful to extend the scope of modularity drawn from Tarrow's usage to include cultural repertoires – recurrent forms of expression, mythic representations, and images that can be employed in different combinations, in a variety of settings, to advance quite different normative and political claims.

For a start, this notion of political-cultural modularity should serve as an antidote to conventional quite static treatments of political culture. Although there are important exceptions,[7] the study of British political culture has customarily relied on an uneasy mix of survey research into political attitudes and bland, often weakly supported, generalizations about "a British political culture" described by the familiar characteristics of homogeneity, consensus, and deference (Kavanagh, 1990; Almond and Verba, 1963; Almond and Verba, 1980). For these observers of political behavior, culture is so firmly habituated and uniformly pervasive that it requires no active agency (see Tarrow, 1994, p. 120). Typically, the attributes of a civic culture – the salutary mix of active and acquiescent orientations that sustain routine democratic participation – are simply taken for granted. Accordingly, there is little recognition of the plasticity of cultural expressions or attention to Beer's important caution that culture is not a "confluence" but a "struggle or at least a debate" (1969, p. xi) with deep-seated and potentially divisive reverberations. Consideration of cultural repertoires and the interplay of competing narratives recasts the conventional anodyne treatments of British or English political culture as moments of cultural representation, with significant normative implications, subject to competing claims.

Secondly, I will use the concept of political-cultural modularity to analyze "the political power of representation itself" (Baker et al., 1996a, p. 7) in identity formation and political mobilization. For those living in

England, as Stuart Hall puts it, "in the shadow of the black diaspora," the rediscovery of "hidden histories" can play a critical political role. Modularity emphasizes the protean appropriation of concepts and scenarios – their reinterpretations in new contexts, their disembedding from "original" or "intended" meanings, their reinvention, all in support of disparate political aims (see Baker et al., 1996a; Baker et al., 1996b; Hall, 1996). When are Muslims in the UK represented – by themselves or external political elites – as "black" or "British," or as an ethnic group as distinct from a religious group? There is a great deal at stake in the strategic application and manipulation of highly charged identity claims; not least, what philosopher and political theorist Charles Taylor (1994) calls the "politics of recognition," to which I will return in chapter 10.

Finally, modularity in political-cultural repertoires helps draw attention to the open-ended and context-dependent combination of identities – a signal feature of contemporary political life. Increasingly, observers recognize that the permeability of borders, which is a *sine qua non* of globalization, produces a growing number of people who define themselves by reference to multiple locations, cultural practices and norms, national attachments, and boundary-crossing identities. In theoretical treatments as well as in common parlance, however, it is difficult to completely jettison the notion of culture as bounded, homogenous, and territorial. Concepts such as "hybrid," "diasporic," and "hyphenated" identities or cultures usefully capture the fragmentary, situational, context-dependent, and fluid character of identity formation and the resulting cultural practices. Nevertheless, all these concepts contain trace elements of essentialism, since they are implicitly constituted by reference to territorially (nationally) defined cultures and circumscribed ethnicities. As the interchangeable use of "hyphenated" and "hybrid" identities suggests (as in British-Pakistanis or French-Algerians), diversity is usually limited to two pre-existing cultural packages, and "cultural diversity" is hence proscribed by a limited menu of pre-given combinations (Caglar, 1997). The concept of modularity should make it possible to move beyond these limiting and somewhat distorting assumptions.

In sum, the notion of modularity in political-cultural repertoires recognizes the struggle and debate at the center of cultural exchanges, whether or not plural identities are implicated. At the same time, the concept of modularity, used this way, explodes the pre-set options often associated with discussions of hybrid or hyphenated identities. Modularity invites experience-based and practice-bound investigations of plural and fluid identities, attention to reinforcing as well as disjunct combinations of identities, and the strategic political implications of identity labeling and identity-based political claims and mobilization. It also helps illuminate the politics of cultural representation and the clash of alternative narratives about core themes in contemporary British social and political life.

Modularity and Normative Dispositions

It is a critical premise of this study that ideological dispositions, interests, political agendas, and specific issue preferences are shaped by personal biographies, collective histories, and shared values, whether commonly understood by reference to class, ethnicity, or gender.[8] Thus, I would argue, integrally connected to the concrete processes of identity formation – the development of a sense of "belonging to" a group – is a framework for understanding social life. I suggest, moreover, that this framework, a means of translating abstract concepts and policy rationales into the "language of experience, moral imperative and common sense" (Hall, 1988, p. 47), involves normative dispositions with potentially significant ramifications for specific policy receptivity and debate.

In contemporary British politics, when it comes to differences of interpretation about nation and community, far more is at issue than electoral politics in a narrow sense or even the viability of alternative models of politics. These issues speak to deeply felt normative concerns and abiding principles: what it means to be British, how social and political life is to be interpreted, who belongs. As we shall see, these resonant and controversial themes generate alternative narratives[9] inspired by the concrete experiences that constitute collective identities, and fraught with political reverberations.

8
National Identities

It is easy to see that the interactive effects of several challenges and disorienting developments have fostered a preoccupation with national identity or identities in the United Kingdom. These include the problematic terrain of race, ethnicity, and nationality; the challenges of redefining political community amidst the pressures for Europeanization associated with 1992, Maastricht, and the "march to Euroland" (Bishop, 1997); and the vexed questions of the relationship of the peoples of the Celtic fringe (the Scots, Welsh, and Irish) to the English. The constitutional reforms in Scotland and Wales as well as the political settlement for Northern Ireland all involve a derogation and complication of UK sovereignty. At least in the short run, they promise to complicate issues of national identity before, one hopes, helping to resolve them (an issue to be taken up in the concluding chapter in challenge 5). In this context, *United Kingdom* seems an increasingly anachronistic conceit, not simply for the monarchical embellishment, but for the pretense that a unified national identity sustains the territorial state.

Political Community: Imagined and Contested

As Benedict Anderson has observed, national identity involves the belief in an "imagined community" of belonging, shared fates, "deep, horizontal comradeship" (1991, p. 7), and affinities among millions of people who do not know each other – and who actually lead quite different and wholly unconnected lives. In the case of the UK, a particularly expansive leap of imagination is necessary to construct national identity as the definite, integral, and bounded conception that Anderson proposes (see

Alexander, 1996, pp. 38–9). The quite basic problem of uncertainty as to who and what might constitute the British nation is underscored by the fact that the United Kingdom of Great Britain and Northern Ireland shares the distinction, along with the former Soviet Union, of "refusing nationality in its naming." As Anderson (1991) observes, anyone who wants to challenge the point has only to ponder what nationality its name could denote: Great Brito-Irish? Questions about brokered sovereignty within the context of the European Union, the commingled historiography of four nations, and the interplay of race and nationality in post-imperial Britain have created doubts about British identity that run deep.

The UK's imperial past clearly created diffuse boundaries of inclusion and nationhood, subject (as we shall see) to extensive redefinition during the postwar and postcolonial period, with continuing dislocating effects on black Britons. Immigration and the political and cultural expression of ethnic minority groups have altered the UK in ways that far transcend the relatively small demographic implications. As ethnicity, intra-UK territorial attachments, and the processes of Europeanization and globalization complicate national identity – as situational identities are shuffled and left unsettled – it becomes increasingly difficult for UK residents to automatically imagine themselves Britons, constituting a resonant national community. What constitutes "Britishness"? Has the UK fragmented into smaller communities that exist side by side, but not necessarily in amiable proximity? These questions are so difficult to answer categorically because British identity, and degrees of inclusion and exclusion, operate on several conceptual, cultural, and territorial frontiers, often with ambiguity, and always subject to political challenges and contested narratives.[1]

J. G. A. Pockock, who helped launch the "four nations or one" historiographical debate, asks what becomes of the definition of national community and "the identity it offers the individual" when sovereignty is "modified, fragmented or abandoned" as it was with the UK's entry into the European Union (1992, p. 364). Hugh Kearney (1991) questions whether the United Kingdom as a political unit comprises four nations or one – and tries to slide past the conundrum by emphasizing the "multi-cultural" as distinct from the "multi-national" history of Britain. Stuart Hall notes that in defining themselves, UK residents say they are "English or Welsh or Indian or Pakistani" (1992, p. 291). Britishness is lost in the assertion of separate territorial or ethnic or cultural identities, based either on nations within the UK or on places of origin or descent outside the UK.

How about English identity as a source of attachment and self-identification? "The sense of identity of the English is almost as difficult to specify as the name of the state," observes Bernard Crick (1991, p. 91), reinforcing Hall's argument. He then explains that "British" is a concept appropriately applied to matters of citizenship and political institutions, and emphasizes, "It is not a cultural term, nor does it apply to any real sense of nation" (p. 97). As Crick observes, for the English it is easy to mistake patriotism for nationalism (a "Britishness" transposed into and experienced as English nationalism). It is important to add, however, that this is a confusion to which ethnic minorities are not prone, especially given the complex interplay between nation and race in rhetorical definitions of Englishness/Britishness and in postwar immigration and nationality policy.

Without digging very deeply into the historical record, it is easy to recognize a quite potent blurring of lineage, race, and nationality that extends from the mid-seventeenth-century historiography of the Norman invasion in 1066 (foreigners oppressing the "Anglo-Saxon race") to Margaret Thatcher's 1982 justification for war against Argentina ("The people of the Falkland Islands, like the people of the United Kingdom, are an island race") (Miles, 1987). To ethnic minority communities, the patriotic appeals during the Falklands War to a truly imaginary part of the UK political community 8,000 miles away emphasized the exclusion felt by ethnic minority individuals right in the heart of England. As one observer noted in the popular press at the time, "Most Britons identify more easily with those of the same stock 8,000 miles away . . . than they do with West Indian or Asian immigrants living next door" (see Gilroy, 1991, pp. 51–2). Thus, one way of imagining the national community appears to privilege *race* (the assertion of common "stock" or ancestry) over *place* (who actually lives in the UK, ethnic identity aside) (see Goulbourne, 1991; Jackson and Penrose, 1994).

As cross-pressures mount and situational identities shift under changing circumstances, a great many narratives of national identity, each of considerable salience, have proliferated in the UK. Recognizing that no representative sample or comprehensive rendering of narratives of British national identity is possible here, I will limit explicit discussion to two that have assumed an important status as narrative and critical counternarrative, and then offer a brief reprise of some politically charged alternatives.

Mythic Englishness as British National Identity

This is the traditional narrative of Englishness that confirms the power of "invented tradition" to "inculcate certain values and norms of behaviour by repetition, which automatically implies continuity with the past" (Hobsbawm, 1992, p. 1). In this case, it is a past of the "sceptered isle" protected from invasion, enjoying a special happy destiny – an image of

Britain's natural advantage of insularity given almost theological force by Shakespeare's famous lines given to the dying John of Gaunt in the play *Richard II* (see Robbins, 1998, p. 31):

> This other Eden, demi-paradise,
> This fortress built by nature for herself
> Against infection and the hand of war,
> This happy breed of men, this little world,
> This precious stone set in the silver sea
> Which serves it in the office of a wall
> Or as a moat defensive to a house
> Against the envy of less happier lands;

By the latter eighteenth century this sense of benign superiority, secured by a purported immunity from invasion, came to inspire a more robust nationalism. English identity was spurred by a rejection of European otherness – Frenchness and Catholicism – heightened by the French revolution and popularized during extensive military campaigns against revolutionary and Napoleonic France (Haseler, 1996). At least in its mythic telling, English national identity became almost indistinguishable from a claim of English exceptionalism and a powerful dose of Euroskepticism.

Central to this narrative, England's gradual evolutionary path contrasts favorably with the radical disjunctures of the continent. This representation emphasizes the critical juncture of the Glorious Revolution of 1688–9: it confirmed the power of Parliament over the monarchy; it also ensured the dominance of the Church of England and ended violent religious conflict, marking the "last successful political coup d'état or revolution in British history" (Black, 1993, p. 6). With the consolidation of the British state consecrated in the Act of Union of 1707, the decisive step was taken to forge a single territorial state in the British Isles. However brutal the process of state building, and however suspect the translation of coerced consolidation as harmonious evolution, the telling and retelling form a cultural repertoire that celebrates continuity, gradualism, and tolerance as the UK's official non-ideological ideology (see Haseler, 1996, p. 22).

It is a United Kingdom of indisputable and metonymic Englishness. Outside of England an indeterminate and often weakly felt Britishness relies on a duality of identities, but in England there is little sense of that. "England offered hospitality, as it were, to institutions identified as 'British' or 'National' – the British Museum or the National Gallery – and took them to be its own," observes Keith Robbins. "There were 'national' museums or libraries of Scotland or Wales but not of England" (1998, p. 284). There was no need for them in England, until issues of national identity came to the fore in the 1970s, since there (and there alone) the elision of Britain and England could be taken for granted.

This England is aptly represented by the Savoy operas of Gilbert and Sullivan, timeless in their appeal and ceaselessly performed to delighted mass audiences – in a comfortable niche between music hall and concert hall – for more than a century. These products of the Victorian era extol an Englishness where foreigners are at best faintly comical, England's imperial greatness is celebrated, and the pageantry of the monarchy becomes increasingly elaborate, contributing nicely to one of the signal inventions of English tradition. Wherever Gilbert and Sullivan's operas are staged, they are about England: a "flag that none dare defy" (*Ruddigore*); the country that "occupies a pre-eminent position among civilized countries" (*Utopia Limited*); the choral affirmation, "For he is an Englishman" (*HMS Pinafore*) (Cannadine, 1992a, 1992b).

This mythic England, and the cultural values it lauds, find expression in the stories of valor and community in London's air raid shelters during German bombing raids in World War II, or in the image of the local bobby. It is aptly rendered in the patriotic and pugnacious figure of John Bull, the eighteenth-century cartoon character who remained a nationalist symbol of England as late as the Second World War (Haseler, 1996). In fact, John Bull has re-emerged recently in new social scientific costume: as a contemporary national identity "type" in a study of British social attitudes intended to identify those respondents who scored high both on *inclusive* aspects of national identity (pride in how the nation functions and/or in its heritage and culture) and on *exclusive* aspects of national identity (protectionism and/or xenophobia). The authors suggest that the John Bulls, who are said to represent a view that was consolidated in the early decades of the nineteenth century, in the aftermath of Britain's victory in the Napoleonic wars, can still claim to represent the "heart of Britain" (Dowds and Young, 1996). I read the study as indicating that this centuries-old character still best embodies traditional England, proud of its national cultural heritage and exclusive in its nationalism.[2]

In an interesting sense, this "official" celebration of Englishness rests on a paradox, typical of myth making: the national identity of the contemporary UK, represented as the England of Shakespeare, Gilbert and Sullivan, and John Bull, is rooted in centuries-old historical tales and cultural artifacts. As a result, the constructed appears natural, reinforced by a mythic appeal – as if the attributes of national identity need no justification beyond simple assertion (see Hobsbawm, 1992, p. 14). Thus, an air of essentialism lends force to the cultural repertoires of sceptered-isle-John-Bull-Englishness.[3] By contrast, counternarratives seem like disputatious upstarts of questionable provenance.

Nation and Migration: Diasporic Identities

The counternarratives of diasporic national identities will be introduced below. First, however, it may be useful to provide the context that constitutes the "collective memory" of black Britons and inspires their images of nation.

Before anyone talked about globalization, the undeniably global phenomenon of colonial and postcolonial migration transformed the lived experiences and vastly complicated the national identities of many thousands of new UK residents and citizens from Africa, South Asia, and the Caribbean. Inevitably, experiences of ethnic minorities have been framed by the politics of citizenship and nationality, driven by perceptions about what ethnic groups "belong" in the UK (and to what degree). For the older members of the ethnic minority communities, as well as for recent immigrants, policies that govern immigration have had the most direct biographical effect, but it is probably fair to say that no ethnic minorities have been spared their formative influences.

It is often remarked that a substantial number of youngsters born in the Caribbean poignantly recall their mothers' departure for England while they were left in the care of an aunt or grandmother, the beneficiary of remittances from abroad, soon to follow into labor-intensive and low-paying jobs in the UK (see G. Lewis, 1993). This collective memory is eloquent testimony to the cross-generational influences of immigration, as the politics of citizenship and nationality have determined the settlement patterns and shaped the opportunities of virtually every ethnic minority family. Even for the increasing majority of ethnic minority Britons who were born in the UK, the collective history of immigration, and certain awareness of the legally sanctioned and racially applied exclusions from political community, continue to shape identity formation and potentially influence ideological dispositions, normative orientations, and political agendas.

Patterns of immigration and changing politics of nationality

As noted in chapter 6, the pattern of immigration and ethnic minority settlement proceeded in a context set by cross-cutting pressures: demand for labor to satisfy the new economic circumstances of postwar reconstruction and economic modernization, on the one hand, and hostility directed against ethnic minority residents and restrictive immigration and nationality legislation, on the other. The intensity of white anger and the crudeness invoked by anti-immigrant politicians should not be forgotten: they undoubtedly comprise an unforgettable element in the collective memories of ethnic minorities in the UK.

If the rampage by white residents in Notting Hill in 1958 remains the most notorious popular expression of resentment directed at ethnic minority groups, the performance of the Conservative candidate Peter Griffiths in the Midlands constituency of Smethwick in 1964 remains the most shocking indicator of the racialized climate of white opinion on the matter. His was the first campaign fought on the issue of race and immigration, and Griffiths reportedly refused to condemn supporters who used the slogan "If you want a nigger neighbour, vote Labour." Griffiths won with a swing to the Conservatives in the constituency of 7.5 percent (against a national swing to Labour of 3.2 percent) and no less a figure than Richard Crossman, Minister of Housing and Local Government in the 1964 Labour government, and a leading intellectual figure in the party, characterized immigration as "the hottest potato" in politics – one on which Labour clearly was not prepared to burn its fingers (Paul, 1997, p. 177). Both Labour and Conservative governments struggled to control immigration, finding ways to "distinguish, in law, between those United Kingdom citizens who in some sense 'belonged' to the United Kingdom itself, and those United Kingdom citizens whose closest ties were in some territory within the Commonwealth" (Rees, 1982, p. 88).

Beginning with the Commonwealth Immigrants Act of 1962, which for the first time introduced controls on the entry of Commonwealth citizens, immigration and nationality policy increasingly operationalized the significance of skin color in the definitions of group identities and "Britishness." The 1962 Act, passed in the face of strong Labour Party opposition, withdrew from most Commonwealth citizens (and from all colonial subjects not of recent British descent) the right to enter and settle in the UK without restriction (instead, new entrants required vouchers, usually tied to specific jobs). The Act was the last significant example of Labour Party resistance to racially suspect exclusionary policies.

After the settlement in the UK of several tens of thousands of ethnic Asians – British subjects and passport holders resident in east Africa, who were displaced by the Africanization policies of the Kenyan government and entitled to relocate in the UK – the Labour government rushed the Commonwealth Immigrants Act of 1968 through Parliament in three days. For the first time, the Act introduced the distinction among UK passport holders between those who had the right to settle in the UK and those who did not. After the invention of a racially loaded concept that came to be called *patriality*, settlement in the UK henceforth required the passport holder to have been born, adopted, or naturalized in the UK – or to have a parent or grandparent who met those conditions. The practical effect of the new doctrine was to preserve the right of settlement for many citizens of the Old Commonwealth, while ending it for many UK passport holders who were resident in the New Commonwealth: in effect, it created a class of persons who were citizens in principle, but in fact stateless, subject to settlement only under a quota system. The 1971 Immigration Act, which in practical terms continues to have the greatest influence on non-European immigration, made the preference for white immigrants even clearer: only patrials and their immediate families, or families of other Commonwealth citizens legally residing in the UK before 1973, retained full rights to live and work freely in the UK; all other Commonwealth passport holders needed work permits that were subject to annual renewals and issued for specific employment opportunities. In contrast, EC citizens could enter freely.

By the early 1970s, the restrictive policies were firmly in place, and immigration from Africa, the Caribbean, and Asia was down to a trickle. Nevertheless, the politics of citizenship and nationality heated up again as the 1979 election approached. In Thatcher's first general election campaign, race and nationality were repoliticized, as the Conservatives invoked the immigration issue for partisan gain (Messina, 1989, pp. 126–49), implying that the increased presence of ethnic minority groups imperiled law and order, and promising to tighten immigration further. In one of the most widely quoted – and controversial – remarks early in the contest, Thatcher exaggerated the rate of immigration from the New Commonwealth or Pakistan and expressed support for those who might be "afraid that this country might be rather swamped by people with a different culture" (Troyna, 1982, pp. 265–6). Although the extent of New Commonwealth and Pakistani immigration throughout the 1970s was minimal, never exceeding 38,000 entrants per year, the anti-immigrant stance was politically potent: Thatcher's support in opinion polls immediately jumped by 9 percent, her immigration policy stole the thunder from the xenophobic National Front, and the Tory stance on nationality and immigration reportedly provided her with the margin of victory in sixteen seats (see Krieger, 1992a, pp. 118–23).

Thatcher's calculated remarks, made for maximum effect on the popular television program *World in Action*, made explicit the underlying assumptions that had governed the politics of race and nationality throughout the postwar period: that differences in culture (color) were threatening to the UK's majority white population, and must be subject to increasingly tight regulation. The Conservatives delivered on their promises of additional restrictive legislation with the 1981 Nationality Act, which further codified the insider versus outsider distinction: those who won rights of settlement in the 1968 and 1971 Acts (patrials) were renamed "British citizens." In addition, two lesser categories of citizenship were formalized (British Dependent Territories Citizenship and British Overseas Citizenship), and neither carried the right of entry or settlement. Although the Act appears to qualify citizenship rights on territorial distinctions, a set of provisions and rulings have emphasized family, blood, and culture over geography in the consummate reconstruction of British national identity (Paul, 1997, p. 182).

At one level, immigration and nationality policy represents a logical adjustment to the loss of empire and receding scope of Commonwealth ties: real Britons have close ties to the UK, proper, and the time has passed when British identity could be reasonably viewed as coextensive with a far-flung empire or commonwealth. At another level, the racialization of policy is unmistakable. Since the 1962 Act, both immigration policy and practice have no longer been shaped as such policies generally have been in postwar Europe, by the rise and fall of labor demand. Rather, a preoccupation with national identity – who is really British? – has redefined immigration policy.

Although references to skin color or different cultures never figured in the wording of any of the Acts, there cannot be much doubt about the cumulative discriminatory effect of the legislation: "each successive measure sought to close the door to dark-skinned potential migrants, while keeping it open to 'whites' from the countries of the Old Commonwealth and South Africa" (Mason, 1995, p. 31). The meaning and political implications of nationality legislation for ethnic minorities have shifted decisively. "Changes in nationality law, by 'constitutionalizing' discriminatory definitions in immigration rules, have both undermined the status of black British citizens born abroad and sealed off future sources of black immigration," noted a researcher at an Asian resource center in Birmingham. "Immigration and nationality are therefore no longer independent issues" (Sondhi, 1983, pp. 255–6). In stark terms, immigration legislation became nationality legislation, progressively transforming the historic distinction between British subjects and aliens, regardless of color, into racial distinctions that denied entry and settlement to those of non-European descent.

As a paradoxical sign of its success, nationality policy *per se* is no longer a hot political issue, and New Labour promises to restore full citizenship to the residents of dependent territories. For white Britons, however, immigration "retains a powerful political undertow in the guise of a fear of multi-culturalism and cultural dilution" (Dowds and Young, 1996, p. 147). Xenophobic concerns remain strong: about two-thirds of UK respondents in a recent social attitudes survey agreed with a statement that the number of immigrants should be reduced, approximately one-half said that immigrants take jobs away from those born in Britain, and about one-quarter said that immigrants increase crime rates (Dowds and Young, 1996).

Diasporic narratives

This history of hostility, invidious restriction, a racializing of citizenship, and xenophobia hauntingly undergirds diasporic national identities, with the result, as Paul Gilroy (1993) puts it, that black and British becomes a lived contradiction. The images that cement John Bull identity underscore the sense of exclusion at the heart of the diasporic narratives, as the boundaries of political community are starkly drawn in racial terms:

> Britons are invited to put on their tin hats and climb back down into the World War II air-raid shelters. There, they can be comforted by the rustic glow of the homogenous national culture that has been steadily diluted by black settlement in the post-war years. That unsullied culture can be mystically reconstituted, particularly amidst national adversity when distinctively British qualities supposedly emerge with the greatest force and clarity. (Gilroy, 1993, p. 24)

In Gilroy's pungent critique, the most powerful cultural repertoires of nationhood, drawn from images of war and collective survival, so casually reprised during the Falklands/Malvinas conflict, represent black settlement and immigration as encroachment. As he explains, Thatcher's inflammatory characterization of striking coal miners as the "enemy within," who were "just as hard to fight and as dangerous to liberty" as the Argentine forces ("the enemy without"), led to the surprising discovery that miners and blacks shared the label of enemy (Samuel et al., 1986; Gilroy, 1991, p. 34). Fifteen years later, the representational force of Thatcher's divisive and exclusionary remark, which was viewed as gratuitously offensive even by Conservatives, has not been blunted. It remains an often repeated theme of the collective history of exclusion, a potent reminder that Fortress England casts those who are marginalized and stoutly independent, especially blacks, as dangerous invaders, who are threats to public safety and English culture (Gilroy, 1993).

The power of narratives: influences on identity formation

The ongoing effort by UK residents and citizens of colonial descent to come to terms with the vast and disjointed collective histories of dispersal and exclusion is often reinforced by the sense of isolation and marginalization that stems from discouraging dead-end jobs and incipient ghettoization. Powerful counternarratives of nation that help make sense of collective histories and personal biographies contribute to the identity formation of blacks in the UK in complex patterns that can only be hinted at here. Below, I distinguish between a universalizing counter-hegemonic identity and more context-dependent situational identities.

Shared counter-hegemonic identity   For some, a drive to recover the past may fuel a desire to construct coherence from necessarily fragmented and distinct collective histories. In this approach, cultural identity becomes "the idea of one, shared culture, a sort of collective 'one true self', hiding inside the many other, more superficial self or artificially imposed 'selves', which people with a shared history and ancestry hold in common" (Hall, 1996a, p. 211). The construction of a narrative of a shared counter-hegemonic identity is inherently fragile. It involves an uneasy balance between the recognition of specific ethnic, national, cultural biographies and group histories and the willingness to have them eclipsed by stretching territorial commonality or inventing a mythic shared geography and common collective history. Edward Said notes the utility of this approach, suggesting that "imaginative geography and history help the mind to intensify its own sense of itself by dramatizing the distance and the difference between what is close to it and what is far away" (1979, p. 55).

In artistic expression, the construction of a common counter-hegemonic identity may take the form of a cultural treatment of the essentialized past, as in the work of Armet Francis, a Jamaica-born photographer who has lived in the UK since childhood. Stuart Hall observes that his photographic representations of the people of the Black Triangle, taken in the US, the UK, Africa, and the Caribbean, attempt "an imaginary reunification" of black people distributed across the globe by slavery, colonization, and diaspora (see Hall, 1990, 1996a). In a similar way, the homogenizing processes of counter-hegemonic identity formation may be observed on the ground, through the transnational force of black American and black Caribbean culture in the UK. In Birmingham and Southall, for example, the everyday language of Asian youth is a cross between Caribbean patois, the vernacular language of American blacks, and the local dialect (Luthra, 1997, p. 29).

Politically, the narrative of common counter-hegemonic identity inspires collective mobilization to advance common interests. This political orientation helped mobilize the broad anti-racist politics of resistance and self-empowerment, especially in the 1980s, in the municipal left campaigns (Gilroy, 1991; Anthias and Yuval-Davis, 1992; Luthra, 1997). In one crucial gesture to underscore the commonality of racism and marginalization in the UK, the Greater London Council cast its central anti-Thatcher, economic development campaign as an anti-racist (rather than class-based) initiative, and placed it under the operational authority of a newly created Ethnic Minorities Committee (chaired by its leader, Ken Livingstone) (see Gilroy, 1991, pp. 136–48). In this process of black identity formation, the imagination transcends finite and enclosed borders, neglects the distinctions of culture and particular ethnicity or origins, and asserts a common, deterritorialized, national identity.

Situational identity formation   The construction of common identity and interests, amidst potent reminders of cultural differences and distinctive political goals, is necessarily a delicate process, fraught with instability and, very probably, a fair degree of uncertainty. Its emphasis on purported commonality of cultural descent (an homogenizing "blackness") or interest (in anti-racist community-based campaigns) may be contrasted to a second process of national identity formation that expresses its truly modular, situational, fluid character.

The Rushdie Affair provides an unusually high-profile example of the politics of situational identities, as ethnic minority groups choose what particular attachment to emphasize for reasons of strategy or need to affirm "belonging" in the face of external pressures.[4] Early in 1989, Ruhollah Khomeini, cleric and leader of the Iranian revolution, called for the murder of Salman Rushdie for his purported defamation of Islam in *The Satanic Verses*. Thereafter, the author received protection from the British authorities while he remained in hiding. Although most community leaders and prominent Muslims disassociated themselves from Khomeini's edict, Muslims in large numbers demonstrated their outrage, called for Penguin Books to withdraw the volume, and urged the government to ban the book. Government ministers, pressed both by popular outrage directed at Khomeini's *fatwa* and Britain's Muslims and by incidents of book burning, invoked indiscriminate descriptions of Muslims as "fundamentalists." At the same time, they raised the specter of threats to law and order by Muslims in the UK (although the demonstrations against the book led to no arrests or injuries), and issued edicts of their own, instructing ethnic minorities "on being British" (Asad, 1990; Lewis, 1994; Modood, 1997).

The Rushdie Affair became a kind of Rorschach test on to which competing interpretations of multiculturalism, Englishness, and ethnic identities were projected (see Ansell, 1997, p. 5). It was a critical example of modularity in political-cultural repertoires, as often mythic representations of normatively loaded terms such as "Islam," "British," and "fundamentalism" were appropriated by all and sundry for very diverse purposes. More important here, it spurred a host of quite contradictory strategies of identity formation with significant political repercussions. In Bradford, where a book burning quickly made the city notorious as Britain's "Islamabad," the Rushdie Affair heightened the tension over context-dependent strategies of ethnic minority representation. Should those who were outraged by Rushdie represent themselves as "Asian," "black," or "Muslim"? How would identity labeling and recognition be manipulated by local authorities? Since in Bradford, as elsewhere, there was little interest in the campaigns against Rushdie's book among non-Muslim Asians, local mobilization emphasized Muslim identity. The Bradford City Council, which had earlier encouraged Muslim mobilization, in the face of the Rushdie Affair withdrew its support from Muslim institutions such as the Council of Mosques, and authorities tried to breathe life into an inclusive, more cooperative, "Asian" identity (Lewis, 1994, 1997; Modood, 1997).

More generally, the Rushdie Affair intensified the context-dependent alternatives in ethnic identification, especially for youth. There is some evidence that this galvanizing event helped mobilize a small militant segment of young Muslims on the edges of community development projects and in Islamic societies at universities, some of whom expressed their growing "Ashrifization" in modes of dress and religious organization, and by emphasizing religious over regional or national identification. Paradoxically, perhaps feeling cornered in response to intense pressures on Muslims to choose to "be British" (or be suspect and marginalized), the Rushdie Affair inspired other young Muslim Asians to represent themselves as British Muslims rather than, say, Pakistanis or Asians (Luthra, 1997, pp. 19–34).

The modularity, contingency, and fluidity of identity formation, focused acutely by high-visibility eruptions like the Rushdie Affair, heighten the importance of shifting scenarios of cultural representation. The melting of religion into ethnicity and ethnicity into nationality in British cultural representation (Baker et al., 1996a), most acutely with reference to Muslims, must be placed in a broader, quite troubling, context. Critical shifts in the politics of race and nation in the UK, inspired by protests against Rushdie's work, occurred against the backdrop of powerful developments in both theory and practice. The "clash of civilizations" perspective, in which Islam replaces communism as the main threat to Western civilization, defined in broad cultural terms (Huntington, 1996), reinforces the view of Muslims as "other" both by reference to white Britons and in comparison to other "Asian" ethnic minorities. At the same time, the broader European political context is set by proliferating xenophobic nationalisms from the rival factions of the Front National in France to Scandinavian anti-immigrant activists to the odious "ethnic cleansing" campaigns of Serbian nationalists (Bjorgo, 1997; Modood, 1997). In the UK, Muslim identity, which begins as a religious identity, is recast as more threatening, as an alien ethnicity cum nationality, far less "English" – and, as a consequence, individuals so labeled are figuratively expelled from the nation (see Baker et al., 1996a).

In a quite different context, one of the most intriguing narratives of diasporic identity formation comes from the observation of youths of African-Caribbean descent, for whom attachments to place and political community may be experienced as transient. For them, nationhood is associated with home, itself an uncertain place and concept. Based on intense fieldwork with small groups of mostly male informants, largely of African-Caribbean descent in London, Claire Alexander argues, following Gilroy (1991), that the ascriptive national identities of black youth tend to be flexible. Their relationship to national identity remains ambiguous, as they straddle boundaries defined by cultural and national communities, often without feeling rooted in either. As Alexander reports, none of her informants, "felt able to describe themselves as 'British', without any further qualification, while 'English' was a label rarely considered appropriate." This is how Alexander describes the ramifications of national identity for one of her informants, admittedly an outlier on this issue:

> Out of those I met, Malcolm was perhaps the least rooted in his identity; although he did not consider Britain to be his home, he also did not locate himself in relation to his parents' island of origin, Jamaica. He had never visited the island and . . . he did not consider this in relation to himself in any significant way, "If I go back there, I can't say that's my home 'cos I wasn't even born there . . . I can't miss what I've never had' . . . For Malcolm, the question of nationhood was one he considered largely irrelevant to his sense of being, of who he is. (1996, pp. 39–40)

Particularly among young people, it seems, the pre-given categories of nation, community, and ethnicity – the forms available in the ready-made modular identity kit – do not satisfy their own designs.[5] In a limited way, these observations of black youth in London challenge Anderson's basic foundational premise that national identity is a primary, almost primordial, and integral attachment. Instead, their ascribed attachments tend to be notably fluid, emphasizing the individual's own perception of place and home over clearly delineated national or cultural communities that are characterized by absolute or bounded membership.

Since Alexander's sample is small and the research is limited in scope to African-Caribbeans in one locale, one should be cautious about generalizing from her findings. A similar pattern of modular, constantly shifting, individually ascribed collective identities has been observed, however, among ethnic minority youth more broadly, amidst other important tendencies: to see their primary identity in terms of place, or to resort to negative identity, or to emphasize self-development goals above all identity claims (Luthra, 1997).

National Identity Unresolved

As one recent study of British social attitudes and the question of nationality identity concluded, "Half a century ago, the term 'British' would have coupled more easily to Empire than to any specific society; Britain, it might now be said, has lost an Empire, and not yet found a nation" (Dowds and Young, 1996, p. 153). There are too many shifting identity claims inhabiting the same territory, amidst deterritorializing (diasporic) claims; there are identity claims for attachment to larger territories (Europe) as well as smaller territories (England, Wales, Scotland, Ireland) than that of the British Isles. Of course, the field of narrative claims to national identity is not covered by discussion of a single pair of narrative and counternarrative alternatives, contrasting the mythic Englishness and diasporic perspectives. Other highly charged narratives abound, often reinforced or implicated by powerful political constituencies.

The "sceptered isle" narrative spawns a variety of avatars. When Englishness is famously depicted only partly in jest as "Parliament, Magna Carta, roast beef, and plum pudding" (Haseler, 1996, p. 21), there is good reason to fear both the loss of sovereign control and the threat to culinary independence embodied in the Single European Act of 1992, Maastricht, and the euro. In this context, it is easy to see the Euroskepticism that contributed to Margaret Thatcher's hasty departure from 10 Downing Street, and which held John Major's premiership hostage, as a modern expression of the *Fortress England* narrative depicted in *Richard II*. This perspective is readily captured in the famously blunt nativist slogan (here offered in its less crude version), "Foreigners start at Calais." That Europeans sense the UK's self-inflicted separation from the continent is made clear in the phrase "11 plus 1," believed to be coined by Jacques Delors, President of the European Commission, which came to describe the British separation from their Community colleagues in the era of swirling debates over Maastricht and the Social Charter (see Cohen, 1994, pp. 28–33).[6]

Extension of this insularity inward, to sharpen the UK borders and narrow the national political community, gives voice to the *New Right* construction of English identity defined by homogenous (white) culture. As Enoch Powell states: "Every society, every nation, is unique: it has its own past, its own story, its own memories, its own ways, its own language or way of speaking, its own – dare I use the word – culture" (Smith, 1994, pp. 129–82; Ansell, 1997, p. 168). This claim of national identity grounded in an exclusionary "way of life" gained credibility with Thatcher's memorable *World in Action* defense of xenophobic fear of the other (where the word "culture" was invoked in this way). The bar marking inclusion was raised quite outlandishly by Norman Tebbit's appeal to cricket, the quintessential icon of English culture. It was not enough, reasoned the Conservative Party chairman, that ethnic minorities, as opposed to Europeans or Americans, share (perhaps exceed) the English passion for the sport and affect English customs, but now, to be above reproach and confirm their national loyalty, they must also root for England in matches (see Alexander, 1996, pp. 2–3; Haseler, 1996, p. 59; Ansell, 1997, p. 5).[7] In the New Right national identity narrative, culture cum race becomes an inviolable barrier to inclusion, confirming that black and British or English are mutually exclusive identities.

These Fortress England and New Right versions, extrapolating and radicalizing moments of the "sceptered isle" narrative, do not, of course, exhaust the options. One has only to review Tom Nairn's classic, *The Break-up of Britain*, to be reminded of the sheer range of alternative narratives of national identity – won, lost, and contested – that emerge from the period of intensified Celtic nationalisms in the 1970s. Nairn's cata-logue, without exhausting the options of appeals to *Celtic Nationalisms*, includes: a narrative of Union based on absorption, not federation; "the troubles" in Northern Ireland as a prelude to radical nationalist move-ments in Wales and Scotland, or alternatively as atavism, as anti-imperialism; Scottish nationalism as belated modernization; "peripheral nationalisms" as the expression of deep-seated incapacities of the British state, exacerbated by Thatcherism, and international competitive pressures, set in the context of a global North–South divide (Nairn, 1981).[8]

As an important alternative to Nairn's menu of Celtic nationalist options, one should add the *Britannic Melting Pot* narrative, clearly articulated by Hugh Kearney, which emphasizes how much is shared by the cultures of the "several states (nations?) . . . that made their appear-ance in the context of British Isles history" (1989, p. 4). From this more benign reading, during the first half of the nineteenth century, England took a leading role due to its superiority in economic and demo-graphic terms (pp. 149–73). Finally, the Good Friday agreements offer a hopeful sign that new, potentially more salutary narratives of national identity as *Negotiated Sovereignty* can be invented, and that traditions of cross-border, cross-community collaboration may displace the bitter legacies of division. For the time being, however, the new accords create an unsettled, although one hopes not destabilizing, period of transition as institutional arrangements and the balance of power are determined.

As the historical record and the narratives reveal, issues of British (English?) national identity are far from settled, the boundaries of inclu-sion and exclusion fluid and vexed, the representations of nation hotly contested, the attachments at once robust and uncertain in political valence and sources of attachment. Beyond the politicization of cate-gories of identity, it is clear that the uncertainty of boundaries extends to conceptual frameworks. It is a signal feature of ethnic minority dias-poras that biographies and collective histories forge complicated cross-border identities. At the same time, in forging attachments and locating a sense of home that cannot in any simple way be defined territorially, and of belonging that is context-dependent, members of ethnic minority groups recognize no sharply drawn distinctions that mark the boundaries of ethnicity, nationality, religion, community, and several other identity characteristics and labels.

Taken together with the transformation of production systems, the evisceration of class agency, and the dispersal of "the working class" into disparate coteries of individuals with distinctive experiences, the "mod-ularization" of collective identities – and motifs for recognizing and rep-resenting those identities – vastly complicates the art of politics. Once individuals are no longer constant in their attachments and attendant definitions of interests, on what fixed points of reference can political leaders or strategists fix their political compass? If identities are context-dependent and situational, and normative claims are neither grounded nor consensual, how should parties orient their policies? Modularity pulls the rug out from under the left versus right distributive bargaining that has broadly shaped postwar European politics, and at the same time, it presents a tremendous challenge to any center-left project to consolidate an enduring social democratic agenda and to reattach politics and interests.

We turn now to a discussion of selected narratives of community, a concept, like nation, that has deep political reverberations and raises critical problems for New Labour, and for almost any model of government that wishes to advance a participatory project.

9

Communities: Actual and Imagined

The perspective of political-cultural modularity emphasizes distinctive ethnic minority attachments. The approach helps to disclose significant differences among ethnic minority cultural practices, even within what outsiders might view as a single "ethnic community." In addition, it recognizes the need for strategic political separation among ethnic minority groups and underscores the political significance of political-cultural repertoires in identity labeling. As Tariq Modood notes, "It is because the public recognition of community identities is so deeply political that it is itself a source of political activity and conflict" (1997, p. 7). The public recognition of an ethnic community, and the way that it is represented, plays a powerful, formative role in organizing group politics framed by collective identities. Alternatively, the appeal to community, in its communitarian ideal, where citizens nurtured in families achieve "the moral power of personal responsibility for ourselves and each other" (Blair, 1996, p. 300), has become a rhetorical mainstay of New Labour, rich in moral and, potentially, institutional and policy implications. These two narratives of community – as figurative construct of essentialized or strategic ethnic unity and metonymy for New Labour's political vision – will be discussed in turn.

Ethnic Minority Communities

As many observers have noted, academics, as well as local political officials and local government administrators, have tended to "conflate culture and spatiality," contributing to a process of inventing a community, in which the residents, themselves, are active strategic participants.

Common sense makes us "map culture on space" and construct a holistic sense of community in which we take for granted the "isomorphism of culture, place and people." The narrative of "the black community" or "the Asian community" is reinforced both by popular discourses of ethnicity that emphasize "roots" and by the practical facts of city life: that local politics and issues of collective consumption require that residents in a neighborhood must organize as such to maximize their options *vis-à-vis* local government (Caglar, 1997, p. 174).

Invented black community

The language of community, whether essentialist or strategic in inspiration, inherently claims a unity that, at the least, temporarily obscures cultural heterogeneity. Often, local authorities are less influenced by preconceived essentialist understandings of who constitutes a given community than by the results of grassroots campaigns, and the negotiation or competition among ethnic groups to determine the identity labeling that almost invariably accompanies local politics in ethnically diverse cities and towns (Modood, 1997). In the UK, the narrative of imagined "black community" has generated a great deal of skepticism. Some direct their criticism at the "race relations industry" emerging in the 1960s – the crisis management approach to race relations. From this perspective, the "community centre" assumes the role of totemic expression of high-handed government policy and archetypal representation of the imagined "black community" constructed from outside (Anthias and Yuval-Davis, 1992; Alexander, 1996). Others who reject the homogenizing narrative of "black community" emphasize the need for ethnic minority peoples of Asian and of African descent in the UK to recognize that antagonism exists. They worry that a tendency to sweep differences under the carpet in service of an imaginary black community may blunt the potential to engage differences – a process that would contribute to improving solidaristic prospects. At the same time, invented unity might distract distinct ethnic groups from separate and potentially more effective political mobilizations (James, 1993). It also obscures complex, historically constituted, and context-dependent patterns of identity formation in actually existing communities. To help reveal these patterns, I offer the case of South Asians in the UK, with specific reference to Manchester Pakistanis.[1]

Modularity in actually existing communities

Any discussion of identity formation among South Asians in the UK could scarcely avoid recognizing the fluidity of boundaries and the complexity of ethnic and national identity formation. Several studies have examined the contextual or situational character of attachments and representations, both from outside and within a group, as they are focused acutely in the local community context (Clarke et al., 1990; Lewis, 1994; Veer, 1995). A host of variables contribute to the intense modularity of community attachments, as the editors of one of the most detailed and knowledgeable studies of South Asians in the UK observed:

> South Asians do not exist as a concrete community. The group is dialecti-
> cally rather than absolutely defined. Ethnic identity is contingent rather
> than categorical . . . South Asians exist as South Asians for some purposes
> but not for others. They exist as South Asians as opposed to West Indians
> or as opposed to whites, but for other purposes they dissolve into their
> sub-groups of nationality, religion, region, language, caste, subcaste or
> *biraderi* [localized marriage-cum-caste descent group]. (Clarke et al., 1990,
> p. 170)

The experiences of the Manchester Pakistani population provide a clear example of the complex process of divisions within an ethnic group in dialectical tension with alternative representational motifs, at least partly imposed from outside. It is also easy to see the practical political implications. In addition to *biraderi* and other aspects of background (such as points of origin and urban or village domicile), specific characteristics of migratory patterns, closely bound up with employment patterns, have contributed to identity formation and group fragmentation.

Pakistani migration to Manchester came in three flows or movements. The first flow involved "traders," who migrated between the 1930s and the 1950s: they were literate, educated, rural or small town Punjabis, who often started as door-to-door peddlers, and in some cases, subsequently became large-scale wholesalers and manufacturers in the clothing and garment trades. The second flow was comprised of "students," who were almost all of higher caste, mostly Punjabis, including Urdu and Gujarati speakers, many with connections to the traders. The most successful of this group returned to occupy elite positions in Pakistan, while many others remained in Manchester and, in time, assumed positions as accountants or doctors, while still others went into business. The third flow, migrating after the first two groups were established, involved "workers," whose backgrounds and circumstances set them apart from the trader and student groups. They were mainly young bachelor men from the West Punjab, with ties to smallholder families and *biraderis* connected to small villages. They came initially as factory workers and to meet the burgeoning demand in the buses and railways. As with the first two migratory flows, caste membership was related to area of origin. In this case, group members came from a variety of castes, including service castes, with the great majority from a set of regionally specific landowning castes.

Similar to most ethnic minority groups and South Asians in other locations in the UK, the Pakistani flows to Manchester followed a pattern of
"chain migration" (Robinson, 1990; Lyon, 1997): earlier migrants of particular *biraderis* and locations followed in the residential and occupational footsteps of their predecessors. Although the initial patterns
established by the three migratory movements have been modified
in subsequent generations, the residential and employment patterns
continue to locate the workers at some remove from the other two
groups. Despite the ability of some from the workers' group to prosper
in the professions and business, it is among this third group that one finds
the highest unemployment and generally lower levels of economic and
occupational success.

Religious differences further divide the Pakistani community along
denominational lines (Sunni, the great majority, Shia and Ahmedia), each
with its own mosque and set of organizations, as well as schools of interpretation. Religious differences have been politicized by a sequence of
sharp ideological disputes, linked to schools of interpretation and religious observation, which have created fierce political rifts. Moreover,
these patterns of religious alliances and divisions among Pakistanis must
be placed within the context of the broader Muslim community in
Manchester, which is divided by national, denominational, ideological,
doctrinal, and organizational lines.

Within this complicated interplay of attachments, material circumstances, cultural values, organizational struggles, ideological differences,
and myriad alliance possibilities, it is not surprising to discover that collective identities are fluid and situational. As Pnina Werbner put it
simply, in her study of unity and division among Manchester Pakistanis,
"there are several salient communal identities which Pakistanis can
choose to highlight, depending on the political context and the particular aims of an association or group" (1990, p. 342). It is interesting to
discover, however, that the selection of identities to highlight follows a
surprisingly straightforward pattern, linking particular issue areas or
events, representational schemes or labels, and political institutions or
arenas.

For example, concern about the provision of ritually slaughtered meat
or proper dress for girls in schools fosters religious identity. In this
context, communal identity as "British Muslims" comes to the fore, and
the Central Mosque becomes the principal institutional arena. When
highlighting national identity – for example, when inviting the Pakistani
Consul or Ambassador to important events, or when the Pakistani
cricket team tours Manchester – the "community" is more likely to
represent itself as "British Pakistanis." In this context, the Pakistani
Community Centre assumes the role of key institutional arena. When
it is necessary to mobilize against racial bias or over resource issues,
Manchester Pakistanis may assume communal identity as members of

the British "Asian" or British "black" community. The latter is the most controversial and purely tactical, the term often being applied with bitterness or irony. When mobilizing in this manner, institutional focus shifts to the City Council Race Sub-Committee.

Thus there are three distinct communities within one, linked through complicated overlapping alliances, in which the influences of the original migratory streams, although diminished, are still present. In this case study from Manchester, we see very complicated, context-dependent, and historically constituted patterns of division and alliance. There is a lot of politics, negotiation, and conflict in the actual communal politics that lie beneath the representation of "community." Paradoxically, the divisions in actually existing communities may help to encourage the undoubted popularity of more solidaristic, homogenizing appeals to community, whether represented as "the black community" or in the more general narrative of community that helps define New Labour's political morality.

New Labour's Normative Community

There is no mistaking the importance of community for New Labour. In fact, it seems clear that, in narratives of community, it finds its moral voice and locates a comfortable third way ethos to guide institutional and policy innovation. For Blair, focus on community – an arena where "we develop the moral power of personal responsibility for ourselves and each other" (1996, p. 300) – captures the salutary blend of individuality balanced by mutuality and interdependence that he considers the core of socialism. Margaret Thatcher was often referred to as a "conviction" politician (see Riddell, 1983, pp. 21–2). It is an appellation not often associated with political leaders in the UK or elsewhere, and a designation not widely applied to Blair, who makes many observers worry that he, like his counterpart, Bill Clinton, is too mindful of opinion polls. The appeal to community, however, reverberates with conviction for Tony Blair.

Blair has long been a member of the Christian Socialist Movement, which, in the aftermath of four consecutive Labour defeats in general elections and in the context of socialism's growing post-cold war disrepute, took as its mission the search for a moral agenda for the Labour Party (see Durham, 1997). In important ways, Blair's Christian socialism provides insight into his moral compass, and that of others in his initial leadership team, such as Jack Straw at the Home Office who, significantly, is in charge of the inter-ministerial committee on the family; the health minister, Paul Boateng; Education Secretary, David Blunkett (see Lloyd, 1997) – and, of course, Blair's predecessor as Labour Party leader, John Smith.

In 1993, the group published *Reclaiming the Ground: Christianity and Socialism* (Bryant, 1993), a revealing window into the Christian Socialist Movement's normative vision, and the evolving narrative of community – and family – that would become the centerpiece of New Labour's political morality. Tony Blair wrote the foreword to the volume, setting the agenda and tone with a straightforward declaration of purpose: "It is a book written by Christians who want to re-unite the ethical code of Christianity with the basic values of democratic socialism." Blair reminded readers that Christianity involves a set of beliefs, such as equality of regard, justice, opportunity, and compassion. But the emphasis could not be more clear for Blair, who suggested that "above all it is about the union between individual and community, the belief that we are not stranded in helpless isolation, but owe a duty to others and to ourselves and are, in a profound sense, dependent on each other to succeed." In a prescient hint of New Labour's policy directions several years down the road, Blair added, "In political terms, this belief in community expresses itself through action collectively to provide the services we need, the infrastructure of society and Government without which modern life would be intolerable." He concluded with a stirring appeal to a reunification of faith and political direction, grounded in conviction, insisting that a "return to what we are really about, what we believe in, would be a healthy journey for our country as well as the Labour Party" (Blair, 1993).

Since Blair is an eclectic thinker, it is likely that his design to modernize New Labour by jettisoning statist institutions and policies, while grounding the political morality in values of equality and community (see Gray, 1997, pp. 14–15), has multiple inspirations. Among these one would include communitarian thinking and renewed interest in the importance for democracy of citizen engagement in a civic community.[2] Of course, the theoretical, institutional, and policy implications would be developed and refined by policy advisors and leading figures within the Labour Party (Brown, 1994; Crouch and Marquand, 1995; Blair, 1996; Mandelson and Liddle, 1996; Mulgan, 1997).

However, within this very interesting document published by the Christian Socialist Movement, one can find all the basic elements for the narrative of community as normative embodiment of New Labour. Particularly in Blair's contribution and that of John Smith (1993), then party leader, the crucial ingredients of a third way political morality are present. Community is established as the moral alternative to the crude individualism of the Thatcherite entrepreneurial culture, on the one hand, and the "Old Labour" collectivism that purportedly crushes individual initiative and rights, on the other hand. At the same time, community emerges as an organizational mid-point between the central state, with its blunt policy instruments and insensitivities, and the neoliberal reliance on *homo economicus*, a soulless profit-maximizing individual, inhabiting a society-less world.

Like Anderson's concept of nations as imagined communities, the narrative of imagined local communities becomes a "highly emotive and potent symbol for both those it envelops and those it excludes" (Alexander, 1996, p. 32). The New Labour narrative of the normative community does not engage complicated boundary issues, and the territoriality and composition of the community as represented by this narrative are never fully examined. What is more, the narrative does not investigate the complexity of identity formation and political mobilization in actually existing communities. Finally, the ability of New Labour to operationalize communitarian principles in the administration of public policy is yet to be established. Despite all these objections, the normative appeal of New Labour's narrative of community has enormous cultural and political force, and lies at the heart of its claim to a third way model of organizing politics.

Modularity, Myths, and Narratives

We often use myth to refer to narratives or stories (our word "myth" comes from the Greek for "word" or "story") that seem fanciful or untrue. At the same time, we use the concept in a more complicated and, I would say, politicized way. It has been said that myths are narratives that help societies pose and potentially resolve basic contradictions in life, as a means of regulating conflicts and sustaining power relations (Barrett, 1992, p. 105). All narratives of nation and community are constructed. They are "imaginary" in Anderson's sense – and therefore mythic in both of these meanings. None of the claims of nationhood ("sceptered isle" or diasporic) or community (essentialist or strategic, when applied by ethnic minorities or New Labour) is either "true" or "untrue." Rather, they are cultural resources with considerable political power: believed by some and received with skepticism by others, strategically manipulated for political aims. The same could be said of other claims of bounded but, within a specified domain, generalized "deep, horizontal comradeship" (Anderson, 1991, p. 7), expressed in group attachments, class most notable among them.

Notions of community and nation help to shape identity formation, how people understand the political world, and how they locate themselves – and their political beliefs and agendas – within it. Different citizens ascribe different values to nation and community, and they draw the boundaries of inclusion and exclusion in both national and more local political communities in various ways. Inevitably, in part due to distinctive collective identity attachments, individuals locate themselves distinctively with regard to those boundaries. They respond quite differently to appeals by New Labour or by any other party to community or to an English way of life, for they understand both the "is" and the "ought" of community and nation in nonstandard ways. It has been said that all politics involves conflicts about values, and that value orientations play a critical role in framing specific political concerns (Dalton, 1996). As a result of what I have termed "political modularity," values and concerns have become increasingly context-dependent, and equivocal, not only due to the "unmaking" and decollectivizing of the working class, but now, in addition, as a result of a "decomposition" in cultural and normative dimensions.

Social democracy operated within the secure boundaries of class agency, distributional politics, and reliable nationhood – expressed in effective policy sovereignty and sustained by what were assumed to be secure, more or less unitary identities and interests that flowed naturally from those solidary attachments. Arguably, none of these conditions any longer obtains to any considerable degree. To the extent that my arguments about modularity in identity formation and related processes of cultural representation are valid, governance is vastly complicated for New Labour as for any center-left project, as the core normative claims and sources of cohesion are jeopardized, and issue preferences become more transitory.

In introducing modular furniture as a metaphor for the transitory commitments that constitute politics nowadays, Gellner emphasized one clear advantage that it has over traditional furniture. It is very difficult to modify old-fashioned furniture, he observed. You have to live with what you brought home from the shop. Changes or additions mean that you must suffer incoherence or make the costly choice to throw the piece out altogether and start again. That is not so with modular furniture, where additions and modifications are possible to respond to new expectations and innovations. Can a revitalized social democracy make the necessary modifications – in its conception of agency, political morality, institutional orientation, and policy approach – to meet the daunting challenges posed by the global age and the disorienting processes of political modularity? This question frames our concluding chapter.

Conclusion

10

Challenges to Contemporary British Government

Gellner rightly emphasizes among the political consequences of modularity that society operates with ever-changing alignments and opinions. The modular individual "is highly variable, not to say volatile, in his activities" (Gellner, 1994, p. 102). I would expand his point to suggest that modularity, along with the decollectivization of class agency that characterizes post-Fordist production systems in the UK, contributes to a thoroughgoing political volatility in which electoral results are but the tip of the iceberg.

In this final chapter, I will first consider the May 1997 election as a window on the UK's deep-seated political volatility. The election, I will suggest, provides corroborating evidence of potential transience or instability in British politics. The sources of this uncertainty amidst consensus may be found in the developmental processes that have "unmade" the British working class, fostered modularity in identity formation, and complicated issues of political-cultural representation, especially concerning nation and community.

Secondly, I propose that for center-left government in the UK to achieve more than transitory success it must reorganize politics and resolve the paradoxes, ambiguities, and tactical evasions implicit in New Labour's model of government. It faces daunting, very possibly intractable, problems.

Viewed this way, the premier challenge of government is to recognize the political consequences of long-term structural developments: the growing political significance of context-dependent modular identities, the solidaristic potential of hybrid production systems, and the constraints imposed – and the political space opened – by brokered national sovereignty. In order to consolidate a grounded modernizing agenda, government must recollectivize politics without recourse either to mythic projections of class unity or to bromide representations of community. It must recognize the actually existing collective as well as the individual basis of political preferences and mobilize emergent left constituencies. By working to reconstitute the critical link between interests, political mobilization, and policy formation in this way – very probably in creative tension with social movement and labor activists – government can explore the outer boundaries of political agency. To help frame this central task of a contemporary center-left project, I introduce an alternative model of government: social democracy for the global age.

Volatility Root and Branch

An intriguing paradox is revealed in the canonical analyses of the British general election of May 1997. On the one hand, it was a landslide, which established nearly twenty records for largest gains, swings, losses, mosts, and firsts (Butler and Kavanagh, 1997; Norris, 1997a; King, 1998a). On the other hand, observers routinely note that New Labour's monumental electoral achievement could all come down like a house of cards (Dunleavy, 1997; Sanders, 1998). Clearly, Blair's victory was of historic proportions, caused by a postwar record swing from the Conservatives to Labour of 10 percent (nearly twice the two-party swing that brought Thatcher to power in 1979) and resulting in the largest number of seats in Parliament won by any party since 1935, the biggest total Labour has ever held, and the largest majority it has ever had. Why should a victory so decisive be viewed, nevertheless, as so perilous?

For a start, the volatility reflected in the election raises the specter of "easy come, easy go" (Dunleavy, 1997), especially since the results indicate very clearly the reduced influence of what have been the two greatest sources of continuity in electoral behavior: class location and attachments to party. Indeed, apart from the dimensions of the Labour victory, nothing about the May 1997 general election could be clearer than the sharp and apparently accelerating decline in the influence of class location on voting behavior and the unprecedented volatility of the electorate.[1] Both "absolute" and "relative" indices confirm that the association between occupational class and voting behavior has weakened very considerably over the last few decades (Sanders, 1998, p. 220).

Likewise, partisan identification has declined significantly. The percentage of British voters who affirm in opinion surveys that they "strongly identify" with either Conservative or Labour has dropped from roughly three-quarters in the mid-1960s to approximately two-fifths today. In addition, the decline in voters who report that they identify "very strongly" with Conservative or Labour has followed much the same pattern. In 1964, each of the main parties could rely on very strong partisan support from about one-fifth of the electorate, while today the figures have dropped to about 10 percent for each (Sanders, 1998).

Not surprisingly, electoral volatility in the UK has increased quite significantly during this period. Throughout the postwar period, the volatility of the British electorate[2] remained well below the average of the nineteen countries of Western Europe. In 1997 the volatility of the electorate more than doubled (Lane et al., 1997; Sanders, 1998), nearly matching the West European average, but without the UK experiencing the sharp upheavals of post-cold war political life – the influx of refugees or the transformation of party identities and systems – that precipitated electoral volatility in some of the other countries. In the absence of the more radical changes in party identifications and systems experienced elsewhere, what accounts for the notable increase in volatility? Why have traditional stabilizing influences on voting behavior (class location and partisan identification) lost so much of their power to affect voter preferences?

It seems clear that, at least to some degree, the most significant and potentially enduring influences on electoral volatility have a common source in the processes of globalization. Without attempting a comprehensive review of all the sources of electoral volatility, I will briefly note three important factors: issue orientations; the shift from "deep-seated" influences, such as class, to "closer" factors, such as consumerist issue preferences; and alternative sources of identity, particularly gender.

Issue orientations

New Labour's calling-card modernization theme combines two closely related but distinct initiatives: ideological repositioning of the party and global refocusing of the tools of statecraft. The shifting of ideological valence and organizational context was emphatically expressed in the elimination of Clause 4 from Labour's constitution, the courting of business, industry, and the City by party leaders, and the pointed distancing of the party from trade unions. The modernizing of government in the context of globalization has involved emphasis on the "core competences" of national government, in tune with "an outward-looking response to globalization." In policy terms, this approach endorses flexibility in the production system to improve competitiveness and attract foreign investment, creates partnerships with business to encourage long-term investment, and supports training, high-technology skill acquisition, and welfare reform to foster a ready and capable workforce (see Dunleavy, 1997, p. 13).

The very success of Blair's effort to transform Labour into New Labour blunted the social basis of party identification. As Norris and Evans (1999) argue, Blair's positioning of New Labour at the center of party competition – flanked by the Conservatives on the right and the Liberal Democrats on the left – has rendered the linkage between class and party more tenuous, sensitive to party image and the appeals of specific policy overtures. The modernization agenda of New Labour resolutely emphasized fiscal responsibility over distributive politics. At the same time, it refocused government on competitiveness in the global context, in which effective state action would increasingly require EU or G7 cooperation in combination with consistent business cooperation. Taken together, the two component parts of New Labour's modernization initiative naturally contributed to the declining electoral salience of class and did nothing to reverse the trend of declining partisanship.

From class actor to policy consumer

Although it is impossible to prove, the decollectivization of class agency emanating from post-Fordist changes in the system of production no doubt contributes to the weakening influence of social class as a variable explaining electoral decisions. As David Sanders aptly observed, "Changing patterns of employment and their . . . consequences for changing class identities appear to have been at the root of declining partisanship – and these are processes which are likely to be reinforced by globalization and future technological change" (1997, p. 73). Policy orientations aside, class identification may have declined in part because managerially imposed flexibility, the diversification of work experiences, and the individuation of labor–management relations weaken workplace solidarity. At the same time, since polling data indicate that nearly one in three (29 percent) semi-skilled and unskilled manual workers (social classes IV and V) report an experience of unemployment in the previous five years and more than one-quarter of all respondents (27 percent) think it likely that they will leave their current employment within a year (Spencer, 1996),[3] the perceived sense of job insecurity associated with post-Fordist flexibility may contribute to the growing salience of more immediate concerns. Who will make it easier to find a good place to live or pay the mortgage, get the health care that a family needs, provide the best education for children – and what role will the government play in underwriting or providing these goods?

Particularly in the early 1980s, many were convinced that questions like these cast a long shadow over politics, both at the electoral and at deeper cultural and normative levels. Consumption politics assumed an important role in reinforcing a Thatcherite ethos and in eroding the collectivist ideals and transforming the civic culture because it seemed to translate political-electoral behavior into the language of experience. It was argued that distinctions based on patterns of consumption (in satisfying housing needs especially, but also in the use of a car, access to an old people's home, medical care, and schooling) influenced political identities and electoral behavior in significant ways (see Saunders, 1986, Dunleavy and Husbands, 1985). Many concluded that at the height of consumption influences on political behavior in the 1983 general election, housing tenure was either a stronger influence on voting than occupational class or, at the least, nearly matched class as the basis of partisanship (Crewe, 1992, pp. 33–6.)

The claims of consumption sector theorists were often overblown (see Krieger, 1992b), and while significant electoral implications faded by the mid-1980s, the precipitous decline in class location and party identification as electoral influences in the 1997 election has provoked new attention to consumption issues in electoral behavior. It seems likely that, in the absence of enduring influences, voters may be acting more like "discriminating consumers," who eye candidates and issues as they would products for purchase, with little brand loyalty. Hence, factors "closer" to the election, such as issue preferences and perceptions of competence, matter more, and "deep-seated factors," such as class or party identification, matter less (Sanders, 1997, 1998).

Alternative sources of identity

What variables, if any, have replaced the traditional influences on voting behavior? One of the most astute observers of British elections, David Sanders, has introduced the possibility that class and party identification may have been replaced by "the growth of alternative sources of identity – apart from class – that have no obvious attachment to the established political parties," including ethnicity, gender, and other increasingly important ways in which people define themselves (Sanders, 1998, p. 221).[4] Gender presents the most interesting case for the electoral influence of alternative collective identities, with potentially significant implications for policy orientations and deeper political agendas.

The issue of a gender gap in voting behavior has long been a mainstay of British electoral studies. The evidence is clear that, with considerable variation, from 1945 to 1992 women were more likely to vote Conservative than were men. The gender gap was greatest in the 1950s, fluctuated in the 1960s and 1970s, nearly disappeared in 1987, and then re-emerged in 1992, when a generational dimension of the gender gap was revealed quite dramatically. The 1992 election saw a limited but significant generation gap favoring the Conservative Party over the Labour Party of 6 percent overall, but the gap actually reversed when analyzed in generational terms. Although there have been important fluctuations, since 1964 a "gender-generation" gap has become well established. The phenomenon was very clear in the 1992 general election. Among younger voters (those under thirty years old), women gave a lead to Labour while men voted strongly for the Conservatives, producing a 14-point gender gap favoring Labour; among older voters (those over sixty-five years old), women were far more inclined to vote Conservative than were their male counterparts, creating a gender gap favoring the Conservatives of 18 points (Norris, 1997b, pp. 133–5).

What happened to the gender gap in the 1997 election – and what are the deeper implications for understanding issues, political agendas, and the organization of politics? The modest all-generation gender gap that was seen in 1992 was closed in 1997, as a greater percentage of women shifted away from the Conservatives (11 percent) than did men (8 percent), with the result that women and men recorded an identical 44 percent tally for Labour (Kellner, 1997; Lovenduski, 1997; Norris, 1997a). The gender-generation gap continued, however, with younger women more pro-Labour than younger men, and the pattern reversing in the older generation. Moreover, one of the most striking features of the 1997 general election was the generational dimension: the largest swing to Labour was among those in the 18–29 age group (+18 percent) and among first-time voters, while there was no swing to Labour among those over sixty-five.

What are the implications of this overlay of gender and generational voting patterns? To be sure, many factors can contribute to both gender and generational patterns of voting, a comprehensive analysis of which lies outside the framework of this study.[5] Recent studies that have attempted to identify the political agendas of women in the UK, however, provide findings that may be quite relevant for understanding the bigger political stakes. They suggest, first, that issues at the top of the list of women's concerns (e.g. child care, the rights and pay of part-time workers, equal pay, support for family care givers, domestic violence) do not feature strongly in the mainstream policy agendas defined by political parties, although they are discussed in documents aimed at women. Secondly, to the extent that women and men care about the same broadly defined issues, women often understand the issues differently than men and express different priorities. For example, while men (and the three major parties) consider unemployment the central employment issue, women emphasize equal pay and pensions, access to child care, and the rights of part-time workers. Thirdly, the research indicates the emergence of distinct sets of issues with special importance for the political agendas of particular groups of women voters. For example, older women are most concerned about pensions and transportation. Due to the over-representation of women in lower-paid, part-time jobs, working women express particular concern about the minimum wage and the treatment of part-time workers. Mothers find the level of child benefit more important than issues of tax cuts. Finally, younger women express quite considerable support for policy innovations that would help them balance the responsibilities of work, family and childcare (Lovenduski, 1997).

In 1997, Labour made a concerted effort to attract female voters and was handsomely rewarded.[6] The unprecedented election of 120 women MPs and the appointment of a significant number of women onto the Labour frontbenches raises hopes that 1997 will mark a critical break-through for women's representation in the Commons and in positions of government leadership. On the matter of women's political concerns, however, the results are far less clear. New Labour did not feature women's political agendas in the campaign (for example, none of the five "deliverable" pledges explicitly addressed their concerns), and they did not deliver on one of the explicit promises they did make: that New Labour's first cabinet would include a Minister for Women (Lovenduski, 1997). In addition, the early dispute over cuts in child benefit for single parents divided Labour MPs, Labour supporters and, reportedly, even policy makers. It also raised some important questions about New Labour's approach to the family, which seemed to privilege marriage and, in the eyes of some, the traditional view that the wife should mother and the father provide the principal financial support for young children (Lloyd, 1997). On the more positive side, in 1998 the government launched a New Deal for Lone Parents, an initiative to provide single parents with children over five years old the opportunity to visit job centers on a voluntary basis, and develop individual plans to improve job search skills and coordinate training and child care (Oppenheim, 1998).

It is probably fair to say, on balance, that Labour did well among women voters less because of any specific pledge (such as a Minister for Women) and more because it made the effort to listen to concerns voiced by women. In adopting a universalist – rather than a "rainbow coalition" – approach, New Labour declined the opportunity to specifically address women's concerns in the famous five pledges or more generally, but Labour stalwarts would insist that they addressed key concerns that women and men shared in talking about health care, crime, and education.

Will the gender gap tilt toward Labour in 1997, driven by the interests and identities of young women, become a case of "easy come, easy go"? New Labour ought not to take it for granted that the gender and generational gaps in 2001 or 2002 will provide the happy auguries that they did in 1997. In the absence of substantial and comprehensive policy achievements that respond to political agendas grounded in women's experiences of work and family life, it is hard to place women decisively in Labour's column. Such policy innovation would require a substantial reconsideration of the way society organizes domestic and work life, and explicit policy attention to the necessary mediations between social needs and the demands of paid work. How much longer should public policy in the UK operate on the gendered assumption of a forty-hour working week with a partner working part-time and willing to take on the necessary domestic tasks (see Sassoon, 1992; Mahon, 1996)? Tax credits for working families and efforts to encourage businesses to adopt more family-friendly policies, however laudable, do not change the basic equation (see Department of Trade and Industry, 1998).

Beyond New Labour

The level of electoral volatility inspires both the search for new influences and the widespread speculation that voting behavior has pulled free of its moorings. As Sanders observes, "It is entirely possible that in modern party politics there are no permanent or even semipermanent electoral coalitions." Without the traditional constraints imposed by partisan and class identities, voters can shift allegiances easily, like consumers, following short-term policy preferences or the most confidence-inspiring management team. If this process comes to describe contemporary party competition accurately, then a landslide victory in 1997 could become a startling defeat in 2001 or 2002 if Labour fails to satisfy the huge numbers of floating voters who appear to determine electoral results (see Sanders, 1998, pp. 221–2).

I have suggested but cannot prove that a new set of influences on voting behavior, all directly or indirectly linked to the complex processes of globalization, contributed strongly to the electoral volatility expressed in 1997 – and may be reshaping explicit or incipient issues and political agendas. Time, future elections, survey research, and new studies will be needed to confirm whether or not (or to what degree) issue orientations, consumerist behavior at the polls, and alternative sources of identity have replaced class location and partisanship as abiding influences on voting behavior. It is too early to know whether issue preferences linked to more disaggregated and varied work experiences and fluid modular identities will pattern electoral behavior or, more importantly for the purposes of this study, shape issue and policy preferences, and make possible – and ultimately necessary – a new organization of politics. But it is not too early to recognize that changes in class agency and political identities, combined with the fragmentation of effective policy control, create challenges for any center-left project that hopes to exert real political traction.

Expressed both in the post-Fordist decollectivization of "male manufacturing" and the fragmentation of labor experiences of women and ethnic minorities, the "unmaking" of the English working class effectively nullifies social democracy. At the same time, the growth of modular identities complicates politics, mandating important revisions in New Labour's model of government. Unlike the add-on coherence that Gellner assumes for modular furniture, the coherence of identities and political dispositions in an era of modularity requires empirical justification. It seems likely that the revocable nature of commitments, the eclectic character of allegiances, and the situational and shifting self-ascription of identities contributes to the instability of politics in several dimensions: not just with reference to class and partisan identifications, but also regarding underlying values and norms, interests, issue preferences, and political agendas.

Viewed narrowly, in vote-maximizing terms, the challenges to New Labour on the electoral battlefront are obvious. In this context of galloping volatility, New Labour's best bet to avoid an "easy come, easy go" reversal of fortunes in the next election is to try to satisfy each of the "new" constituencies in Labour's broad band of support where Labour benefited from the greatest swings: homeowners, women, voters in southern England, and the middle classes (Sanders, 1998). Of course, this goal is much easier said than done, but on present evidence of the competitive strength of the Conservatives and Liberal Democrats, success may well be achievable.

Perhaps less obvious but more profound are the deeper challenges to innovation and political integration in a global era of brokered national policy sovereignty, amidst unsettling issues about identity and political direction. As the historic Good Friday document and the government's territorial constitutional agenda, more generally, make clear, Tony Blair's New Labour exhibits the potential to go well beyond a play-it-safe approach. At its best, convictions and ambitious goals drive New Labour beyond a nominal agenda of staying in government. Moreover, in a sense, the challenges described below build on New Labour's modernization themes, urging more resolute attention to the "core competences" component of its modernization strategy (what I referred to above as the global refocusing of the tools of statecraft).

That said, the risk taking of New Labour occurs within a circumscribed framework of government (as analyzed in chapter 2) and is driven by a different reading of the imperatives of globalization (see Held, 1998). The outlines of policy and mobilizational strategies below presuppose more robust alternatives to marketization and individuation than what New Labour would countenance. They also ascribe a more context-dependent and less universalist logic to the principles of social justice, and they accord far more attention to the politics of race and ethnicity. For better or worse, core features of the regime characteristics of New Labour are settled, critically among them the decollectivization of working-class agency and a rejection of interest-based or group-based politics in favor of a middle-down arithmetic coalition. The gap between New Labour and the model of politics that is immanent in these challenges is too great: it would therefore be futile to direct these challenges explicitly to New Labour (although New Labour serves as their dramatic foil). They are intended instead for a wider community of interest in the prospects of European social democracy.

Challenge 1: Enhance competitiveness while recollectivizing labor and transforming systems of production

The UK has assumed a specialized profile within EU Europe as a producer of low-technology, low-value-added products through the use of a comparatively low-paid, segmented, decollectivized, and easily dismissed workforce. As noted in part II, extensive research in Europe points to the competitive advantages of post-Fordist production systems that include more human-centered and collaborative forms of work organization, and which make extensive use of a highly skilled workforce with broad problem-solving capabilities. Although the research is not conclusive, it strongly suggests that a commitment to modernize industry in accordance with a "best practice" standard means, at the very least, the open-minded consideration of alternative models of production. Accordingly, the government's skill acquisition initiatives should include targeted support for training suited to more collaborative and participatory models of production (including cross-training and system-wide understandings of production). In addition, business leaders should receive encouragement and support to experiment with alternative production orientations.

Any center-left project must categorically reject the premise that the economic processes of globalization tie the hands of government or that they mandate a linear trend toward forced flexibility. Modernization and competitiveness involve concerted efforts to bring labor into more collaboration in order to enhance the prospects for the organizational innovation that is necessary for effective technological innovation. In addition, concerted efforts are warranted to reverse the risky tendency toward promoting a single "low end" national production system. It is likely that most of the benefits of attracting world-class corporations through FDI and of utilizing Japanese management practices to reinforce and legitimize the pre-existing preferences of British managers have already been achieved. In addition, as noted in chapter 4, the UK's "wait and see" approach to the single currency provides opportunities for short-term competitive advantages and reflection about how best to cushion the effects of downturns and to prepare for the expected adoption of the euro in the future.

New Labour's policy generals run the usual risks of fighting the last war, which leaves them with poor strategic positioning for the next war. The last war, the struggle with unions over shopfloor power, is over. The next battle is under way: to develop the most propitious mix of local systems of production to succeed in an era of perpetual, fast-paced innovation and global competition. Who would want to face intense global competition with an insecure, fragmented workforce, one that lacks the organizational capacity not only to resist managerial prerogative, but to contribute to innovation? Wouldn't it be far better to have a workforce that is ready and able to assist in ongoing product, process, and organizational innovation as well as in comprehensive problem solving during the inevitable – and perpetual – processes of "debugging" that are endemic to contemporary cutting-edge production?

Competitiveness for the sake of competitiveness, locked into a neoliberal iron cage, misreads the strategic direction of post-Fordism and forsakes the normative claims of a center-left project. The centrifugal logic of post-Fordist production, driven by plant-specific adjustments in response to fast-paced technological and market changes, demands workers who can rescue huge capital investments and reduce down-time with accurate and knowledgeable interventions. To make the most of shopfloor knowledge and experience, management, for its own sake, must erode the distinction between shopfloor and office, reduce decision-making hierarchies, and coordinate production collaboratively (see Gordon and Krieger, 1993, 1998).

Innovative management recognizes these imperatives, but in the absence of counterpressures, it is understandably inclined to buy worker involvement in exchange for individualized rewards, such as bonuses, productivity schemes, training programs, and career advancement (see Mahon, 1991). New Labour accepts this framework without demur and, in large measure, British unions have followed suit. They have contributed to a thoroughgoing decollectivization of agency, in which unions become service providers for their members and defenders of workplace rights (mainly individual rights) codified in legislation. As Chris Howell puts it, by "responding to the individualization of industrial relations with a parallel individualization of the relationship between a union and its members," trade unions have contributed to their own demise (Howell, forthcoming).

In accepting this approach, all the key political actors – management, government, and unions – squander a critical opportunity to modernize the industrial relations system. As a result of this shortsightedness, management may lose strategic capacities, but for labor and Labour the political stakes are even higher. As one observer put it, "it is only when unions are able to negotiate the terms of worker involvement on a *collective* basis, i.e. in return for the right collectively to control working conditions, training opportunities, working hours and the like, that flexible automation can be seen as a historically progressive alternative to Fordist relations in production" (Mahon, 1991, p. 299). Post-Fordist economies can head in two directions: toward a model of a few good core jobs and a vast casualized majority; or a more democratic, solidaristic, egalitarian, and participatory alternative. New Labour has opted for the first, while the second should be at the heart of a center-left project.

In political terms, the processes of decollectivization of labor and evisceration of class agency, if left unchecked, run the risk of irretrievably severing the ties between interests and politics, with the twin results that electoral volatility, paradoxically, becomes an enduring feature of British politics and the notion of core constituencies is lost. The institutionalized capacities of trade unions linked to party, in combination with the distributive bargaining and solidaristic ethos of the welfare state, organized Old Labour politics. What will be the comparable institutional basis for the organizational politics of New Labour? It is too early to be certain, but thus far there is little indication that "community" or the projected "radical reform" of the welfare state holds the potential for constituting an alternative set of interests or political agency. New Labour now appears to be unreasonably detached from the experiences of everyday working life – on the shopfloor or in shops, banks, and catering establishments. It is concerned too little with the basic needs of workers for secure employment and a reasonable level of participation in decisions about production. It is all but contemptuous of collective agency and solidaristic work traditions. In hastening the "unmaking" of the working classes in the UK and projecting a political agenda that is free of "special interest" ties to the trade union movement, New Labour has done its part to hasten the demise of the collective institutions of labor. To what end?

Challenge 2: Design social policy that is responsive to the actually existing organization of production and social life

As with the organization of production, the modernization of social policy means critically evaluating and, where appropriate, adopting "best practice" European standards. In the design of social policy, this approach involves comprehensive provision of child care and a basic reformulation of the welfare state to bring it in step with the contemporary facts of economic and social life. As noted above, I believe that New Labour has established its credentials as an advocate of managerial prerogative and British industry, and has won the war to consolidate a model of production that assumes a flexible workforce as the prerequisite for successful competition: the main challenges of welfare reform, therefore, lie elsewhere.

Most significantly, the challenge of modernizing social policy involves revisiting what I called in chapter 5 the work–welfare–family nexus. There is a popular campaign to redesign the Bretton Woods institutions under the slogan "Fifty Years is Enough" – the same, adding a few years, could be said of the Beveridge Report. It is time to categorically dispel the lingering gendered "male breadwinner" vestiges of Beveridge. These are expressed in a mix of benefit rules and normative expectations of British social policy that persist in outdated gendered constructs, in spite of the everyday realities of women's labor force participation. With regard to pensions, the government should consider ways to provide more generous support for those with interrupted careers and low-wage jobs, a profile in which women, of course, are overrepresented. This would require specific coverage plans for "carers" that recognize how difficult it is for them to maintain contributions (for example, at retirement the Exchequer should supplement contributions to satisfy deficits and fulfill eligibility requirements) (Campbell, 1998). Instead the government's new pension plan, published in December 1998, promises to turn SERPS, in effect, into a program for the poor only, and New Labour has taken new steps to implement the 1996 Tory decision to reduce by half the benefit that can be passed onto the surviving spouse.

With reference to what I consider the most critical issue of family policy – child care provision – the British case is the most incoherent in Europe, and will probably remain so despite New Labour's National Child Care Strategy. Both general labor force participation rates and those for mothers with children are high in comparative European terms, yet there is extremely low public provision of child care. The challenge is clear: to narrow the gap between child care supply and demand through concerted public policy that fully recognizes both women's active labor market participation and the child care responsibilities of both parents, whatever the household form. It is clear enough that these issues are high on women's political agendas, especially for the all-important younger generation who swing the gender gap toward the center-left. To refocus the welfare state to recognize women's lives as they actually are and to help close the gap between child care demand and supply is well within the "core competences" of national government. In meeting this challenge, no household form, including two-parent, married-couple families, should be normatively privileged. This should be the case even if a set of policy initiatives quite reasonably focuses on the particular set of problems in balancing work and child care responsibilities which are most often (but by no means exclusively) faced by households constituted this way.

As should be clear by now, there is a radical edge – in conception, design, and mobilization – that goes beyond the specific policy orientations. In the coordination of domestic life and social policy, as in the organization of production, society has not come to terms with the pre-eminent fact of women's massive participation in paid labor (see Sassoon, 1992). Both the welfare state and the system of production operate as if every full-time worker has a wife. Nearly everyone observes that most women have part-time jobs (while fewer than one in fifteen men work part time) and perceives that neoliberal support for one-sided managerial flexibility has a disparate gender impact: it produces a distinctive pattern of casualized, insecure, lower-paid employment for women. While the Labour government offers minor ameliorative adjustments that leave intact these structural dispositions, British unions tend to view these concerns instrumentally, as the inspiration for recruitment strategies aimed at women (Howell, forthcoming). The political space remains open for a more grounded politics (one in touch with the actually existing organization of domestic and productive life) to make the most of this extraordinary strategic and emancipatory opportunity.

Can a political orientation emerge in the UK, akin to "wage earner feminism" in Sweden, which sees in the particular needs of women workers the basis for robust across-the-board mobilization (Mahon, 1991, 1996)? Women may have the most to gain from a more democratic and participatory post-Fordist alternative, from a struggle against the endemic casualization of work, and from a recognition of the organic connection between work and domestic life. They also might benefit the most from demands for pay equity and political parity, and the changes that wage-earner feminism could inspire in welfare, labor market, and industrial relations policy. But they would hardly be alone in achieving desirable results. Of course, complications would inevitably arise between men and women and among ethnic cultures about gender roles, the nature of family responsibilities, and the priorities of work and family. I am willing to bet, however, that a wage-earner feminist agenda would be a fine starting point for exploring alliance strategies shaped by modular identities and grounded in the needs that emerge from the everyday strains of reconciling work and family life.

Challenge 3: Extend political recognition to modular communal identities

It has been argued, first, that "nonrecognition" of some identities or the "misrecognition" of others can cause harm to minority groups and, secondly, that the politics of recognition presents a basic challenge to the principle of equal representation for all (Taylor, 1994). As Amy Gutmann poses the question, "Can citizens with diverse identities be represented as equals if public institutions do not recognize our particular identities, but only our more universally shared interests . . . ?" She then concludes that a "secure cultural context" has become a basic interest that should be embraced by liberal democratic states (see Parekh, 1993; Gutmann, 1994, pp. 3–4).

There are no easy answers to what it would take to provide a secure cultural context for ethnic minorities in the UK, but political recognition of cultural particularity – of the vitality and formative importance of diverse, context-dependent, situational, diasporic identities as they exist, rather than as they are instrumentally labeled – would be an important first step. As noted in part IV, cultural representation is a potent force. The appeal to community in its communitarian abstractions of equality and commonality expresses a quite powerful message of misrecognition to ethnic minorities. It ignores their personal biographies and collective memories of immigration and nationality, settlement and employment; it effaces the damage inflicted by the Rushdie Affair and the depiction of ethnic minorities as "the enemy within." Extending political recognition to communal identities would therefore, in an important way, concretize a narrative of normative local communities and reduce its exclusionary implications.

Extending the politics of recognition might also open the dialogue about "community" in a way that would make it possible to operationalize egalitarian principles more effectively in actually existing communities. Specifically, recognition would help to focus much needed attention on ways in which public policy might remedy endemic patterns of inequality in employment opportunities, whether public or private, and in the provision of services. In the end, however, the recognition of "public ethnicity" and support for multiculturalism mean little unless they are backed by policy and resource commitments and tackle practical questions. Why have Muslim schools not won public funding as routinely as Jewish and Christian schools have (the first two Muslim schools were only granted official status in 1998) (Lewis, 1997; Modood, 1997); and why are Muslims, by contrast to Sikhs and Jews, not considered an ethnic group, thereby being left unprotected by anti-discrimination legislation (Modood, 1994)? How might the development of housing policy be influenced by concrete analysis of distinctive ethnic housing patterns, including such factors as residential settlement, household formation, household need and actual demand patterns, preferences in housing tenure, the interplay of housing markets and agencies, perceptions by housing agencies, and the overall picture of housing investment and finance (Sarre et al., 1989; Smith, 1989; Harrison, 1995; Law, 1996)? What mechanism can be found for effective, participatory, and fair-minded ethnic negotiation about local politics, education, business, religion, and race relations (see Lewis, 1997)?

Problems and policy dilemmas abound. It is difficult to target minority group needs without violating the individual rights of nonminority individuals. In addition, policy dilemmas grow with an awareness that different ethnic minority groups have very different goals, aims, and values – and that well-meaning policies may clash (it may be difficult or impossible, for example, to reconcile equal schooling for girls with the traditional views of gender roles that characterize some ethnic minority perspectives) (see Modood, 1994). Finally, there is no easy solution to the problem of ethnic minority representation: tendencies for fragmentation and organizational conflicts pose grave problems for the organization and representation of interests. Who can speak for the "community" (Yalçin-Heckman, 1997)? Finally, as should also be clear by now, the matter of representation is vastly complicated by modular politics, which implies shifting identity agendas and fluid alliance strategies.

Paradoxically, these problems increase the degree of difficulty, but intensify the need for an assertive politics of recognition. Such a perspective, nourished by public debate and backed by substantial resources and innovative policy initiatives, can help secure the cultural contexts of ethnic minorities. At the same time, it can promote a more nuanced approach to the organization of interests, enhance the political integration of ethnic minorities, and redress the very significant problem of extensive (although varied) group-based inequalities in opportunities and outcomes.

Challenge 4: Constitute British identity amidst competing territorial, ethnic, and supranational attachments and a complex patchwork of shared institutional authorities

The Blair government's most radical and potentially far-reaching innovations are a set of constitutional changes that redistribute power and renegotiate governing authority. In a variety of ways, they reduce the historic concentration in the Westminster Parliament (see Holliday, 1997). In effect, these reforms surrender the *ancien régime* and construct a more modern, democratized, post-imperial, quasi-federal constitutional architecture. The character of the political dynamic unleashed by this constitutional agenda is impossible to anticipate. It seems very likely, however, that devolution in Scotland, Wales, and Northern Ireland, with all the asymmetries, experimentation and divisiveness that these processes will entail, will create a political momentum of its own that no one can easily control (see Holliday, 1997; Marquand, 1998). To this mix must be added the mounting pressure that the UK faces to participate in the single currency, as the most important EU member not to be in the initial euro-11 group, and the complex cross-pressures of nationality and ethnicity discussed in chapter 8.

Increasingly, the problem of sovereignty, which begins as a fairly limited issue of effective control over policy, will rapidly become politicized at many levels and, perhaps, structural. How will ethnic minority

Britons react to the formation of representative institutions in the UK and the increasing power of the European Union when devolution privileges another kind of national identity, and they remain cool, at best, to European initiatives (see Modood, 1997; Alibhai-Brown, 1998)? What will prevent a Scottish Parliament from "transforming a benign modernization-move" into a "reappearance (albeit one-legged) of sovereignty," spurred by a Scottish National Party that wishes for nothing less than a separate Scottish state (Nairn, 1997, p. 9)? Will aspirations by politicians, say, in Yorkshire to acquire the Brussels deal-cutting potential of their ministerial betters in Scotland or in German *Länder* fuel a movement for devolution of powers in alternative power centers throughout the UK (see Marquand, 1998)?

The complicated interplay of principles of subsidiarity and UK sovereignty in the emerging institutional architectures at the level of nation (English, Welsh, Scottish, Irish/Northern Irish), state (United Kingdom), and region (European Union) presents a tremendous set of challenges to cohesive government. There is no easy solution to the interregional divisions of interest that drive devolution. Moreover, despite strong signals that the question has shifted from whether to when, the UK faces a complicated set of trade-offs in its decision to join the single currency.

From the start, the challenges should be faced squarely. Unlike Germany's Helmut Kohl, who paid the price in the September 1998 election for remaining in denial (at least publicly) about the profoundly dislocating consequences of unification, Blair should come clean on all these vexed issues of sovereignty and identity, which is quite different than announcing a National Changeover Plan or all but officially endorsing entry. Thus far, in my view quite unreasonably, the government has opted to play down the political significance of the euro. Blair and his followers lay the groundmark for success in the "yes" campaign that emerged in 1998, despite government assurances that the promised referendum will not be held until after the next general election. All the while, the Chancellor of the Exchequer, Gordon Brown, repeatedly assures listeners that the decision on entry into the single currency will be based on how high the euro scores on a series of economic tests.

He is at least half right. The economic considerations are complicated, and a "wait and see" approach seems sensible on economic criteria. Even if one applies a discount rate to the more dire doom-and-gloom projections of irreversible loss of sovereignty and a quick slide toward a federal Europe (see Lloyd, 1998), it is true that a decision to join the euro area does involve significant concessions. If and when it joined, the UK would lose the power to set short-term interest rates (and differences in longer-term interest rates narrow considerably); likewise, it would be unable to adjust its exchange rate against other countries participating in the single currency. Moreover, the significance of these restrictions would be enhanced by the fact that the UK's economic cycle has been out of line with those of its continental counterparts (Miles, 1997). Bringing the UK into the euro would probably involve, therefore, some initial shocks as increased interest rates trigger inflationary pressures, to which the UK could not respond by devaluation.

Like all members of the euro area, the UK would lose some critical instruments for cushioning the economy from external shocks (Joffe, 1997) or, for example, for protecting the competitiveness of firms in weaker regions (Armstrong, 1998). So long as the UK is regarded as a "sympathetic 'out'" – concerned to cushion its economy from paying the price for its idiosyncrasies, but committed to economic integration and cooperative in its dealings with the euro-11 – then the negative consequences of the "wait and see" approach are diminished (Miles, 1997). Of course, such a sympathetic approach in expectation of joining later would also reduce the benefits of staying out, since policy decisions would largely replicate the terms of the EMU Stability and Growth Pact, and monetary policy would mimic that of insiders (most importantly, there would be something close to a fixed euro–sterling exchange rate).

In the end, the posture of a euro-agnostic waiting exclusively for economic proof stretches credulity. New Labour is a politically savvy, strategically deft government. All decisions are political decisions, and the decision about the euro invites delay because it is crucial and involves high-wire risk management. Although support for the single currency initially increased after the euro's launch, polls still showed a solid majority opposed. In addition the volatility of the currency as well as the crisis in the European Commission will probably revitalize the "no camp." Moreover, as the economic benefits of delay evaporate and tension with members inevitably rises, the larger political cost of nonparticipation in the single currency will increase dramatically. As one observer put it, New Labour recognizes that "the British state can realise its century-long aim of continuing to punch above its weight in world affairs only through close and cooperative involvement in the developing European Union" (Marquand, 1997, p. 336). Clearly, from 1999 onwards, membership in the Euro Club is the entry ticket to top-tier EU influence, and the UK cannot sustain equivalent influence as a free-rider.

If I am right that the drive for European influence will lead Blair's Britain to join the euro area, we are compelled to ask a basic follow-up question: what sort of influence can we expect? Will the UK use its added influence to render Europe (as the Bundesbank and the European Central Bank would have it) a region where domestic price stability is paramount and macroeconomic stimulus to spur growth and job creation is forbidden? Although with Lafontaine's departure, it has lost its leading advocate, there is growing resistance on the continent to the EU's

"market-monetarist austerity policies." Many leading European economists reckon that EMU, like economic orthodoxies of the 1930s, will
drive high levels of unemployment even higher. Political observers add
that increased unemployment and resulting social dislocation threaten
to intensify social polarization, which already finds expression in tough
immigration and asylum policies, xenophobic movements, and a "fortress
Europe" mentality (Gill, 1998, p. 6). The UK defends the orthodoxy of
the central bankers. It almost goes without saying that this is not the progressive influence that one would expect from a center-left government.
Equally relevant here, this perspective cuts against the project of building a wide and deep allegiance to the UK *qua* nation-state as a bulwark
against the inevitable chaos of subordinate and superordinate sover-
eignties that the country will face for the foreseeable future.

How well is the UK positioned to withstand at one and the same time
the pressures of devolution and supranational federation? A European
state that projects its influence in powerful regional arenas for deregulated labor markets and against social protection makes a weak case for
its transcendent legitimacy in Brussels, not to mention Scotland. A
regime that refuses to build true coalitions based on collective interests,
institutions, and needs has little to call on when push comes to shove.
This concern is real enough when scandals and internecine battles
embroil the cabinet, as they did with Peter Mandelson's resignation in
December 1998, or when the inevitable recessionary pressures make it
far harder for the government to toe the fiscal line and, at the same time,
deliver its promises on health care and education. How much more will
the deficit in organized support be felt when the stakes transcend everyday politics?

The destabilizing potential – or at least the potential for resistance
and sheer confusion – associated with all these complications of
sovereignty is heightened by the "thinness" of British identity. Can the
UK get past "cricket tests" for national loyalty, the perceived contradiction between "black and British," the dissonant value claims of diasporic
and John Bull identities, and the fundamental uncertainty about the
relationship between ethnic group, nation, and state? Endemic
divisions over boundaries and the normative dimensions of Britishness,
on the one hand, and fast-paced changes in institutional and constitutional arrangements, on the other, present a formidable context in
which to construct a coherent and integrated British identity. At stake is
nothing less than the constitutional arrangements and the political
mobilization necessary to bind together a multinational, multiethnic
state (see Brown, 1998). In this era of unprecedented tendencies for sub-
division into smaller single-ethnic nations, on the one hand, and larger
supranational regional associations, on the other, nothing should be
taken for granted.

Challenge 5: Reconnect politics to interests
and collective attachments

In an important way, this challenge summarizes the other four and frames the fundamental mission of any progressive, politically integrative model of politics. I have argued that prospects for class-wide agency have been immensely weakened as the experience of work has become increasingly individuated, the collective organizations of labor have been very substantially weakened, and "the working class" has subdivided almost infinitely within distinctive ethnic and gender patterns. At the same time, the UK faces a more circumscribed and brokered sovereignty within the context of the European Union, devolution, and the Northern Ireland peace agreement. The commingled historiography of four nations, the interplay of ethnicity and nationality in the post-imperial UK, the unresolved tensions over the representation of nation and community, and the nonrecognition or misrecognition of ethnic minorities all create doubts about British identity. Class, identity, state, and nation are all in flux, subject to what I have called modular politics, and each is highly context-dependent.

The volatility and plasticity of political identities in the UK stretches nearly to breaking point the integral connection between political projects and abiding interests – a process that threatens social democratic politics in particular and raises broader questions about volatility and accountability in liberal democracies. Can a center-left political project resolve these dilemmas?

Traditional social democratic politics operated on the assumption that the collective representatives of business and labor were exactly that. However limited in their capacities to coordinate action in a disciplined manner, they existed to aggregate the preferences of constituencies with committed single-identity voices. Likewise, and more importantly, the capacity of political parties to perform the functions of choice, aggregation, and consensus building was framed by traditional distributive politics. Social democratic politics, like all distributive bargaining, could always "split the difference," but this framework cannot resolve the nonmaterial aspects of disputes over boundaries and inclusion in the political community framed by nationality or ethnicity; nor can it easily address different visions of the family and the organization of domestic life.

The transformation of actually existing systems of production, motivated by global competitive pressures for perpetual innovation and deindustrialization, on the one hand, and modularity in collective identities, on the other hand, presents political parties, especially Labour and Conservative, with a conundrum. In an important way, these political parties, in particular, have been restricted by their legacy of narrow fields of vision as they remained trapped within traditions that largely confined political appeals to a left–right continuum of distributive alternatives. Break through these restrictions in a manner analyzed by Kitschelt, switch to what I have called the strategic adjustment model of social democracy, and electoral gains are the order of the day. But what happens to politics when the hegemonic center-left party decisively shifts strategic orientations away from class and distributive politics, when it distances itself from core constituencies and institutions defined by class or socioeconomic status and fosters only nominal electoral coalitions?

It is dangerous to draw lessons from a single illustration, but in the aftermath of the British general election of May 1997, all deep-seated connections between constituencies and parties seemed stretched almost beyond recognition. It is one thing to risk a narrowly defined class-based electorate; quite another, it would seem, to encourage a generalized collapse of party partisanship and the historic linkages between enduring interests and party programs. To the extent that my claims for the importance of modularity in collective identities hold, this process of delinkage may prove to be a persistent trend, pushing party strategies and systems into a new era of volatility.

If true, the British party system and the terms of electoral competition have moved even further away from "class-mass" parties than Otto Kirchheimer anticipated. New Labour has overshot the catch-all parties, which still presupposed a model of party politics framed by rather firmly located constituencies with abiding collective interests, located within a context of distributive bargaining over material needs that are shaped by class position. Kirchheimer, after all, spoke of the possibility of parties making strategic appeals to different class-based constituencies when they could find "enough community of interest" and when interests did not "adamantly conflict." He used the example of a party smoothing over relatively small differences in group interests: for example, between groups of white-collar and manual workers, both of whom might be won over by vigorous efforts to cushion the shocks of automation. In the end, Kirchheimer cautioned that the catch-all party "cannot hope to catch all categories of voters" (1966, p. 186). In its adamant rejection of all group-based politics, New Labour appears to be attempting exactly that feat.

The decollectivization of labor and the processes of modular identity formation undermine the classic role of political parties as purveyors of choice and mechanisms for the programmatic aggregation of interests. In this global post-collectivist era, parties are limited by the sheer difficulty of assimilating and organizing diverse and shifting political dispositions, issue preferences, and policy agendas on incommensurable scales. Nevertheless, a party with progressive aspirations should work to defeat the prospects of perpetual volatility and provide a coherent political agenda that reconnects politics to group-based needs and abiding interests, understood in both material (class) and cultural (communal) terms. Acceptance of the first four challenges would imply a commitment to meeting the broader challenge to reconnect politics with interests grounded in lived experiences.

I propose that these five challenges, and in particular the challenge to reconnect politics to needs, interests, and attachments, mark the path to a truly significant new organization of politics, one consonant with revitalized social democracy for the global age.

Social Democracy for a Global Age

As the set of five challenges above illustrates, contemporary politics presents government with profound dilemmas and vexing alternatives. I have argued that nothing less is at stake than the basic organization of politics in the UK, and it should be clear by now that New Labour is not about to resolve the paradoxes it has both inherited and created, nor to meet the challenges discussed above.

New Labour cannot resolve the fundamental antinomy between the conservatism of its economics, expressed in neoliberal monetary, fiscal, and industrial relations projects, and the radicalism of its institutional and constitutional politics. As a result, it is unwilling to recognize that a democratic participatory project cannot reasonably be built on casualized and insecure labor, robbed of agency and denied voice. As Marquand observes, "employee subordination may be compatible with citizen empowerment," but it is a yawning paradox at the heart of the New Labour project. "Good citizens debate, argue and question . . . [a]nd they cannot switch off their citizen selves when they go to work" (1997, p. 336). New Labour requires them to do just that – an explicit denial of the historic demands of *social* democracy (and the EU norm) that representation and participation must extend to the workplace.[7]

With reference to EU affairs, the UK's increasingly suspect "wait and see" posture on the single currency is a policy in search of a rationale. If the government is moved to procrastinate out of post-imperial sentimentality about sterling and fear of confronting sceptered-isle-John-Bull-Englishness, then its stance is unworthy of a center-left government. If its delay is motivated in part out of concern to preserve the instruments of policy, in order to cushion UK citizens from external shocks, then why is the government so loath to use these instruments while it has them, to advance measured redistributive goals and pursue targeted efforts to reduce the group inequalities of ethnic minorities?

In the end, by opting for a middle-down aggregation of voters rather than a grounded interest-based coalition, New Labour faces the basic dilemma of mobilizing support for a wide-ranging modernizing agenda with no organized collective agency waiting in the wings. All models of social democracy confirm the inherent empirical and normative link between material interests and politics (indeed, conservative and right politics confirm this as well). By explicitly breaking this historic linkage, New Labour hopes to resolve the core dilemma that it extracts from the history of the Labour Party: "how to construct a broad-based and enduring social coalition capable, not just of giving it a temporary majority in the House of Commons, but of sustaining a reforming government thereafter" (Marquand, 1991, p. 207; quoted in Blair, 1995). It may well achieve the goal of sustained leadership (without the benefit of a grounded social coalition), but at considerable cost. In the end, Blair's heady modernizing project evades more than it transcends left and right, and it fails to meet the critical challenges of politics in the global age.

I suggest that a determined response to these challenges requires consideration of a new model of government. Table 10.1 compares Social Democracy for the Global Age, New Labour, and the institutional-collectivist model of social democracy.

This new alternative model of a revitalized social democracy follows directly from the discussion above of the five challenges facing contemporary British government.[8] Agency is rooted in a claim that, as a consequence of modular politics and the decomposition and individuation of class, core constituencies in the traditional sense (defined territorially or by class position and socioeconomic status) no longer animate politics. If identities and interests are context-dependent, so too is political agency. The model argues for the vital place of decentralized workplace mobilization that insists on a role in shaping the contours of a progressive post-Fordist alternative. It suggests, at the same time, a robust modular identity alliance strategy that engages diversity and commonality in a wage-earner-feminist strategy to face the fundamental challenges of the social organization of productive and social life.

It follows that policy formation should pursue a problem-solving rather than constituency-serving approach, at least in the conventional sense. Thus, the policy approach of Social Democracy for the Global Age responds to needs and political agendas that emerge from the actually existing organization of production and social life. It emphasizes recognition of the fragmented and context-dependent interplay of experiences of work and diverse identity attachments and their associated norms and values. Industrial relations, employment, labor market, and training policies, as well as research and development, should emphasize the competitive advantages of progressive post-Fordist alternatives. Social policy should be focused on a thoroughgoing reinvention of the work–family nexus. Nothing short of a thorough redesign of caring policies to facilitate the non-gendered distribution of work and family time is required. We will know that we have done enough when there is a random distribution of women and men in part-time employment, and full parity and

Table 10.1 Comparison of institutional-collectivist social democracy, New Labour, and Social Democracy for the Global Age

	Institutional-collectivist social democracy	New Labour	Social Democracy for the Global Age
Agency	Class actors mobilized by party and peak associations	Middle class down, middle England electoral coalition	Recollectivization of labor; alliance strategies shaped by wage-earner feminism and modular politics
Policy approach	Postwar settlement, Keynesianism, and welfare state	"Third Way," Keynesianism, and business partnership	Solidaristic and egalitarian post-Fordist alternative; social policy focused on work–family nexus and targeted redistributive measures
Institutional orientation	Range in economic governance, social welfare, and labor regimes	Constitutional reform, reversal of statist centralization, and local participation	Political integration, articulated centralization, and subsidiarity
Political morality	Equality, class abatement, and collectivism	Equality, stakeholder society, Christian socialism, communitarianism, rights and responsibilities	Politics of recognition; connect politics to identities and interests; constitute British identity within multicultural Europe

comparable worth are achieved. The same measures should be applied to the work experience of ethnic minorities compared to that of whites. Until the disparate impact of the global processes of deindustrialization is neutralized and discriminatory practices are ended in employment and services, targeted redistributive efforts should be implemented to narrow the endemic patterns of inequality.

In a similar vein, the institutional orientation emphasizes political integration of diverse groups, operationalized through a carefully artic-ulated framework of centralized authority and subsidiarity. The unpre-dictable political dynamic unleashed by devolution should be welcomed for its participatory fervor and likely rejection, especially in Scotland, of neoliberal and paternalistic economic and social policies. At the same time, following the European approach to structural adjustment and regional development, the UK should introduce comparable "country of regions" initiatives that sustain powerful institutional ties between nations, regions, and the UK. A contemporary social democratic UK would fully "join Europe," participate in the single currency, and use its influence to recollectivize politics, improve employment prospects, posi-tively address issues of asylum, immigration, and European citizenship, and reduce the problems of xenophobia and social dislocation that have plagued European integration.

Finally, according to this model, the normative claim of government (political morality) extends and deepens the rights and equal treatment of groups through a politics of recognition. It asserts the need to recon-cile the discordant and exclusionary representations of nation, to narrow the gap between imaginary images and actually existing communities, in all their complexity, and through the agency, policy, and institutional ini-tiatives discussed above to constitute a more substantive and purposeful sense of British identity.

Does it lie within the power of political agency to resolve the many dilemmas that would plague any effort to reconnect politics to needs, interests, and collective attachments in this way? The answer is by no means certain, but it is clear that no social democratic project can fail to take up the challenge.

Notes

Preface

1 Unless otherwise indicated, I use "New Labour" as a synonym for the British Labour Party during the period of Tony Blair's leadership and as a descriptor for UK government policy during his premiership. Of course, no party or government operates as a unitary actor and even within Blair's initial cabinet several key figures – including John Prescott (Deputy Prime Minister), Robin Cook (Foreign Secretary), and David Blunkett (Education and Employment Secretary) – were not associated with the New Labour strand within the Labour Party. Distinctions among currents within the Labour Party and the Blair government are important and useful objects for analysis (see Shaw, 1996; Panitch and Leys, 1997; Shaw, 1998), but are of only limited concern in this study. The routine use of the term "New Labour" does not indicate acceptance of any particular characterization of the historic legacy of the Labour Party or the distinctions between "old" and "new" claimed by adherents.

2 For an exception, see Giddens (1998).

Chapter 2 New Labour: Regime Characteristics, Strategic Options, Dilemmas

1 Kitschelt argues that effective social democratic parties forge electoral coalitions based on new socioeconomic constituencies formed by the "clustering of preferences" linked to "the actual combination of everyday life experiences shared by large groups in advanced capitalism" and characterized by six social-structural attributes: ownership, public or private sector employment, international or domestic sector employment, task structure of jobs, education, and gender (1994, pp. 20–7).

2 It should be noted, however, that New Labour has set up a taskforce called the Heartlands Project to revitalize Labour's traditional core constituencies (see Williams, 1998).

3   For a discussion of "arithmetic politics," see Krieger (1986, p. 86). The American New Deal coalition presents a classic alternative of a cross-class coalition of diverse elements defined by interests, policy agendas, and institutional resources for political agency (see Finegold, 1993).

4   These categories are drawn from the Registrar-General's Classification of Occupations: A – higher professional, managerial and administrative (e.g. company directors, doctors); B – intermediate professional, managerial and administrative (e.g. junior management, teachers); C1 – supervisor, clerical and other non-manual (e.g. bank tellers, administrative assistants). For a fuller description of the Registrar-General's scheme and alternative definitions of class applied to electoral behavior see Norris, 1997b, pp. 99–147.

5   I am grateful to Chris Howell, who made me aware of this article and provided the text.

6   Other significant commitments made to the trade union movement, including the introduction of a minimum wage and the opt-in on the Social Charter, are less directly relevant to the question of political agency, and will not be considered here. For a comprehensive review of the evolution of the relationship between the Labour Party and trade unions and the specifics of New Labour's policy toward organized labor, see Howell (1998). My discussion of these themes and of *Fairness at Work* closely follows Howell's account.

7   It should be added that this bold policy initiative positions the UK well, if and when the government decides that the UK ought to participate in the single currency. Issues concerning the decision whether, when and why to join the single currency will be discussed in chapter 10 (challenge 4).

8   For an original and potentially influential approach to family policy, see Giddens (1998, pp. 89–98).

9   This is exclusively a heuristic exercise: I make no claim that Blair or his associates were explicitly influenced by any of the academic writing discussed in the analysis of alternative models of social democracy, although such familiarity may be assumed among the broader intellectual and policy networks associated with New Labour.

10   This observation, of course, is aimed more at Blair than Kitschelt, whose treatment of the British case in *The Transformation of European Social Democracy* antedates Blair's leadership of the Labour Party and the shift to New Labour. Few anticipated the radical departure that Labour would take from its traditional emphasis on distributive politics, and Kitschelt was not among them; nor does he anticipate the growing importance of the communitarian dimension in British politics. See Kitschelt (1994, 178–81).

11   For an argument that Blair has converted Labour into a new brand of Liberalism, see Beer (1997).

Chapter 3   Social Democracy, Class, and National Policy Sovereignty

1   Unless otherwise noted, the term "social democracy" refers to social democracy as understood by the institutional-collectivist model developed in chapter 1, with the postwar period through the mid-1970s providing the

empirical referent. In this context, the term is used interchangeably with center-left politics.

2 It should be noted that the term "class" was subject to widely varying interpretations, including occupation within a manual/non-manual divide, ownership of the means of production and control over other people's labor in the workplace, and even private/public cleavages in consumption. The precise meaning was often left unspecified in accounts of the class basis of British social democracy, but the manual/non-manual distinctions (usually referred to as "occupational class") are the most commonly applied, especially in electoral studies: professional/managerial (AB); routine non-manual (C1a); skilled manual (C1b/C2); unskilled manual (D/E).

3 The assumptions of national policy sovereignty and the categorical distinction between domestic politics and international affairs are, of course, not limited to social democracy. Although comparisons with other regimes lie beyond the scope of this study, it can reasonably be claimed that the high demands for bargaining and the mobilization of support by organized interests associated with the politics of the postwar settlement make the costs of non-sovereignty higher in social democratic polities than in other regimes.

4 The principles and policy orientations of the British welfare state will be discussed in chapter 5.

5 The relationship between identity politics and class formation, the emergence of modular politics, and their implications for the organization of politics will be discussed in part IV.

6 Following Anthony Giddens, "structure" is used to denote a system of generative rules and resources, understood within a dualism of agency and materiality (praxis). As Giddens puts it, applying the term "duality of structure," rules and resources "are drawn upon by actors in the production of interaction, but are thereby also reconstituted through such interaction." This understanding presupposes the "mutual dependence" of structure and agency, asserting that "the structural properties of social systems are both the medium and outcome of the practices that constitute those systems," and are therefore both enabling and constraining (Giddens, 1979, pp. 49–95).

7 For a useful summary of competing schools of interpretation about globalization (the "hyper-globalisation school" versus globalization skeptics) and a thoughtful alternative approach to the globalization of economic activity, see Perraton et al. (1997).

Chapter 4   Globalization, Post-Fordism, and the British Model

1 The related effects of "deindustrialization" and new technologies on the division of labor, and the gendered and ethnic distribution of work experiences, will be discussed in part III.

2 For a detailed discussion of the distinctions between internationalization, multinationalization, and transnationalization, and for analysis of the implications of globalization for emergent production systems, see Gordon (1995).

3 For an excellent review of this literature and discussion of varied European research traditions that address the emergence of alternative production

systems, see Charles (1995). The discussion that follows draws extensively on collaborative work with Richard Gordon (e.g. R. Gordon, 1993, 1995).

4 There is considerable debate about the decisions leading to the closings and their greater significance. Was Uddevalla, in particular, a "noble experiment in humanistic manufacturing" that could not be justified once Volvo began to suffer heavy losses in 1992? Alternatively, was the Uddevalla alternative to lean production a highly productive and commercially viable model that was not permitted to succeed? This important debate, which is a microcosm of debates in the EU over the competitive viability of APS, goes beyond the terms of the discussion here. For discussion of alternative management strategies and production concepts at Volvo and the broader implications of the rise and decline of work reorganization efforts, see Berggren (1992).

5 Many additional factors that contribute to the UK's structural competitiveness and help shape work organization could be considered, among them the support of government for R & D, industrial policy, the provision of education and training, and specific patterns of industrial financing. For comprehensive overviews of these themes, see Buxton et al. (1994a) and Coates (1996).

6 It should be noted that roughly half of this difference in labor productivity can be attributed to the tendency of FDI to locate in technologically more advanced industries (OECD, 1996).

7 The discussion intentionally neglects the more holistic definition of Japanization understood to encompass broader organizational and cultural principles (permeated or full Japanization). For a critical analysis of alternative definitions of Japanization and the application of the concept to UK industry, see Ackroyd et al. (1988).

8 It is noteworthy that since the sale of Rover, BL's successor company, to BMW in 1994, none of these firms is indigenous to the UK. Hence the notion of a "British" motor industry now has extremely limited meaning.

9 For an insightful account of this Fordist scenario in Nissan Sunderland and one that influences this more general treatment, see Garrahan and Stewart (1992).

Chapter 5   Women, Work, and Social Policy

1 No criticism of Thompson is intended on this point. In an aside (referred to as an "apology") to Scottish and Welsh readers, Thompson explains that his neglect of Scottish and Welsh histories of working-class formation is due to his caution in generalizing beyond the English experience and his conviction that the experiences of the Welsh and, in particular, the Scottish are very different from those of the English in the matter of class formation. It is interesting to note that in this aside Thompson emphasizes cultural differences. See Thompson (1966, p. 13).

2 This terminology is drawn from Erik Olin Wright. What follows is influenced by Wright's analysis of temporality, class structure, and class consciousness, particularly the important distinctions between structural and processual approaches, and his analysis of the "trajectory of experiences" in what he

calls the "temporal aspects" of class analysis. My analysis, nonetheless, rejects any notion of unalloyed class consciousness or class interests defined by reference to objective structural class locations. See Wright (1997).

3   Thompson's argument that class "happens" subjects him to a claim that his view of class formation may be excessively agency-oriented at the expense of structural factors. For a useful review of this argument, see Porpora (1985). As the preceding discussion of post-Fordist systems of production should indicate, I hope to integrate processual and structural accounts of class and class formation (see Wright, 1997).

4   At points, Thompson seems to recognize this: for example, when he suggests that "class is a cultural as much as an economic formation" (1966, p. 13). However, the cultural elements of class formation are not fully developed and the priority of class over alternative systems of identity seems to be taken for granted.

5   It should be emphasized that the Employment Department survey on reasons for taking part-time jobs did not include a question that would reveal what role insufficiencies in child care provision may have played in the preference scheme; nor did the survey group respondents by parenting status (i.e. presence or absence of children, number, age, etc.). Therefore, it is impossible to draw any reliable inferences about why respondents "did not want a full-time job." The raw data do suggest some themes for further inquiry, however: 36.2 percent of males and 79.9 percent of females (88.0 percent of married, but only 45.4 percent of non-married) reported this preference. The gap between the preferences of men (undifferentiated in the survey by marital status) and single women is quite narrow (9.2 percent), while the gap between married and unmarried women is sizable (42.6 percent). The relative significance of child care concerns, conditions of need, gendered social roles, and perhaps generational life-cycle variables invite further study and clarification. The survey is reported in Central Statistical Office (1994).

6   I do not wish to imply that these findings demonstrate that the importance of a feminization effect is particular to the financial sector. In fact, researchers found similar patterns in the printing industry, electronics, and plastics processing, and suggested that the pattern might apply generally where there is an overlap between men's and women's work at the industry level (there appears to be little overlap at the level of individual firms). See Craig et al. (1985).

7   Esping-Andersen's work has been taken to task for its neglect of unpaid domestic labor and the importance of caring work, as well as for an implicit "gender-blindness" (the claim that women "disappear from the analysis once they disappear from the labor market"). See, for example, J. Lewis (1993) and Duncan (1996).

8   "Social security" has a broader definition in the UK than in the US, referring to the basic system of contributory and non-contributory benefits to provide financial assistance (not services directly) for the elderly, sick, disabled, unemployed, and others similarly in need.

9   Except where otherwise noted, this discussion of Thatcherism and women follows closely from Lovenduski and Randall (1993, pp. 40–54).

10   This discussion will take as its point of departure a single model: a woman who is in a more or less permanent domestic partnership with a man, engaged in paid part-time or full-time work for most of her life, with one or more children. I select this model, recognizing that it is a simplification of an increasingly diverse range of household and family arrangements, for two reasons: first, it corresponds to the great majority of households and therefore holds particular political significance; secondly, it helps expose tensions between class and gender experiences and identities in an especially interesting way for the broader argument of this book. It is important to add that this model holds no prescriptive or normative connotations. See Sassoon (1992, p. 161).

11   It should be noted that the high proportion of women in part-time paid labor may partly offset the demand for state-provided child care, although that same condition of employment increases the financial strains associated with the need to purchase child care provision.

Chapter 6   Ethnic Minority Groups: Employment and Settlement Patterns

1   Although the term "New Commonwealth" is justified by the fact that the countries so designated gained independence after World War II, by contrast to the Old Commonwealth countries of Australia, Canada, and New Zealand, it is a euphemism for countries of the former British empire whose populations are predominantly black. The usage is almost unavoidable, and will be applied to refer to ethnic minority communities. See Mason (1995, p. 130).

2   In the UK as elsewhere, the terminology used in discussing ethnic and racial diversity is itself a complicating factor in analysis and one subject to considerable controversy. Until relatively recently, political emphasis on issues of immigration and nationality meant that official estimates of ethnic minority populations were based on the place of birth of persons born outside the UK – a framework (apart from other objections) that was inherently flawed by its increasingly limited applicability over time, as a growing proportion of the ethnic minority population came to be born in the UK. After considerable debate and the consideration of alternative schemas, the 1991 Census, for the first time, asked respondents to classify themselves in terms of ethnicity, with reference to the following categories: White; Black-Caribbean; Black-African – Other (please describe); Indian; Pakistani; Bangladeshi; Chinese; Any other ethnic group (please describe). These categories were adopted by the Commission for Racial Equality. Subsequently, the same or similar categories were introduced in Labour Force Surveys and in General Household Surveys. I recognize that terms such as minority, ethnicity and race are potentially misleading, even offensive, although their usage is almost unavoidable. Unless otherwise indicated, my usage will try to conform with my understanding of social-scientific treatments of the subject in the UK: the term "ethnic minority" or "ethnic minority group" or "ethnic minority community" will be used to refer to peoples whose recent origins lie in the former British colonies in the Indian subcontinent, the Caribbean, and Africa, emphasizing the diversity of distinctive ethnic cul-

tures and experiences; occasionally the term "black" will be used to refer to all ethnic and racial minorities, when the emphasis is on a broad-based discrimination or exclusion based on skin color and, particularly, when ethnic minority authors elect this terminology; general references to ethnic diversity include white people. These concepts, used for ethnic identification and analysis of race and ethnicity in the contemporary UK, will be used here without intending any normative implications, and it is hoped that the contexts will render the meanings clear. The usage closely follows that of David Mason (1995), who analyzes the terminological issues with considerable clarity.

3   Data indicate that mortality rates over the past two decades for ethnic minorities have been higher than those of whites, but that the gap appears to be narrowing. Analysis of the factors contributing to this disparity, whether epidemiological or related to socioeconomic status, falls outside the framework of this study, but it should be noted that differential mortality rates would necessarily affect the age distribution of distinct demographic groups (see Luthra, 1997, pp. 250–68).

4   This figure includes the first six months of 1962, before the beginning of immigration controls.

5   This bimodal employment pattern also applies to men of Chinese descent.

6   These figures refer to self-employment as a proportion of all in employment, and are based on the 1990 Labour Force Survey.

7   Although the study was first published in 1995, the findings are based on a 1990 survey and associated field research.

8   The West Yorkshire study carefully compares the responses of Pakistani and white women in an effort to challenge myths and stereotypes.

Chapter 7   Modularity, Identities, and Cultural Repertoires

1   It should be noted that Gellner uses the term "modular man." I substitute the term "modular politics" both to efface any gendered connotation and to focus attention on broader systemic processes rather than on voluntary acts.

2   The claim that modularity affirms the social construction of categories of identity should not be read as an endorsement of the unrestricted plasticity sometimes implied by postmodernism (see Gilroy, 1993).

3   Quoted in Hobsbawm (1996).

4   For especially helpful treatments of the theoretical implications and a useful synthesis of recent scholarship from which these points are largely drawn, see Cohen (1994, pp. 204–5); Baker et al. (1996a); and Modood (1997).

5   It should be noted that Patterson refers exclusively to ethnicity, although the analysis seems more broadly applicable to an extensive range of collective identities.

6   Tarrow attributes the application of modularity and the concept of repertoires applied to contentious collective action to the work of Charles Tilly (see, for example, Tilly, 1993).

7   For notable exceptions, see Sinfield (1989); Gilroy (1991); Hebdige (1991); and Gilroy (1993).

8   Other sources of identity, such as those located in sexuality, religion, and disability, among others, warrant comparable consideration but lie outside the focus of this study.

9   I use the term "narrative" with caution, as a specific translation of abstract normative concepts, political doctrines, or policies into a language of experience and common sense. I assume that at least most of the time the interpretations behind these narratives are influenced by concrete experiences and can be meaningfully generalized by reference to collective identities, although other factors of course contribute to these interpretations. Thus, by contrast to some uses of the concept by postmodernists, I locate narratives within social scientific argument and in the context of normative claims. For useful elaborations of questions of narrativity, see Rosenau (1992) and Sommers (1992).

Chapter 8   National Identities

1   For development of the notion of "frontiers" and a comprehensive and interestingly theorized account of the dimensions of British identity, including the application of the notion of "fuzzy logic" to frontiers of British identity, see Cohen (1994).

2   The authors state that, depending on how the question is posed, other types may have a stronger claim to represent the "heart of Britain" (see Dowds and Young, 1996).

3   It should be noted that John Bull as icon of Englishness has no "Jane Bull" counterpart, happy or otherwise. Indeed, the whole narration of this traditional story of national identity tends to exclude Englishwomen or frame them as patriotic accessories to male valor, thereby sustaining a masculine, as well as an ethnocentric, version of Englishness (see Cohen, 1994, pp. 13–14).

4   The strategic political differentiation and use of alternative identity representations or labels occurs routinely, especially in community-based or city politics, and not only at moments of crisis or as a result of special circumstances of visibility and threats of exclusion. This more routine application of modular identities will be discussed in chapter 9, with reference to the Pakistani community in Manchester.

5   Partha Chatterjee offers a parallel observation about anti-colonial and postcolonial nationalisms. Chatterjee objects to the pre-given limits that Anderson bestows upon forms and expressions of anti-colonial nationalisms, the imposition of which robs the movements of powerful, liberating expression. "If nationalisms in the rest of the world have to choose their imagined community from certain 'modular' forms already made available to them by Europe and the Americas," asks Chatterjee, "what do they have left to imagine?" (1996, p. 216). Chatterjee argues that the capacity of anti-colonial nationalisms to imagine and construct their own domain of sovereignty expressed in "spiritual culture" is a fundamental feature of anti-colonial struggles that has been overlooked by Anderson, as well as others.

6   The formulation, of course, brings to mind the "4 + 1" talks leading to the unification of Germany, a reference that may add to the humor of the "11 + 1" phrase and sharpen its political edge.

7   For an extremely interesting analysis of the complex issues of colonial and postcolonial loyalty and national identity formation in India, which places Tebbit's unfortunate "cricket test" in context, see Appadurai (1997, pp. 89–113).

8   This list includes a sample of the great variety of narratives and interpretations of national identity and nationalism discussed by Nairn. I do not mean to imply his analytic or normative endorsement of the claims, some of which he clearly rejects: for example, the atavistic and anti-imperialist accounts of the struggles in Northern Ireland (Nairn, 1981, pp. 216–55).

Chapter 9   Communities: Actual and Imagined

1   Except where otherwise indicated, the account of Manchester Pakistanis is drawn from Werbner (1990).

2   Any serious evaluation of communitarian theory and discussion of social capital and civic engagement lies beyond the scope of this study. For an excellent selection of communitarian thinking, see Etzioni (1995). John Gray provides a very influential interpretation of communitarianism in the UK and clearly illuminates its potential as an alternative to collectivist ("Old Labour") and New Right perspectives (Gray, 1995, 1997). Robert D. Putnam sparked enormous interest in civic community (see Putnam, 1993, 1995), which has been applied to the UK or located within British debates in several important contributions, including Boswell (1990), Sullivan (1995), and Hall (1997).

Chapter 10   Challenges to Contemporary British Government

1   For more detailed analysis of the decline in class voting and analysis of other elements of volatility in the May 1997 general election, see Butler and Kavanagh (1997); Dunleavy (1997); Norris (1997); Sanders (1998).

2   Volatility is defined here by the Pederson volatility index, which measures net changes in voter support for political parties by adding together the net change in each party's share of the vote between national elections.

3   It should be noted that expectations of job leaving combine voluntary and involuntary departures and that the author concludes from the survey data that there is little indication of increasing anxiety about layoffs (Spencer, 1996).

4   Sanders acknowledges that difficulties of measurement make it hard to be certain about the significance of these identity influences (1998, p. 221).

5   Excellent reviews of the influence of both factors may be found in Dalton (1996) and Norris (1997b, 1999).

6   Especially notable were the extensive efforts to improve women's prospects for selection as candidates, pursuant to the goal set at 1992 annual conference that half the seats where MPs were retiring and half of the most winnable seats should be contested by female candidates. In addition to specific policy statements, the appointment of a series of Shadow Ministers for Women, who worked hard to mobilize support through women's networks and organizations, contributed to Labour's success in reversing the

gender gap. For a detailed account of the efforts by Labour, as well as the Conservatives and Liberal Democrats, to attract women voters, see Lovenduski (1997).

7   For a compelling theoretical argument for the extension of the principles of representative democracy to the enterprise, see Dahl (1985).

8   Inevitably, the model is only a spare outline at this stage, intended as an invitation for further discussion.

References

Ackroyd, Stephen, Gibson Burrell, Michael Hughes and Alan Whitaker 1988: The Japanisation of British industry? *Industrial Relations Journal*, 19(2), 11–23.

Alexander, Claire E. 1996: *The Art of Being Black: the creation of black British youth identities*. Oxford: Clarendon Press/Oxford University Press.

Alibhai-Brown, Yasmin 1998: Nations under a groove. *Marxism Today*, November/December, 47.

Allen, Sheila and Carol Wolkowitz 1987: *Homeworking: myths and realities*. London: Macmillan Education.

Almond, Gabriel A. and Sidney Verba 1963: *The Civic Culture: political attitudes and democracy in five nations*. Princeton, NJ: Princeton University Press.

Almond, Gabriel A. and Sidney Verba 1980: *The Civic Culture Revisited*. Boston, Mass.: Little, Brown.

Anderson, Benedict 1991: *Imagined Communities: reflections on the origin and spread of nationalism*. London and New York: Verso.

Ansell, Amy Elizabeth 1997: *New Right, New Racism: race and reaction in the United States and Britain*. New York: New York University Press.

Anthias, Floya and Nira Yuval-Davis 1992: *Racialized Boundaries: race, nation, gender, colour and class and the anti-racist struggle*. London and New York: Routledge.

Appadurai, Arjun 1997: *Modernity at Large: cultural dimensions of globalization*. Minneapolis, Minn., and London: University of Minnesota Press.

Armstrong, Harvey 1998: What future for regional policy in the UK? *Political Quarterly*, 69(3), 200–14.

Aronowitz, Stanley 1992: *The Politics of Identity: class, culture, social movements*. New York and London: Routledge.

Asad, Talal 1990: Multiculturalism and British identity in the wake of the Rushdie Affair. *Politics and Society*, 18(4), 455–80.

Bagilhole, Barbara 1996: Kith not kin: the effects on women as givers and receivers of voluntary care in Britain. *European Journal of Women's Studies*, 3, 39–54.

Baker, Houston A., Jr, Stephen Best, and Ruth H. Lindeborg 1996a: Introduction: representing blackness/representing Britain – cultural studies and the politics of knowledge. In Houston A. Baker Jr, Stephen Best, and Ruth H. Lindeborg (eds), *Black British Cultural Studies: a reader*. Chicago, Ill., and London: University of Chicago Press, 1–15.

Baker, Houston A., Jr, Manthia Diawara, and Ruth H. Lindeborg (eds) 1996b: *Black British Cultural Studies: a reader*. Black Literature and Culture. Chicago, Ill., and London: University of Chicago Press.

Bakker, Isabella 1988: Women's employment in comparative perspective. In Jane Jenson, Elisabeth Hagen, and Ceallaigh Reddy (eds), *Feminization of the Labour Force: paradoxes and promises*. Cambridge: Polity Press, 17–44.

Barrett, Michèle and Mary McIntosh 1982: *The Anti-Social Family*. London: Verso.

Barrett, Stanley R. 1992: *The Rebirth of Anthropological Theory*. Toronto: University of Toronto Press.

Beer, Samuel H. 1969: *British Politics in the Collectivist Age*. New York: Vintage.

Beer, Samuel H. 1982: *Britain Against Itself: the political contradictions of collectivism*. New York: Norton.

Beer, Samuel H. 1997: Britain after Blair. *Political Quarterly*, 68(4), 317–24.

Bell, Daniel 1975: Ethnicity and social change. In Nation Glazer and Daniel P. Moynihan (eds), *Ethnicity: theory and experience*. Cambridge, Mass.: Harvard University Press, 141–74.

Benyon, John and Adam Edwards 1997: Crime and public order. In Patrick Dunleavy, Andrew Gamble, Ian Holliday, and Gillian Peele (eds), *Developments in British Politics 5*. New York: St Martin's Press, 326–41.

Berger, Suzanne and Ronald Dore (eds) 1996: *National Diversity and Global Capitalism*. Cornell Studies in Political Economy. Ithaca, NY, and London: Cornell University Press.

Berggren, Christian 1992: *Alternatives to Lean Production: work organization in the Swedish auto industry*. Ithaca, NY: ILR Press.

Best, Michael H. 1990: *The New Competition: institutions of industrial restructuring*. Cambridge: Polity Press.

Bien, Melanie 1997: A woman's place is in the workplace – but pay her more. *The European*, 11–17 December, 35.

Bishop, Graham 1997: The march to Euroland. In Paul Temperton (ed.), *The Euro*. Chichester: Wiley, 7–19.

Bjorgo, Tore 1997: "The invaders," "the traitors" and "the resistance movement": the extreme right's conceptualisation of opponents and self in Scandinavia. In Tariq Modood and Pnina Werbner (eds), *The Politics of Multiculturalism in the New Europe: racism, identity and community*. London and New York: Zed Press, 54–72.

Black, Jeremy 1993: *The Politics of Britain 1688–1800*. Manchester and New York: Manchester University Press.

Blair, Tony 1993: Foreword. In Christopher Bryant (ed.), *Reclaiming the Ground: Christianity and Socialism*. London: Spire/Hodder and Stoughton, 9–12.

Blair, Tony 1995: Lecture at a commemoration organised by the Fabian Society to mark the fiftieth anniversary of the 1945 general election. London: Labour Party.

Blair, Tony 1996: *New Britain*. Boulder, Colo.: Westview Press.

Blair, Tony 1997: No return to the strike-bound 70s. *Daily Mail*, March, 26, 7.

Boswell, Jonathan 1990: *Community and the Economy: the theory of public co-operation*. London and New York: Routledge.

Brodner, Peter 1986: Skill based manufacturing vs. "unmanned factory" – which is superior? *International Journal of Industrial Ergonomics*, 1, 145–53.

Brown, Archie 1998: Asymmetrical devolution: the Scottish case. *Political Quarterly*, 69(3), 215–23.

Brown, Gordon 1994: The politics of potential: a new agenda for Labour. In David Miliband (ed.), *Reinventing the Left*. Cambridge: Polity Press, 113–22.

Bryan, Beverly, Stella Dadzie, and Suzanne Scafe 1985: *The Heart of the Race: black women's lives in Britain*. London: Virago.

Bryant, Christopher (ed.) 1993: *Reclaiming the Ground: Christianity and socialism*. London: Spire/Hodder and Stoughton.

Butler, David and Dennis Kavanagh 1997: *The British General Election of 1997*. Basingstoke: Macmillan.

Buxton, Tony, Paul Chapman, and Paul Temple (eds) 1994a: *Britain's Economic Performance*. London and New York: Routledge.

Buxton, Tony, Paul Chapman, and Paul Temple 1994b: Introduction. In Tony Buxton, Paul Chapman, and Paul Temple (eds), *Britain's Economic Performance*. London and New York: Routledge, 1–8.

Caglar, Ayse S. 1997: Hyphenated identities and the limits of "culture." In Tariq Modood and Pnina Werbner (eds), *The Politics of Multiculturalism in the New Europe: racism, identity and community*. London and New York: Zed Press, 169–85.

Campbell, Mary 1998: Pensions: redressing the balance. *Political Quarterly*, 9(1), 15–22.

Cannadine, David 1992a: The context, performance and meaning of ritual: the British monarchy and the "invention of tradition," *c.*1820–1977. In Eric Hobsbawm and Terence Ranger (eds), *The Invention of Tradition*. Cambridge: Cambridge University Press, 101–64.

Cannadine, David 1992b: Gilbert and Sullivan: the making and un-making of a British "tradition." In Roy Porter (ed.), *Myths of the English*. Cambridge: Polity Press, 12–32.

Central Statistical Office 1994: *Social Trends 24*. London: HMSO.

Chamberlayne, Prue 1993: Women and the state: changes in roles and rights in France, West Germany, Italy and Britain, 1970–1990. In Jane Lewis (ed.), *Women and Social Policies in Europe: work, family and the state*. Aldershot: Edward Elgar, 170–93.

Charles, Tony 1995: The new division of labour in Europe. In Wolfgang Littek and Tony Charles (eds), *The New Division of Labour: emerging forms of work organisation in international perspective*. Berlin: Walter de Gruyter, 235–61.

Chatterjee, Partha 1996: Whose imagined community? In Gopal Balakrishnan (ed.), *Mapping the Nation*. London and New York: Verso, 214–25.

Church, Roy 1994: *The Rise and Decline of the British Motor Industry*. Cambridge: Cambridge University Press.

Clarke, Colin, Ceri Peach, and Steven Vertovec 1990: South Asians in contemporary western countries and the Middle East: introduction. In Colin Clarke, Ceri Peach, and Steven Vertovec (eds), *South Asians Overseas: migration and ethnicity*. Cambridge: Cambridge University Press, 167–96.

Coates, David (ed.) 1996: *Industrial Policy in Britain*. Basingstoke: Macmillan.

Cohen, Robin 1994: *Frontiers of Identity: the British and the others*. London and New York: Longman.

Craig, Christine, Elizabeth Garnsey, and Jill Rubery 1985: Labour market segmentation and women's employment: a case-study from the United Kingdom. *International Labour Review*, 124(3), 267–80.

Crewe, Ivor 1992: Labour force changes, working class decline, and the labour vote: social and electoral trends in postwar Britain. In Frances Fox Piven (ed.), *Labor Parties in Postindustrial Societies*. New York: Oxford University Press, 20–46.

Crick, Bernard 1991: The English and the British. In Bernard Crick (ed.), *National Identities: the constitution of the United Kingdom*. Oxford: Blackwell, 90–104.

Crompton, Rosemary and Kay Sanderson 1994: The gendered restructuring of employment in the finance sector. In Alison MacEwen Scott (ed.), *Gender Segregation and Social Change: men and women in changing labour markets*. Oxford: Oxford University Press, 271–300.

Crosland, C. A. R. 1952: The transition from capitalism. In R. H. S. Crossman (ed.), *New Fabian Essays*. New York: Praeger, 33–68.

Crosland, C. A. R. 1963: *The Future of Socialism*. New York: Schocken Books.

Cross, Malcolm 1992: Black workers, recession and economic restructuring in the West Midlands. In Malcolm Cross (ed.), *Ethnic Minorities and Industrial Change in Europe and North America*. Cambridge: Cambridge University Press, 77–93.

Crouch, Colin and David Marquand (eds) 1995: *Reinventing Collective Action: from the global to the local*. Oxford: Blackwell.

Crouch, Colin and Wolfgang Streeck 1997: Introduction: the future of capitalist diversity. In Colin Crouch and Wolfgang Streeck (eds), *Political Economy of Modern Capitalism: mapping convergence and diversity*. London: Sage, 1–18.

Dahl, Robert A. 1985: *A Preface to Economic Democracy*. Berkeley, Calif.: University of California Press.

Dale, Jennifer and Peggy Foster 1986: *Feminists and State Welfare*. London: Routledge and Kegan Paul.

Dalton, Russell J. 1996: *Citizen Politics: public opinion and political parties in advanced industrial democracies*. Chatham, New Jersey: Chatham House.

Dankbaar, Ben 1994: Sectoral governance in the automobile industries of Germany, Great Britain, and France. In J. Rogers Hollingsworth, Philippe C. Schmitter, and Wolfgang Streeck (eds), *Governing Capitalist Economies: performance and control of economic sectors*. New York: Oxford University Press, 156–82.

Daye, Sharon J. 1994: *Middle-Class Blacks in Britain: a racial fraction of a class group or a class fraction of a racial group?* New York: St Martin's Press.

Deacon, Alan 1998: The green paper on welfare reform: a case for enlightened self-interest? *Political Quarterly*, 69(3), 306–11.

Department of Trade and Industry 1998: *Fairness at Work*. London: DTI Web site: http://www.dti.gov.uk/.

Dicken, Peter 1992: *Global Shift: the internationalization of economic activity*. New York: Guilford Press.

Dowds, Lizanne and Ken Young 1996: National identity. In Roger Jowell, John Curtice, Alison Park, Lindsay Brook, and Katarina Thompson (eds), *British Social Attitudes: the 13th report*. Aldershot: Dartmouth Publishing Co., 141–60.

Driver, Stephen and Luke Martell 1998: *New Labour: politics after Thatcherism*. Cambridge: Polity Press.

Duncan, Simon 1996: The diverse worlds of European patriarchy. In Maria Dolors García-Ramon and Janice Monk (eds), *Women of the European Union: the politics of work and daily life*. London and New York: Routledge, 74–110.

Dunleavy, Patrick 1997: Introduction: "new times" in British politics. In Patrick Dunleavy, Andrew Gamble, Ian Holliday, and Gillian Peele (eds), *Developments in British Politics 5*. New York: St Martin's Press: 1–19.

Dunleavy, Patrick and Christopher T. Husbands 1985: *British Democracy at the Crossroads: voting and party competition in the 1980s*. London: Allen and Unwin.

Durham, Martin 1997: "God wants us to be in different parties": religion and politics in Britain today. *Parliamentary Affairs*, 50(2), 212–22.

Elger, Tony and Peter Fairbrother 1992: Inflexible flexibility: a case study of modularisation. In Nigel Gilbert, Roger Burrows, and Anna Pollert (eds), *Fordism and Flexibility: divisions and change*. New York: St Martin's Press, 89–106.

Esping-Andersen, Gøsta 1985: *Politics Against Markets: the social democratic road to power*. Princeton, NJ: Princeton University Press.

Esping-Andersen, Gøsta 1990: *The Three Worlds of Welfare Capitalism*. Cambridge: Polity Press; Princeton, NJ: Princeton University Press.

Etzioni, Amitai (ed.) 1995: *New Communitarian Thinking: persons, virtues, and communities*. Charlottesville, Va: University Press of Virginia.

Feldstein, Martin 1998: Europe's new challenge to America. *New York Times*, 7 May, A35.

Finegold, Kenneth 1993: New Deal coalition. In Joel Krieger (ed.), *Oxford Companion to Politics of the World*. New York: Oxford University Press, 626–7.

Finer, Catherine Jones 1997: Social policy. In Patrick Dunleavy, Andrew Gamble, Ian Holliday, and Gillian Peele (eds), *Developments in British Politics 5*. New York: St Martin's Press, 304–25.

Forbes, Ian 1994: Gender, race and inequality. In Philip Allan, John Benyon, and Barry McCormick (eds), *Focus on Britain 1994*. Chicago, Ill.: Fitzroy Dearborn, 193–200.

Foreman-Peck, James, Sue Bowden, and Alan McKinley 1995: *The British Motor Industry*. Manchester and New York: Manchester University Press.

Freeman, Richard B. and Lawrence F. Katz 1994: Rising wage inequality: the United States vs other advanced countries. In Richard B. Freeman (ed.), *Working under Different Rules*. New York: Russell Sage Foundation, 29–62.

Gardiner, Jean 1985: Women, recession, and the Tories. In Stuart Hall and Martin Jacques (eds), *The Politics of Thatcherism*. London: Lawrence and Wishart, 188–206.

Garrahan, Philip and Paul Stewart 1992: *The Nissan Enigma: flexibility at work in a local economy*. London: Mansell.

Garrett, Geoffrey 1998: *Partisan Politics in the Global Economy*. Cambridge: Cambridge University Press.

Gellner, Ernest 1994: *Conditions of Liberty: civil society and its rivals*. New York: Penguin.

Giddens, Anthony 1979: *Central Problems in Social Theory: action, structure and contradiction in social analysis.* Berkeley, Calif.: University of California Press.

Giddens, Anthony 1990: *The Consequences of Modernity.* Cambridge: Polity Press; Stanford, Calif.: Stanford University Press.

Giddens, Anthony 1991: *Modernity and Self-Identity: self and society in the late modern age.* Cambridge: Polity Press; Stanford, Calif.: Stanford University Press.

Giddens, Anthony 1998: *The Third Way: the renewal of social democracy.* Cambridge: Polity Press.

Gill, Stephen 1998: European governance and new constitutionalism: economic and monetary union and alternatives to disciplinary neoliberalism in Europe. *New Political Economy*, 3(1), 5–26.

Gilroy, Paul 1991: *"There Ain't No Black in the Union Jack."* Chicago, IU.: University of Chicago Press.

Gilroy, Paul 1993: *Small Acts: thoughts on the politics of black cultures.* London: Serpent's Tail.

Goldthorpe, John H. (ed.) 1984; *Order and Conflict in Contemporary Capitalism: studies in the political economy of western European nations.* Oxford: Oxford University Press.

Gordon, Ian 1995: The impact of economic change on minorities and migrants in western Europe. In Katherine McFate, Roger Lawson, and William Julius Wilson (eds), *Poverty, Inequality, and the Future of Social Policy.* New York: Russell Sage Foundation, 521–42.

Gordon, Linda 1990: The new feminist scholarship on the welfare state. In Linda Gordon (ed.), *Women, the State, and Welfare.* Madison, Wis.: University of Wisconsin Press, 9–35.

Gordon, Richard 1993: Fordism. In Joel Krieger (ed.), *The Oxford Companion to Politics of the World.* New York: Oxford University Press, 307–9.

Gordon, Richard 1995: Globalization, new production systems and the spatial division of labor. In Wolfgang Littek and Tony Charles (eds), *The New Division of Labour: emerging forms of work organisation in international perspective.* Berlin: Walter de Gruyter, 161–207.

Gordon, Richard and Joel Krieger 1992: *Anthropocentric Production Systems and US Manufacturing Models in the Machine Tool, Semiconductor and Automobile Industries.* Brussels: FAST/Commission of the European Communities.

Gordon, Richard and Joel Krieger 1993: *Technological Change, Production Organization and Skill Formation in the US Machine Tool, Semiconductor and Auto Industries.* Washington, DC: US Department of Labor.

Gordon, Richard and Joel Krieger 1998: Investigating differentiated production systems: the US machine tool industry. *Competition and Change*, 2, 1–27.

Goulbourne, Harry 1991: *Ethnicity and Nationalism in Post-Imperial Britain.* Cambridge: Cambridge University Press.

Government, HM 1942: *Social Insurance and Allied Services.* Report by Sir William Beveridge. London and New York: HMSO/Macmillan.

Grant, Wyn 1998: *Evaluating New Labour.* Baltimore, Md: Council for European Studies.

Gray, John 1995: *Enlightenment's Wake: politics and culture at the close of the modern age.* London and New York: Routledge.

Gray, John 1997: *Endgames: questions in late modern political thought.* Cambridge: Polity Press.

Gutmann, Amy 1994: Introduction. In Amy Gutmann (ed.), *Multiculturalism: examining the politics of recognition.* Princeton, NJ: Princeton University Press, 3–24.

Hall, Peter A. 1986: *Governing the Economy: the politics of state intervention in Britain and France.* New York: Oxford University Press.

Hall, Peter A. (ed.), 1989: *The Political Power of Economic Ideas: Keynesianism across nations.* Princeton, NJ: Princeton University Press.

Hall, Peter A. 1997: Social Capital in Britain. Bertelsmann Stiftung Workshop on Social Capital, Berlin.

Hall, Peter A. and Sidney Tarrow 1998: Globalization and area studies: when is too broad too narrow? *Chronicle of Higher Education,* XLIV(20), B4–5.

Hall, Stuart 1988: *Thatcherism and the Crisis of the Left: the hard road to renewal.* London and New York: Verso.

Hall, Stuart 1990: Cultural identity and diaspora. In Jonathan Rutherford (ed.), *Identity: community, culture, difference.* London: Lawrence and Wishart, 222–37.

Hall, Stuart 1992: The question of cultural identity. In Stuart Hall, David Held and Tony McGrew (eds), *Modernity and Its Futures.* Cambridge: Polity Press in association with the Open University, 273–325.

Hall, Stuart 1996a: Cultural identity and cinematic representation. In Houston A. Baker, Jr, Manthia Diawara, and Ruth H. Lindeborg (eds), *Black British Cultural Studies: a reader.* Chicago, Ill., and London: University of Chicago Press, 210–22.

Hall, Stuart 1996b: New ethnicities. In Houston A. Baker, Jr, Manthia Diawara, and Ruth H. Lindeborg (eds), *Black British Cultural Studies: a reader.* Chicago, Ill.: University of Chicago Press, 163–72.

Harrison, M. L. 1995: *Housing, "Race," Social Policy and Empowerment.* Aldershot: Avebury.

Haseler, Stephen 1996: *The English Tribe: identity, nation and Europe.* New York: St Martin's Press.

Hay, Colin 1998: That was then, this is now: the revision of policy in the "modernisation" of the British Labour Party, 1991–97. *New Political Science,* 20(1), 7–33.

Hay, Colin and Matthew Watson 1998a: The discourse of globalisation and the logic of no alternative: rendering the contingent necessary in the downsizing of New Labour's aspirations for government. Paper presented at the annual conference of the Political Studies Association, University of Keele, Keele.

Hay, Colin, and Matthew Watson 1998b: Labour's economic policy: studiously courting competence. In Gerlad R. Taylor (ed.), *The Impact of New Labour.* London: Macmillan.

Hebdige, Dick 1991: *Subculture: the meaning of style.* London and New York: Routledge.

Held, David 1995: *Democracy and the Global Order: from the modern state to cosmopolitan governance.* Cambridge: Polity Press; Stanford, Calif.: Stanford University Press.

Held, David 1998: Globalisation: the timid tendency. *Marxism Today,* November/December, 24–7.

Hobsbawm, Eric 1992: Introduction: inventing traditions. In Eric Hobsbawm and Terence Ranger (eds), *The Invention of Tradition*. Cambridge: Cambridge University Press, 1–14.

Hobsbawm, Eric 1996: *The Age of Extremes: a history of the world, 1914–1991*. New York: Vintage.

Holliday, Ian 1997: Territorial politics. In Patrick Dunleavy, Andrew Gamble, Ian Holliday, and Gillian Peele (eds), *Developments in British Politics 5*. New York: St Martin's Press, 220–40.

Hollingsworth, J. Rogers and Robert Boyer (eds) 1997: *Contemporary Capitalism: the embeddedness of institutions*. Cambridge Studies in Comparative Politics. New York: Cambridge University Press.

Hollingsworth, J. Rogers, Philippe C. Schmitter, and Wolfgang Streeck (eds) 1994: *Governing Capitalist Economies: performance and control of economic sectors*. New York and Oxford: Oxford University Press.

Howell, Chris 1997: Constructing industrial relations: the British state and industrial relations reform since 1890. Paper presented at the annual meeting of the American Political Science Association, the Sheraton Washington Hotel.

Howell, Chris 1998: From New Labour to no Labour? The Blair government in Britain. Paper presented at the annual meeting of the American Political Science Association, Boston, Mass.

Howell, Chris (forthcoming): Unforgiven: the crisis of British trade unionism. In George Ross and Andrew Martin (eds), *The End of Labor's Century?* Providence, RI: Berghahn.

Huber, Evelyn and John D. Stephens 1998: Internationalization and the social democratic model: crisis and future prospects. *Comparative Political Studies*, 31(3), 353–97.

Humphries, Jane and Jill Rubery 1988: Recession and exploitation. In Jane Jenson, Elisabeth Hagen, and Ceallaigh Reddy (eds), *Feminization of the Labour Force: paradoxes and promises*. Cambridge: Polity Press, 85–105.

Huntington, Samuel P. 1996: *The Clash of Civilizations and the Remaking of World Order*. New York: Simon and Schuster.

Hutton, Will 1995: *The State We're In*. London: Vintage.

Ingram, Peter 1991: Changes in working practices in British manufacturing industry in the 1980s. *British Journal of Industrial Relations*, 29(1), 1–13.

Jackson, Peter and Jan Penrose (eds) 1994: *Constructions of Race, Place and Nation*. Minneapolis, Minn.: University of Minnesota Press.

James, Winston 1993: Migration, racism and identity formation: the Caribbean experience in Britain. In Winston James and Clive Harris (eds), *Inside Babylon: the Caribbean diaspora*. London: Verso, 231–87.

Jenson, Jane 1988: The limits of "and the" discourse. In Jane Jenson, Elisabeth Hagen, and Ceallaigh Ready (eds), *Feminization of the Labour Force: paradoxes and promises*. Cambridge: Polity Press, 155–72.

Jessop, Bob, Kevin Bonnett, Simon Bromley, and Tom Ling 1988: *Thatcherism: a tale of two nations*. Cambridge: Polity Press.

Joffe, Josef 1997: The euro: the engine that couldn't. *New York Review of Books*, XLIV, 26–31.

Johnes, Geraint and Jim Taylor 1996: The labour market. In M. J. Artis (ed.), *The UK Economy: a manual of applied economics*. Oxford: Oxford University Press, 286–329.

Kahn, Peggy 1997: Employment restructuring and gender in British National Health Service support work. Unpublished.

Kamerman, Sheila B. 1996: Gender role and family structure changes in the advanced industrialized West: implications for social policy. In Katherine McFate, Roger Lawson, and William Julius Wilson (eds), *Poverty, Inequality, and the Future of Social Policy: western states in the new world order.* New York: Russell Sage Foundation, 231–56.

Katznelson, Ira 1986: Working-class formation: constructing cases and comparisons. In Ira Katznelson and Aristede R. Zolberg (eds), *Working-Class Formation: nineteenth-century patterns in western Europe and the United States.* Princeton, NJ: Princeton University Press.

Kavanagh, Dennis 1990: *British Politics: continuities and change.* Oxford: Oxford University Press.

Kearney, Hugh 1989: *The British Isles: a history of four nations.* Cambridge: Cambridge University Press.

Kearney, Hugh 1991: Four nations or one? In Bernard Crick (ed.), *National Identities: the constitution of the United Kingdom.* Oxford: Blackwell, 1–6.

Kellner, Peter 1997: Why the Tories were trounced. *Parliamentary Affairs*, 50(4), 616–30.

Kern, Horst and Michael Schumann 1987: Limits of the division of labour: new production and employment concepts in west German industry. *Economic and Industrial Democracy*, 8, 151–70.

Kesselman, Mark and Joel Krieger (eds) 1997a: *European Politics in Transition.* Boston, Mass.: Houghton Mifflin.

Kesselman, Mark and Joel Krieger 1997b: Introduction. In Mark Kesselman and Joel Krieger (eds), *European Politics in Transition.* Boston, Mass.: Houghton Mifflin, 1–37.

King, Anthony 1998a: The night itself. In Anthony King (ed.), *New Labour Triumphs: Britain at the Polls.* Chatham, NJ: Chatham House, 1–13.

King, Anthony 1998b: Why Labour won – at last. In Anthony King (ed.), *New Labour Triumphs: Britain at the polls.* Chatham, NJ: Chatham House, 177–207.

King, Desmond and Mark Wickham-Jones 1998: Training without the state? New Labour and labour markets. *Politics and Society*, 26(4), 439–55.

Kirchheimer, Otto 1966: The transformation of the western European party systems. In Joseph LaPalombara and Myron Weiner (eds), *Political Parties and Political Development.* Princeton, NJ: Princeton University Press, 177–200.

Kitschelt, Herbert 1994: *The Transformation of European Social Democracy.* New York: Cambridge University Press.

Krieger, Joel 1986: *Reagan, Thatcher and the Politics of Decline.* New York: Oxford University Press.

Krieger, Joel 1992a: Britain. In Mark Kesselman and Joel Krieger (eds), *European Politics in Transition.* Lexington, Mass.: D. C. Heath, 27–127.

Krieger, Joel 1992b: Class, consumption, and collectivism: perspectives on the Labour Party and electoral competition in Britain. In Frances Fox Piven (ed.), *Labor Parties in Postindustrial Societies.* New York: Oxford University Press, 47–70.

Krieger, Joel 1992c: Manufacturing technologies and the micropolitics of production: a framework for US–European comparisons. Paper presented to the eighth international conference of Europeanists, Chicago, Ill.

Lane, Christel 1995: *Industry and Society in Europe: stability and change in Britain, Germany and France.* Aldershot: Edward Elgar.

Lane, Jan-Erik, David McKay, and Kenneth Newton 1997: *Political Data Handbook: OECD countries.* Oxford: Oxford University Press.

Law, Ian 1996: *Racism, Ethnicity and Social Policy.* London and New York: Prentice Hall/Harvester Wheatsheaf.

Layton-Henry, Zig 1984: *The Politics of Race in Britain.* London: Allen and Unwin.

Lee, Simon 1996: Manufacturing. In David Coates (ed.), *Industrial Policy in Britain.* Basingstoke: Macmillan, 33–61.

Lehner, Franz 1992: *Anthropocentric Production Systems: the European response to advanced manufacturing and globalisation.* Luxembourg: FAST/Commission of the European Communities.

Lewis, Gail 1993: Black women's employment and the British economy. In Winston James and Clive Harris (eds), *Inside Babylon: the Caribbean diaspora in Britain.* London: Verso, 73–96.

Lewis, Jane 1993: Introduction: women, work, family and social policies in Europe. In Jane Lewis (ed.), *Women and Social Policies in Europe: work, family and the state.* Aldershot: Edward Elgar, 1–24.

Lewis, Jane 1998: "Work," "welfare" and lone mothers. *Political Quarterly*, 69(1), 4–13.

Lewis, Philip 1994: *Islamic Britain: religion, politics and identity among British Muslims: Bradford in the 1990s.* London and New York: I. B. Tauris.

Lewis, Philip 1997: Arenas of ethnic negotiation: cooperation and conflict in Bradford. In Tariq Modood and Pnina Werbner (eds), *The Politics of Multiculturalism in the New Europe: racism, identity and community.* London and New York: Zed Press, 126–46.

Lipschutz, Ronnie 1992: Reconstructing world politics, emergence of global civil society. *Millennium*, 21, 389–411.

Lloyd, John 1997: A benefit cut in search of a policy. *New Statesman*, 19 December, 12–13.

Lloyd, John 1998: Interview: David Owen. *New Statesman*, 13 February, 18–20.

Lord, Christopher 1996: Industrial policy and the European Union. In David Coates (ed.), *Industrial Policy in Britain.* Basingstoke: Macmillan, 212–37.

Lovenduski, Joni 1997: Gender politics: a breakthrough for women? *Parliamentary Affairs*, 50(4), 708–19.

Lovenduski, Joni and Vicky Randall 1993: *Contemporary Feminist Politics: women and power in Britain.* Oxford: Oxford University Press.

Luthra, Mohan 1997: *Britain's Black Population: social change, public policy and agenda.* Aldershot: Arena/Ashgate.

Lyon, Wenonah 1997: Defining ethnicity: another way of being British. In Tariq Modood and Pnina Werbner (eds), *The Politics of Multiculturalism in the New Europe: racism, identity and community.* London and New York: Zed Press, 186–205.

McFate, Katherine 1995: Introduction: western states in the new world order. In Katherine McFate, Roger Lawson, and William Julius Wilson (eds), *Poverty, Inequality, and the Future of Social Policy: western states in the new world order.* New York: Russell Sage Foundation, 1–26.

Mahon, Rianne 1991: From solidaristic wages to solidaristic work: a post-Fordist historic compromise for Sweden? *Economic and Industrial Democracy*, 12(3), 295–326.

Mahon, Rianne 1996: Women wage earners and the future of Swedish unions. *Economic and Industrial Democracy*, 17(4), 545–86.

Maier, Charles S. 1987: *In Search of Stability: explorations in historical political economy*. Cambridge: Cambridge University Press.

Mandelson, Peter and Roger Liddle 1996: *The Blair Revolution: can New Labour deliver?* London: Faber and Faber.

Markovits, Andrei S. and Philip S. Gorski 1993: *The German left: red, green and beyond*. Cambridge: Polity Press; New York: Oxford University Press.

Marquand, David 1988: *The Unprincipled Society: new demands and old politics*. London: Jonathan Cape.

Marquand, David 1991: *The Progressive Dilemma*. London: Heinemann.

Marquand, David 1997: After euphoria: the dilemmas of New Labour. *Political Quarterly*, 68(4), 335–8.

Marquand, David 1998: The Blair paradox. *Prospect*, May, 19–24.

Marshall, T. H. 1950: *Citizenship and Social Class*. Cambridge: Cambridge University Press.

Marx, Karl 1963: *The 18th Brumaire of Louis Bonaparte*. New York: International Publishers.

Mason, David 1995: *Race and Ethnicity in Modern Britain*. Oxford: Oxford University Press.

Mayer, Tom 1994: *Analytical Marxism*. Thousand Oaks, Calif.: Sage.

Messina, Anthony M. 1989: *Race and Party Competition in Britain*. Oxford: Clarendon Press.

Miles, David 1997: The UK and the euro. In Paul Temperton (ed.), *The Euro*, Chichester: Wiley, 51–64.

Miles, Robert 1987: Recent Marxist theories of nationalism and the issue of racism. *British Journal of Sociology*, 38(1), 24–43.

Miliband, Ralph 1994: *Socialism for a Sceptical Age*. London and New York: Verso.

Modood, Tariq 1994: Ethnic difference and racial equality. In David Miliband (ed.), *Reinventing the Left: new challenges for the left*. Cambridge: Polity Press, 86–100.

Modood, Tariq 1997: Introduction: the politics of multiculturalism in the new Europe. In Tariq Modood and Pnina Werbner (eds), *The Politics of Multiculturalism in the New Europe: racism, identity and community*. London and New York: Zed Press, 1–25.

Morris, Jonathan 1994: The Japanization of industry: a review of developments in the UK and Canada. In Jorge Niosi (ed.), *New Technology Policy and Social Innovations in the Firm*. London: Pinter, 173–86.

Morris, Jonathan and Rob Imrie 1992: *Transforming Buyer–Supplier Relations: Japanese-style industrial practices in a western context*. Basingstoke: Macmillan.

Morris, Jonathan, Max Munday, and Barry Wilkinson 1993: *Working for the Japanese: the economic and social consequences of Japanese investment in Wales*. London: Athlone.

Mulgan, Geoff (ed.) 1997: *Life After Politics: new thinking for the twenty-first century*. London: Fontana.

Munday, Max 1990: *Japanese Manufacturing Investment in Wales*. Cardiff: University of Wales Press.

Nairn, Tom 1981: *The Break-Up of Britain*. London: Verso.

Nairn, Tom 1997: Sovereignty after the election? *New Left Review*, 224, 3–18.

Nana, Chavi 1997: Differentiated success: Indians and Pakistanis in modern day Britain. Wellesley College, unpublished.

Nolan, Peter and David Harvie 1995: Labour markets: diversity in restructuring. In David Coates (ed.), *Economic and Industrial Performance in Europe*. Aldershot: Edward Elgar, 125–39.

Norris, Christopher 1990: *What's Wrong with Postmodernism: critical theory and the ends of philosophy*. Baltimore, Md: Johns Hopkins Press.

Norris, Pippa 1997a: Anatomy of a Labour landslide. *Parliamentary Affairs*, 50(4), 509–32.

Norris, Pippa 1997b: *Electoral Change in Britain since 1945*. Oxford: Blackwell.

Norris, Pippa 1999: A gender-generation gap? In Geoffrey Evans and Pippa Norris (eds), *Critical Elections: British parties and voters in long-term perspective*. London: Sage, forthcoming.

Norris, Pippa and Geoffrey Evans. 1999: Conclusion: was 1997 a critical election? In Geoffrey Evans and Pippa Norris (eds), *Critical Elections: British parties and voters in long-term perspective*. London: Sage, forthcoming.

OECD 1996: *OECD Economic Surveys: 1995–1996*: United Kingdom. Paris: OECD.

Office for National Statistics 1997a: *Overseas Direct Investment 1996*. London: The Stationery Office.

Office for National Statistics 1997b: *Social Trends 27*, London: The Stationery Office.

Office for National Statistics, Social Survey Division 1997: *Living in Britain: results from the 1995 General Household Survey*. London: The Stationery Office.

Ohmae, Kenichi 1991: *The Borderless World: power and strategy in the interlinked economy*. New York: Harper Perennial.

Ohmae, Kenichi 1995: *The End of the Nation State: the rise of regional economies*. New York: Free Press.

Oliver, Nick and Barry Wilkinson 1992: *The Japanization of British Industry: new developments in the 1990s*. Oxford: Blackwell.

Oppenheim, Carey. Welfare reform and the labour market: a "third way"? Labour in Government: The "Third Way" and the Future of Social Democracy. Minda de Gunzburg Center for European Studies, Harvard University, 13–15 November 1998.

Ostner, Ilona 1993: Slow motion: women, work and the family in Germany. In Jane Lewis (ed.), *Women and Social Policies in Europe: work, family and the state*. Aldershot: Edward Elgar, 92–115.

Ostner, Ilona and Jane Lewis 1995: Gender and the evolution of European social policies. In Stephan Leibfried and Paul Pierson (eds), *European Social Policy: between fragmentation and integration*. Washington, DC: The Brookings Institution, 159–93.

Panitch, Leo and Colin Leys 1997: *The End of Parliamentary Socialism: from New Left to New Labour*. London and New York: Verso.

Parekh, Bhikhu 1993: The cultural particularity of liberal democracy. In David Held (ed.), *Prospects for Democracy: north, south, east, west*. Cambridge: Polity Press, 156–75.

Patterson, Orlando 1983: The nature, causes, and implications of ethnic identification. In C. Fried (ed.), *Minorities: community and identity*. Berlin: Springer-Verlag, 25–50.

Paul, Kathleen 1997: *Whitewashing Britain: race and citizenship in the postwar era*. Ithaca, NY, and London: Cornell University Press.

Perraton, Jonathan, David Goldblatt, David Held and Anthony McGrew 1997: The globalisation of economic activity. *New Political Economy*, 2(2), 257–77.

Phizacklea, Annie 1990: *Unpacking the Fashion Industry: gender, racism, and class in production*. London and New York: Routledge.

Phizacklea, Annie and Carol Wolkowitz 1995: *Homeworking Women: gender, racism and class at work*. London, Thousand Oaks, Calif., New Delhi: Sage.

Pierson, Paul 1994: *Dismantling the Welfare State? Reagan, Thatcher, and the politics of retrenchment*. Cambridge: Cambridge University Press.

Piore, Michael and Charles Sabel 1984: *The Second Industrial Divide: possibilities for prosperity*. New York: Basic Books.

Pockock, J. G. A. 1992: History and sovereignty: the historiographical response to Europeanization in two British cultures. *Journal of British Studies*, 31(4), 358–89.

Pontusson, Jonas 1988: Swedish social democracy and British labour: essays on the nature and condition of social democratic hegemony. Cornell University, Center for International Studies, Occasional Paper no. 19.

Pontusson, Jonas 1992: *The Limits of Social Democratic Power: investment politics in Sweden*. Ithaca, NY, and London: Cornell University Press.

Porpora, Douglas V. 1985: The role of agency in history: the Althusser–Thompson–Anderson debate. *Current Perspectives in Social Theory*, 6, 219–41.

Przeworski, Adam 1985: *Capitalism and Social Democracy*. Cambridge: Cambridge University Press.

Przeworski, Adam 1993: Socialism and social democracy. In Joel Krieger (ed.), *The Oxford Companion to Politics of the World*. New York: Oxford University Press, 832–9.

Przeworski, Adam and John Sprague 1986: *Paper Stones: a history of electoral socialism*. Chicago, IU., and London: University of Chicago Press.

Przeworski, Adam and Michael Wallerstein 1982: The structure of class conflicts under democratic capitalism. *American Political Science Review*, 76, 215–38.

Przeworski, Adam and Michael Wallerstein 1988: Structural dependence of the state on capital. *American Political Science Review*, 82, 11–31.

Putnam, Robert D. 1993: *Making Democracy Work: civic traditions in modern Italy*. Princeton, NJ: Princeton University Press.

Putnam, Robert D. 1995: Bowling alone: America's declining social capital. *Journal of Democracy*, 6(1), 65–78.

Ramsey, H. 1991: The commission, the multi-national, its workers and their charter. *Work, Employment and Society*, 5(4), 541–66.

Rees, Tom 1982: Immigration policies in the United Kingdom. In Charles Husband (ed.), *"Race" in Britain*. London: Hutchinson, 75–96.

Reich, Robert 1991: *The Work of Nations*. New York: Simon and Schuster.

Reynolds, Paul and David Coates 1996: Conclusion. In David Coates (ed.), *Industrial Policy in Britain*. Basingstoke: Macmillan, 241–68.

Riddell, Peter 1983: *The Thatcher Government*. Oxford: Martin Robertson.

Robbins, Keith 1998: *Great Britain: identities, institutions and the idea of Britishness*. London and New York: Longman.

Robinson, Vaughan 1990: Boom and gloom: the success and failure of South Asians in Britain. In Colin Clarke, Ceri Peach and Stephen Vertovec (eds), *South Asians Overseas: migration and ethnicity*. Cambridge: Cambridge University Press, 269–96.

Rosenau, Pauline Marie 1992: *Post-Modernism and the Social Sciences*. Princeton, NJ: Princeton University Press.

Rubery, Jill 1989: Labour market flexibility in Britain. In Francis Green (ed.), *The Restructuring of the UK Economy*. Hemel Hempstead: Harvester Wheatsheaf, 155–76.

Sadler, David 1992: *The Global Region: production, state policies and uneven development*. Oxford: Pergamon.

Said, Edward 1979: *Orientalism*. New York: Vintage.

Samuel, Raphael, Barbara Bloomfield, and Guy Boanas (eds) 1986: *The Enemy Within: pit villages and the miners' strike of 1984–5*. History Workshop Series. London and New York: Routledge and Kegan Paul.

Sanders, David 1997: Voting and the electorate. In Patrick Dunleavy, Andrew Gamble, Ian Holliday, and Gillian Peele (eds), *Developments in British Politics 5*, New York: St Martin's Press, 45–74.

Sanders, David 1998: The new electoral battlefield. In Anthony King (ed.), *New Labour Triumphs: Britain at the polls*. Chatham, NJ: Chatham House, 209–48.

Sarre, Philip, Deborah Phillips and Richard Skellington 1989: *Ethnic Minority Housing: explanations and policies*. Aldershot: Avebury.

Sassoon, Anne Showstack (ed.) 1992: *Women and the State: the shifting boundaries of public and private*. London and New York: Routledge.

Sassoon, Anne Showstack 1992: Women's new social role: contradictions of the welfare state. In Anne Showstack Sassoon (ed.), *Women and the State: the shifting boundaries of public and private*. London and New York: Routledge, 158–88.

Saunders, Peter 1986: *Social Theory and the Urban Question*. New York: Holmes and Meier.

Schmitter, Philippe 1974: Still the century of corporatism? *Review of Politics*, 36(1), 85–131.

Seyd, Patrick 1998: Tony Blair and New Labour. In Anthony King (ed.), *New Labour Triumphs: Britain at the polls*. Chatham, NJ: Chatham House, 49–73.

Sharp, Margaret and William Walker 1994: Thatcherism and technical advance – reform without progress? In Tony Buxton, Paul Chapman, and Paul Temple (eds), *Britain's Economic Performance*. London and New York: Routledge, 397–429.

Shaw, Eric 1996: *The Labour Party since 1945*. Oxford: Blackwell.

Shaw, Eric 1998: New Labour and the politics of welfare reform. Paper presented to the eleventh international conference of Europeanists, Baltimore, Md.

Sinfield, Alan 1989: *Literature, Politics, and Culture in Postwar Britain*. Berkeley and Los Angeles, Calif.: University of California Press.

Smith, Anna Marie 1994: *New Right Discourse on Race and Sexuality: Britain, 1968–1990*. Cambridge: Cambridge University Press.

Smith, John 1993: Reclaiming the ground – freedom and the value of society. In Christopher Bryant (ed.), *Reclaiming the Ground: Christianity and socialism*. London: Spire/Hodder and Stoughton, 127–42.

Smith, Susan M. 1989: *The Politics of "Race" and Residence: citizenship, segregation and white supremacy in Britain*. Cambridge: Polity Press.

Sohinger, Jasminka and Daniel Rubinfeld 1993: European labor markets: the eastern dimension. In Lloyd Ulman, Barry Eichengreen, and William T. Dickens (eds), *Labor and an integrated Europe*. Washington, DC: The Brookings Institution, 271–85.

Sommers, Margaret F. 1992: Narrativity, narrative identity, and social action: rethinking English working-class formation. *Social Science History*, 16(4), 591–630.

Sondhi, R. 1983: Immigration and citizenship in postwar Britain. In C. Fried (ed.), *Minorities: community and identity*. Berlin: Springer-Verlag, 255–68.

Spencer, Peter 1996: Reactions to a flexible labour market. In Roger Jowell, John Curtice, Alison Park, Lindsay Brook, and Katarina Thompson (eds), *British Social Attitudes: the 13th report*. Aldershot: Dartmouth Publishing Co., 73–91.

Steinmo, Sven, Kathleen Thelen, and Frank Longstreth (eds) 1992: *Structuring Politics: historical institutionalism in comparative analysis*. Cambridge Studies in Comparative Politics. New York: Cambridge University Press.

Streeck, Wolfgang 1991: On the institutional conditions of diversified quality production. In Egon Matzner and Wolfgang Steeck (eds), *Beyond Keynesianism: the socio-economics of production and full employment*. Aldershot: Edward Elgar, 21–61.

Streeck, Wolfgang 1997: German capitalism: does it exist? Can it survive? *New Political Economy*, 2(2), 237–56.

Sullivan, William M. 1995: Re-inventing community: prospects for politics. In Colin Crouch and David Marquand (eds), *Reinventing Collective Action: from the global to the local*. Oxford: Blackwell, 20–32.

Tarrow, Sidney 1994: *Power in Movement: social movements, collective action and politics*. New York: Cambridge University Press.

Tawney, R. H. 1931: *Equality*. New York: Harcourt, Brace and Co.

Taylor, Charles 1994: The politics of recognition. In Amy Gutmann (ed.), *Multiculturalism: examining the politics of recognition*. Princeton, NJ: Princeton University Press, 25–73.

Temple, Paul 1994: Overview: the agents of change – notes on the developing division of labour. In Tony Buxton, Paul Chapman, and Paul Temple (eds), *Britain's Economic Performance*. London and New York: Routledge, 345–72.

Thompson, E. P. 1965: The peculiarities of the English. In Ralph Miliband and John Saville (eds), *Socialist Register 1965*. New York: Monthly Review Press, 311–62.

Thompson, E. P. 1966: *The Making of the English Working Class*. New York: Vintage.

Tilly, Charles 1993: Contentious repertoires in Britain, 1758–1834. *Social Science History*, 17, 253–80.

Titmuss, Richard 1958: *Essays on the Welfare State*. London: Allen and Unwin.

Treasury, HM 1997: *Recent Overseas Investment Statistics*.

Troyna, Barry 1982: Reporting the National Front: British values observed. In Charles Husband (ed.), *"Race" in Britain: continuity and change*. London: Hutchinson: 259–78.

Veer, Peter van der (ed.) 1995: *Nation and Migration: the politics of space in the South Asian diaspora*. South Asia Seminar Series. Philadelphia, Pa: University of Pennsylvania Press.

Webster, Juliet 1996: *Shaping Women's Work: gender, employment and information technology*. London and New York: Longman.

Werbner, Pnina 1990: Manchester Pakistanis: division and unity. In Colin Clarke, Ceri Peach and Steven Vertovec (eds), *South Asians Overseas: migration and ethnicity*. Cambridge: Cambridge University Press, 331–47.

Wickens, Peter 1987: *The Road to Nissan: flexibility, quality, teamwork*. Basingstoke: Macmillan.

Williams, John 1998: Keeping the Heartlands happy. *New Statesman*, 6 March, 18–20.

Wilson, Elizabeth 1977: *Women and the Welfare State*. London: Tavistock.

Wilson, Wiliam Julius 1987: *The Truly Disadvantaged: the inner city, the underclass, and public policy*. Chicago, Ill., and London: University of Chicago Press.

Wolin, Sheldon S. 1988: On the theory and practice of power. In Jonathan Arac (ed.), *After Foucault: humanistic knowledge, postmodern challenges*. New Brunswick, NJ: Rutgers University Press, 179–201.

Womack, James P., Daniel T. Jones, and Daniel Roos 1990: *The Machine that Changed the World*. New York: HarperCollins.

World Bank 1995: *World Development Report 1995: workers in an integrating world*. New York: World Bank/Oxford University Press.

Wright, Erik Olin 1985: *Classes*. London: New Left Books/Verso.

Wright, Erik Olin 1997: *Class Counts: comparative studies in class analysis*. Cambridge: Cambridge University Press.

Yalçin-Heckman, Lale 1997: The perils of ethnic associational life in Europe: Turkish migrants in Germany and France. In Tariq Modood and Pnina Werbner (eds), *The Politics of Multiculturalism in the New Europe: racism, identity and community*. London: Zed Press, 95–110.

Zeitlin, Jonathan 1995: Why are there no industrial districts in the United Kingdom? In Arnaldo Bagnasco and Charles Sabel (eds), *Small and Medium-Sized Enterprises*. London: Pinter, 98–114.

Index